The Germany which em[...] divided politically and geographically, disrupted economically, and torn ideologically between denying or excusing the Nazi horror and trying to exorcise it. To give a truthful picture of the social and political situations, a group of young former soldiers distributed a newspaper, *Der Ruf* [The call]. At first, some of its contributors, led by Hans Werner Richter, were inspired by a belief in the effectiveness of literature to change society and wanted to confront the past. In 1947, after *Der Ruf* was banned, Richter called together a circle of friends to read from their writings while seated in the dreaded "electric chair" and to receive criticism silently. By the second meeting they had dubbed themselves "Group 47," a definite format and ritual was established, and attendance by exclusive invitation grew rapidly. For two decades the group offered a periodic meeting ground for German-language writers from all over the world, and it has served as an initiator of new trends and a barometer of changing literary tastes and social conditions.

Siegfried Mandel presents here the essential and exciting history of Group 47. There are so many important writers connected with the group—indeed, its members have been called the makers of modern German literature—that Professor Mandel has divided his study into chapters covering each genre produced rather than individual authors.

Fiction was the first form writers turned to. Mandel considers salient features of the works of Hans Werner Richter, Martin Walser, Günter Grass, Uwe Johnson, and recent Nobel Prize winner Heinrich Böll, and includes discussion of many lesser writers.

Postwar poetry. Mandel explains, was directed toward the purgation of sentimentality and imprecision, and every conceivable poetic form was tried: neo-Dadaism, neosurrealism, satire, analytical poetry, and poetry of virtuosity. Günter Grass wrote poems of fantasy: Karl Krolow, Helmut Heissenbüttel, and Hans Magnus Enzenberger considered poetry a form of superior amusement. Other major poets discussed are Günter Eich, Ingeborg Bachmann, Paul Celan, and Johannes Bobrowski.

Mandel finds Group 47 involved in three dramatic genres: the radio play, the documentary, and the stage. He sees the radio play as a unique form of the fifties which provided an excellent field for experimentation and social expression by writers known for other work. Documentary theater, such as Peter Weiss's *Marat/Sade,* chooses politically and socially inflammatory material and, as Mandel shows, has enlivened the awareness of critical issues as no other form has been able. Not until the 1960s did Group 47 members take more than a sporadic interest in writing for the stage. The new plays, too, reflect sharp political controversies. As significant examples of the new dramatists, Mandel chooses Martin Walser, Wolfgang Hildesheimer, Günter Grass, and Peter Handke.

Group 47 is, therefore, a history of an influential body of postwar literature and its aesthetics and ideology, and also a critical study of many individual authors. Students and scholars of German, European, and general contemporary literature will find Professor Mandel's book richly rewarding for its range and comprehensiveness in these categories.

Siegfried Mandel is Professor of English and Comparative Literature at the University of Colorado. He is the author of *Rainer Maria Rilke: The Poetic Instinct* and editor and contributor to *Contemporary European Novelists,* both published in the Crosscurrents series. He is the author of several other books on literary thought, science, and symbolism. Professor Mandel has contributed articles, features, and reviews to *Criticism,* the *Saturday Review,* the *New York Times Book Review,* the *Denver Quarterly, Comparative Literature Studies,* and other publications.

Harry T. Moore is Research Professor at Southern Illinois University, Carbondale. Among his recent books are *E. M. Forster, Twentieth-Century French Literature, Twentieth-Century German Literature,* and *Age of the Modern,* a collection of his critical analyses and miscellaneous writings. He is coauthor of *D. H. Lawrence and His World.*

Crosscurrents / MODERN CRITIQUES

Harry T. Moore, *General Editor*

GROUP 47

The Reflected Intellect

Siegfried Mandel

WITH A PREFACE BY

Harry T. Moore

SOUTHERN ILLINOIS UNIVERSITY PRESS
Carbondale and Edwardsville

FEFFER & SIMONS, INC.
London and Amsterdam

For Irwin and Selma
who shared the experience

Library of Congress Cataloging in Publication Data

Mandel, Siegfried.
    Group 47: the reflected intellect.

(Crosscurrents/modern critiques)
    Bibliography: p.
    1. Gruppe Siebenundvierzig. I. Title.
PT405.M33   830'.9'00914   73–8698
ISBN 0–8093–0641–7

Contents

Preface

Imagine a Continental country laid waste by artillery and aerial bombardment, its cities jagged ruins—with most of the rest of the world pointing out that the inhabitants brought the destruction on themselves; which was essentially true, though there were some drastic oversimplifications of the matter: a Norwegian woman who had won the Nobel Prize thought that the people of this land were, and always had been, brutes in victory or in attempts at victory, but whiners in defeat; and that they should all be exterminated was an opinion spoken out in England by a man of high rank (no, not Churchill); and then consider some of the younger writers of the devastated country organizing an important literary movement. Its participants would for the most part accept the fact of the Continental country's recent evilness, would often write perceptively about it, and would grow into strength as the nation itself did in rejoining what is so frequently called the civilized community.

Of course we all know that in Nazi times there were plenty of people of the kind we sometimes called "good" Germans; there were a great many of them, despite all the really dominent types, in the Nazi years; at that time some of the non-Nazi Germans went abroad (as Thomas Mann did), some went underground, some quietly went into a state known as inner emigration, and a few even spoke out, as the author Ernst Wiechert did—an attitude which put him into Buchenwald for five months in 1938.

Then, after the war, some brilliant young writers formed

Group 47, whose origin is described later in this volume. Among the young postwar writers who became the big stars of Group 47, Uwe Johnson (born in 1934) was too young to serve in Hitler's army. But two of the others did, including Günter Grass, who during the war was in the Luftwaffe, was wounded, and was taken prisoner. Heirich Böll was also wounded and captured. These last two men have dealt with the war in their fiction, Grass in a wildly comic-satiric vein. The three of them, like other members of the Group, have also given the world a detailed picture of readjustment to a new life. The Group 47 people—novelists, poets, dramatists, essayists—are among the most exciting authors existing anywhere today. Böll has recently won the Nobel Prize, and he was an excellent choice among the somewhat younger writers of the world (he was born in 1917); his nearest rival among his contemporaries would be Günter Grass. Of course there are some older authors whom the Nobel Committee, with its awards to Bucks and Steinbecks, should consider: Lewis Mumford, for example, and Thornton Wilder. But Böll was, in most ways, a good choice.

The award to him emphasizes the achievements of Group 47; its founder, the journalist and novelist Hans Werner Richter, deserves mention—and Siegfried Mandel writes about him in this book, which is the 117th volume of the Crosscurrents/Modern Critiques series.

Professor Mandel has also written an earlier book for the series, a study of the greatest of twentieth-century German poets, Rainer Maria Rilke. It is a most valuable study for many reasons, among them its detailed treatment of various last-phase poems of Rilke which earlier commentators had neglected. Further, Dr. Mandel has edited, again for the Crosscurrents series, a volume on Contemporary European Novelists, to which he contributed a chapter on "The German Novel: In the Wake of Organized Madness" (Wallace Fowlie wrote on the French novel, and other experts dealt with the genre in relation to still other countries). Professor Mandel yet further demonstrated the versatility and range of his interests and thinking when he prepared for the Dell Publishing Company his notable Dictionary of Science.

As Siegfried Mandel says in the Acknowledgments to the present book, he wrote it at my suggestion. It was certainly one of the best imaginable suggestions, as the reader will discover in the early pages, which are merely a beginning that leads toward a rich fulfillment. For the author presents not only the history of Group 47, but also the ideas behind it, as well as the critical judgments which make this book so excellent. Dr. Mandel (who served in the U.S. Army Intelligence in the Second World War) made one of his return journeys to his native country in order to obtain first-hand material for this volume. Earlier, I said that the book is excellent; it is also unique, in English, for the thoroughness of its treatment. It seems to me to be one of those rare accomplishments, a first-rate work of literary history illuminated by first-rate criticism.

HARRY T. MOORE

Southern Illinois University, Carbondale
February 22, 1973

Acknowledgments and Aims

Several years ago Harry T. Moore suggested that I undertake a study of Group 47, a group which became a legend in its time. Some have called its existence mythical and its definition impossible. As one punster has remarked in the style of Gertrude Stein, "Group 47, a group which is no group, is a group which is. . . ." This study hopes to complete the implications of that sentence. Group 47 has not been bashful about publicizing itself as a literary metropolis, invisible yet likely to meet anywhere in or outside of Germany. Indeed, for two decades it offered a periodic meeting ground for German-writing authors from all over the world, within Europe, and the divided Germanies. Originally it consisted mainly of young soldiers who returned from World War II and had ambitions of making their way as writers. Through the years, it also afforded reunions with those who returned from exile after the demise of the Third Reich, with those who chose to stay in exile, and with the fairly large number of writers who became expatriates in the fifties and sixties. During the course of my research the halo which surrounded the group gradually disappeared and my respect increased for the passionate dedication to literature by the individuals and the diversity of their writing. When the group accepted an invitation to meet in 1966 at Princeton University, publishers insisted that those authors who were flying should distribute themselves over as many planes as possible lest an accident detroy the makers of modern German literature. The exaggeration is slight because all one needs to do is expand the roster of group authors by at most ten names to achieve inclusiveness.

In his autobiography, Jakov Lind mentions the frustrating relationship between word and world, between writing and understanding. He poses the questions, "How can the picture in front of one's eyes be drawn with words? How can the intellect reflect itself in letters?" It is precisely these questions that inform the writings of Group 47, and hence they prompted the subtitle of my book. Group 47 is high-powered intellectually with enough doctorate holders among its writers and critics to make any distinguished university envious. Their knowledge and use of world traditions and comparative literature are equally impressive. One hallmark then of their writing and polemics is the reflecting and reflected intellect; yet, to some extent, it also explains a frequent lack of spontaneity, despite inventiveness, and a dominant occupation with polish and craft.

Publication dates appear after titles; works untranslated—as far as information was available to me—and literal titles are given in brackets. Except where noted, translations are my own. In order to illustrate points of discussion, my aim has been to paraphrase faithfully the texts quoted. Perhaps the reader will be encouraged to take the originals in hand, especially the poetry which often resists translation. For the rendering of the selections from Ingeborg Bachmann's poetry, I am indebted to the advice of Aaron Kramer, a sensitive poet and friend.

A faculty fellowship by the Graduate Council on Research and Creative Work of the University of Colorado assisted me immeasurably in my work by making it possible to spend time in Europe; my appreciation is extended to the Council for its support.

SIEGFRIED MANDEL

University of Colorado
January 1973

Group 47

1

A Call to Letters and an
Invitation to the Electric Chair

Group 47 is a paradox. It is one man, Hans Werner Richter, and at the same time an expanding and contracting constellation identifiable by several constant stars. The group has given its members a publicity platform, and reciprocally some of its members have brought the group an international reputation. Group 47 was conceived, nurtured, fathered, and brought to prominence by Richter, a person of single-minded political idealism, a tenacious social vision and dedication to basic German interests, an unparalleled flair for publicity and its exploitation, and with an iron-cool temperament seemingly devoid of sentimentalism. Anyone who might have had more endearing qualities or lesser egocentricity than Richter would surely have failed to keep alive for more than two decades a loosely-knit association of writers who periodically exhibited their wares (which pleased or antagonized fellow participants and the public), engaged in critical debate over socio-literary-aesthetic issues, and assisted in revitalizing all forms of literary expression inside and outside the fluid group. It kept alive because it never hardened into a school of style or inflexible ideology. At times it initiated new trends, but more often it was a barometer of changing literary tastes, social conditions, and political climates.

Drawing upon his own background, Richter lately has written reminiscence stories, *Blinder Alarm* [False Alarm] (1970) — sketches whose style has moved away from his early realistic novels to a lyrical, ironic prose. The Baltic island of

Usedom, and the town of Bansin where he was born in 1908, was populated by fishermen, masons, locksmiths, and peasants from interior villages, and from the time of Kaiser Wilhelm II to the postwar Russian occupation it reflected in a microcosm the experience of much of Germany in all its political periods; little has changed physically, except that presently a few miles away is a barbed wire border with Poland. A sense of nationality reigned supreme, yet his father returned from World War I a Social Democrat (a rare phenomenon in his town) and with stories that told not of glory but of his endless task of emptying bedpots. During Nazi times, his family had to suffer indignities and social ostracism because he did not play along with new political trends. When the second war came contrary to his expectations, he advised his five sons to behave unobtrusively in the army, to be neither heroic nor cowardly, and never to volunteer for anything; they survived the war. He was against war but for the honoring of soldiers, a distinction which made an impact on his son, Hans Werner.

In Berlin, the young Richter started to learn the book trade, joined the Communist party in 1930 and left it in 1933, migrated to Paris but after a year of starvation returned to Berlin under the watchful eyes of the Nazis. After the war started he was recruited into the German infantry for duty in France and Italy and eventually gave himself up to the Americans at Monte Cassino. Again, he began to concern himself seriously with political questions while a German prisoner of war at Camp Ellis in the United States. Because the American officers interfered little in the internal affairs of the prisoner camps, some of the German *Wehrmacht* officers and noncoms cooperated with terrorists who wanted to keep alive the dedication to Nazism and who used discipline and sometimes murder to keep dissenters in line and to prohibit debate. Reeducation came slowly and was speeded up when the defeat of Germany became a certainty. To open a truthful picture of the military and political situations, a POW newspaper was distributed during the winter of 1944 and lasted into early 1946. Along the line, one of the editors of this newspaper, called *Der Ruf* [The call], was a lawyer, Walter Mannzen, and he was joined by Richter and by Alfred Andersch, among others. When Andersch was released soon after the war, he founded another *Der Ruf* in August 1946 in Munich, with the subtitle "Independent newsleaf of the new generation." Richter made contributions from the start, and with the fourth issue they continued jointly to edit the periodical until April 1947 when the American military government in Bavaria banned further publication under Andersch-Richter auspices.

The issues raised in *Der Ruf* and the solutions firmly advocated have importance in their historical context and carry over into the thinking of what later was Group 47. Some of the fellow POWs, who had worked with both men before, renewed their contributions to the newsleaf. *Der Ruf* found considerable resonance among subscribers in all four zones of occupation and its circulation rapidly rose above 100,000. Within a short time, there also was talk of a political *Ruf* party. Mainly, the newsleaf was politically oriented, but it also contained general cultural articles, fiction and poetry, and journalistic reports which intended to gauge the actual condition of German life and peoples' mentalities. The dual purpose of the newsleaf was to become the voice of the silent generation, the young homecoming soldiers, and to influence the political direction of Germany. In some respect the arguments put forward had jelled during the times of the old POW publication and then received renewed polemical force. The core propositions were the following: the freedom and unity of Germany, a social-humanistic foundation for the new political structure of Germany, a unified socialist Europe, no imposition of the idea of collective guilt upon the German people, and no unnecessary humiliation of Germans. Among other points, *Der Ruf* wanted Germans to play a role in all peace deliberations, called for the speedy return of German prisoners of war from camps all over the map, urged the use of German revolutionary courts—instead of the Nuremberg trials—to deal with Germans who had committed crimes against Germany, and proposed a bridging role or middle position for Germany between East and West.

The contents of the articles which appeared in *Der Ruf*

merit more than the mere gloss which critics have accorded
them since they reveal attitudes free of the disguises that
marked other publications during the postwar era in regard
to political, economic, social, and cultural problems. Writers
for the publication discarded all niceties and taboos, spoke
plainly and often aggressively. Although Germany had capitulated unconditionally, these writers bent no knees to
the military government and warned that only a just peace
would have durability. Other than the precondition for a
united Germany, the revision of eastern boundaries, and
retention of the 1937 geographical status quo, many of the
proposals fitted into a somewhat fuzzy blueprint. A recurrent
theme is the call for a humanistic socialism which would
democratize socialism and socialize democracy and the
search for a third way which would be indigenously German.
Richter felt that the time was ripe for socialism because the
capitalistic order had been weakened by two imperialistic
wars and periodic crises while the middle-class supporters
of capitalism had been demoralized by Fascist experiments;
the whole system was in its decline. Theoretically, the proletariat should be the carrier of future developments but he
seemed paralyzed by the magnitude of the tasks though the
goal was close. Richter saw irony in the fact that when the
liberal middle-class elements needed underpinning from the
Left in 1933, it was lacking, while during the postwar years
it was forthcoming. The tragedy of the German working
class, thought Richter, lay in the lack of effective leadership
yesterday and today. *Der Ruf*'s socialism envisaged freedom
of political and social choice, including acceptance or rejection of religion, instead of Marxist determinism.

From Paris to Moscow, Communists were particularly
upset with Richter's sharp letter, published in *Der Ruf*
(February 15, 1947), which struck at M. Marcel Cachin,
one of the oldest members of the French Communist party.
Cachin had said publicly that the Nazi spirit still prevailed
in Germany, that Germans had no regret nor showed pen-
ance, that Nazis still were in key positions, and that American and British interests were abetted by the rebuilding of
industries in their sectors. Richter responded by accusing

M. Cachin of being a traitor to international socialism and reminded him of the boundless disillusion suffered by socialists at the 1939 Stalin-Hitler pact, the alliance between a Fascist Germany and Russia. He recalled further Cachin's defeatist role in urging French workers to lay down their arms when the Germans invaded France. More specifically, Richter noted that Cachin's demand for dismantling factories would pauperize the German worker. Richter condemned Cachin for nationalist and revenge tactics which attempted to internationalize instead of socializing the rich industrial Ruhr, for wanting to dismantle factories instead of unionizing them, for encouraging workers to dynamite the Hamburg dock industry rather than turning it over to the workers. Cachin's allegiance was to Moscow while Richter favored a new socialistic approach; he thought that it would be a mistake to restore the political parties which exhibited their weaknesses during the Weimar regime of the twenties. The various plans to dismember Germany, as well as Churchill's ideas of decentralized provincialities, were rejected by *Der Ruf* writers. Instead of Churchill's balance-of-power orientation, Richter called for a socialized Europe, a United States of Europe in which Germany would play a cooperative and equal role. Reiterated was the idea that Germany's political hopes for the future would rest on the young homecoming generation and their joining hands with socialist forces throughout Europe. The journalist Nicolaus Sombart expressed the hope that the young Frenchmen would put aside any Clemenceau-like hatreds that resulted in the Versailles Treaty and in return Germans would never again tolerate a Hitler among them.

The socialist economy, as broached, regarded the private ownership of the means of production as obsolete and absurd as slavery; a planned economy and technology were essential. A prescription for healing Germany was given by Mannzen, who proposed to free the economy from the chains of the profit motive and the market mechanisms; socialistic planning was to control the economy. While Germany appreciates American economic assistance and wants the good will of the world, Richter wrote, "Young

Germany knows that its future state will be proletarian, but it is not ready to live in a state of beggary." Of course, as Andersch pointed out, the economy and society would need to be reconstructed in order to foster changes that would eliminate the physical and psychic effects of aerial bombings of German cities, to help millions of Germans made homeless in the East, to eliminate the blight of black markets, to end the Babylonian captivity of soldiers, to reverse the paralysis of industries and cities in ruins, to still the voices of hunger and despair. Actually, German industry was not destroyed: about eighty percent was relatively undamaged.

Most of the writers for *Der Ruf* neither spoke softly nor entirely hid a big stick; many battled defensively against the resentment that broke in waves over Germany after the war. An example of countering foreign criticism was set by Walter Kolbenhoff (b. 1908), who won a prize from the POW *Der Ruf* in 1946 and continued to contribute to the new one. The occasion was a book written by Nobel Prize winner Sigrid Undset, translated from a Norwegian manuscript as *Return to the Future* (1942; *Wieder in die Zukunft*, 1944, published in German simultaneously in New York and Zürich). Just before the German march into Norway, she fled to the United States and there learned that her son had been shot by the Germans. As a patriot and mother, her distaste for anything German became unrelenting: "German brutality is boundless whenever they are masters; but when luck turns against them, they beg and whine for mercy. . . . Can anyone doubt that we will again hear such lamentations should the Allies succeed in winning the war against the attackers of free states." She thought, too, that there had been no change over the past thousand years in the *Herrenvolk* or master-race mentality of the Germans. Kolbenhoff made emotional concessions to Mrs. Undset's grief and then launched into admonishments: "Your forefathers, also, Mrs. Undset, once were brutal and unpleasant robbers." Hate should not be directed against those who resisted Hitler, wrote Kolbenhoff, not against the millions of innocent German children who are not responsible for the stupidities of their parents. He reminded

Mrs. Undset of Germany's cultural contributions (as if the glories of Weimar allow an absolving of the barbarities in nearby Buchenwald) and the contributions to the socialist movement of Europe. "Other Europeans also suffer from political infantilism," but the best part of the German nation, comments Kolbenhoff, is attempting to find a new way, and the good forces will prevail: "The only solution of the problem is that we achieve union with the life of other nations." He concluded with the optimistic assessment that Germans would seize their "third chance." There is no record of any reply or forgiveness by Sigrid Undset, who had cause to remember, among other things, the destruction by German bombers of the town of Lillehammer where she lived in a house which had been built in the year 1000.

Many of the contributors to *Der Ruf* worked hard to absolve the soldiers of the German *Wehrmacht* from any dishonor; through their contributions to the newsleaf they wanted to restore the pride of the homecomers and their hopes. Alfred Andersch was particularly fulsome in extolling the "astounding military deeds of the young Germans in this war" as against the deeds of the somewhat older Germans who were being tried in Nuremberg; their deeds "stand in little relation to one another." "The warriors at Stalingrad, El Alamein, and Cassino, to whom even their opponents paid respect, are innocent of the crimes at Dachau and Buchenwald"; their defeat was honorable, wrote Andersch, and "the real enemies of the young soldiers who braved death on all European and African fronts are the political and military criminals. . . . the nation will again have its honor when these traitors are defrocked." *Der Ruf* contributors expressed anger and concern for the six million, mostly young, German soldiers who two years after the war were still in POW camps, doing reconstruction work in Russia, especially in Siberia, felling trees in Canada, mining and working in France and North Africa; they complained about medical attention, food, and housing comforts (which were somewhat unlike those they enjoyed when they were occupiers). Perhaps *Der Ruf* was unaware that sixty percent of Russian POWs in German hands never returned home.

As for the home front, Andersch indicted official and public indifference to the POWs: "Sorrow and empathic suffering is confined to circles of close relatives, to the mothers robbed of millions of sons. . . . women and girls turn their backs to the apparently hopeless lot of those behind barbed wires." A former student and POW, Friedrich Minssen, in looking around, felt that 1946 had not brought a new start, that despite the help of the Allies "our calorie rations are lower than that since the beginning of the war . . . and are not significantly higher than what they were in the German concentration camps"; economic stagnation, hunger, and despair are the signs of peace. The writers for *Der Ruf* resented foreign reporting about the mean, petty, grubbing, and degrading postwar life in Germany, but they too were distressed by the facts. In whatever sphere they felt vulnerable to criticism, they built up defensive arguments which solidified down to the idea that Germans were guilty only in degree; others were guilty too, other nations were imperialists too. They pointed to the appeasement policies of the Western powers during the thirties, symbolized by Neville Chamberlain, which allowed Hitler to have his way, to the inhuman treatment of minorities by Poland and particularly the virulent anti-Semitism of the Soviets, and to other sins by Germany's neighbors. Dietrich Warnesius, a free-lance writer, sharply noted, "I do not subscribe to the idea that the German nation is the only instigator of all crimes in this epoch." He pointed out also that Germans were no better or worse than others, which, however it is taken, is a significant revision of the *Herrenvolk* theory of the Third Reich. To the argument that Germany must be ready to cede territories because it lost the war, it was suggested that this might-is-right notion was practiced by Hitler but should not be turned against post-war Germany. In other words, there was a defensive argument for every hostile foreign feeling, real or anticipated.

As proof that *Der Ruf* did not shut the door to friendly disagreement, it published the personal observations of Stephen Spender, the English poet. Possibly also this was an indirect opening to the international discussions which

Richter hoped would link the young Germans to figures such as Arthur Koestler, Ignazio Silone, André Malraux, all of them anti-Fascists and anti-Stalinists, yet of the intellectual Left. Spender was well acquainted with the German as well as the French scene and did not minimize the difficulties of developing cooperative working attitudes between Germans and the rest of Europe. Germans still felt that France's fall was deserved morally and factually; they felt that France's part in the occupation of Germany was unearned and unfair since she had been beaten. The French novelist Vercors, who had founded an underground newspaper during the German occupation, had written an essay in 1945, "Are there decent Germans?" Although his answer was not encouraging and was in line with sentiments of many Frenchmen, Spender did manage to see some hopeful signs of a new chapter in Franco-German relations. Spender, unlike the writers for *Der Ruf*, was suspicious of any new German youth movement: "the young Germans of today are the most tired, unknowledgeable, and intellectually poverty-stricken generation group today." Further, he feared that the German universities were becoming asylums for ex–army officers with nationalistic sympathies. He did find on university rolls the names of German university professors of undoubted integrity, and of the older generation, but as for the rest he was cautious. For one thing, he was disturbed by some who, though they claimed to be anti-Nazi nationalists, still clung to racial theories that stressed the incompatibility between Caucasians and Asians, and the inevitability of East-West conflicts. Certain articles in *Der Ruf* admitted that some university elements still paid homage to the National Socialist madness but that one should not have expected university professors to have set a better example than other segments of German society which swayed with the times; among the scores of professors who could not pass the eighteen-month denazification process were some whose dismissal possibly was unjust. Andersch claimed that the information used by the military authorities should have been made public: "Let the people know." He and others strongly urged the return of émigré scholars to

German universities, although there would be social and intellectual difficulties. They could not foresee, however, that the gulf was rarely to be bridged in the future; voluntary émigrés, by and large, gained the taint of "deserters." Some writers made the realistic assessment that Germans at that time were interested in material rather than cultural CARE packages.

Spender also put his finger on another problem, namely, the "astonishing lack of sensitivities to realities in the attitude of most German intellectuals" who glossed over everything casually as if nothing had ever happened. If this is too great a generalization, it is offset by the repetitious and woebegone insistence in most of *Der Ruf* articles that the world ought to recognize how much the Germans had suffered. It seems to me that some of the writers who tried to reestablish the moral equilibrium of Germans adduced arguments and made appeals to the very sentiments which had caused arrogant attitudes toward their European neighbors. Anyone acquainted with the colloquial strata of German life and expression even before the Third Reich knows of the currency of contempt in which the Italians, French, Poles, Czechs, Russians, and non-German Europeans were held. In no inconsiderable way did such ingrained outlooks influence war actions and German occupation policies, including the systematic genocide practiced especially in Poland, which along with other Eastern countries was marked as a slave state; the readiness to denigrate was turned against those who were defined as nonpersons or decadent people or inferior nations. There were signs of postwar German shock at the revelations of the enormity of crimes committed as a consequence of the so-called German nationalist awakening during the Third Reich. The possibility of spiritual regeneration and profound soul-searching, despite or because of half-empty bellies or the fear of retribution, was never greater. But the finger-pointing technique of *Der Ruf* writers continued with questions directed to the German public by W. M. Guggenheimer, for instance, as to "why are we not disturbed by such ugly behavior as the Italians hanging Mussolini and his girlfriend on meat-hooks, but are only ashamed and disturbed at descriptions of what happened in German concentration camps?" Such mischievous logic and juxtapositions were to be carried to extremes later in the neo-Fascist newspaper *Soldatenzeitung*, which specializes in showing other peoples to have been worse than the Nazis. Precisely such defensive illustrations may account for the argument I heard advanced by some German students that the English were responsible for the first concentration camps during the Boer Wars, that in modern times the Turks, Poles, French, and Russians were also guilty of massacres, as if one crime mitigates another.

The glorification of German soldiers in *Der Ruf* was amplified to extremes in many directions afterward, most spectacularly through a book ingenuously called *The Unloved German*, which became a German best-seller in 1963. Its author, Dr. Hermann Eich, an editor-journalist who learned to perfect his trade as an official of the foreign press section of the Nazi government, made a case for the kindly German soldier as a gay, childish, and children-loving tourist who saved national monuments, raised sanitary and dietary levels in occupied areas, sparing the unfortunate population "the worst," and only made stern reprisals when partisans violated German commandments of war and sportsmanlike rules. In other words, the armed burglars treated their chosen hosts with consideration. When these well-treated hosts presented their bill after the war, Eich was moved to remark, "The true picture of the German occupation from 1939 to 1945 has been obscured by the understandable need of the liberated countries to secure themselves a good place in the queue for reparations." Such cynicism and contempt were far from the intent of those writing for *Der Ruf*, yet others were tempted to abuse the basic premises advocated.

Subject also to misunderstanding was the unity of postwar Europe envisaged by *Der Ruf*. It seemed that some Germans were short on memory while other Europeans could not shake the memory, still fresh, of devastation wrought by two wars unleashed by Germany. The word *unification*, though tempered by the idea of socialistic humanism and national integrity, still carried with it unwitting reminders of the German aim of complete European colonization—from Flanders to the Urals—by Nazi tacticians who used the army as their instrument. *Der Ruf* came on too early and too strong with idealistic slogans which appealed to masses of homefarers, who wanted salve for their wounds. Also it created suspicions of unrelenting German nationalism; it created fears of renewed militarism —an unjust charge in view of the idealistic insistence on worldwide disarmament; it antagonized Communists who liked neither the Cachin letter nor the powerful excerpt-reprints of Arthur Koestler's exposé of Stalinist trials in his novel *Darkness at Noon*; and *Der Ruf*, with its recalcitrant attitudes, disturbed the military government. Pressures mounted against the continuation of this publication, so that in April 1947, with the seventeenth issue still in press, the publication's editors were put out of business because of their "untrustworthy criticism." Yet, given the independent temperament of its writers, *Der Ruf* could not have been less controversial than it was.

Much of the reportage and the fiction published in *Der Ruf* carried the same sociopolitical tone evident in the articles. By and large, they described the apathy of much of the public and the difficulties in turning away from a past which seemed better or no worse than the present. It may have been optimistic to expect too soon a profound rejection of the racial and ideological messages steadily propagated by the schools and mass media during the past thirteen years. Obviously literature can assist in the reorientation of readers by tone and example, without being propagandistic, but it was to take some time before such possibilities became realizable. In some instances, the theoretical and actual groundwork was poured for a postwar literature. Gustav René Hocke (b. 1908) combined the best features of academic and journalistic training in his incisive article "Deutsche Kalligraphie oder: Glanz und Elend der modernen Literatur" [German calligraphy or the glory and misery of modern literature] (*Der Ruf*, November 1946). He called for a new sensitivity to style and clarity of expression, a discarding of the aestheticized language and the subterfuges of those who went into an "inner migration" during the

Hitler years, a rejection of the endemic bureaucratese, newspaper and platform rhetoric of the old dictatorship; along with others of *Der Ruf* Hocke insisted on a new, honest, and realistic prose suited to the times. The turn to a realistic simplicity was made, but often the style and content of literature bore an uneasy, tentative, and groping relationship. Human miseries were recorded in sharp matter-of-fact style in stories, but in poems subjective feelings gave a tone of special pleading.

Richter had gathered poems by some thirty German POWs in a volume called *Deine Söhne, Europa* [Your sons, Europe] (1947), which exhibited the trend toward the new simplicity of style but also were shot through with unrestrained elegiac self-pity and recountings of the horrors visited upon Germans during the war and the deprivations endured in prison camps. If these poets or would-be poets could see no suffering other than their own and of those closely related to them, how could it be otherwise for a less articulate and equally self-preoccupied public? The old refrain appears:

We suffer hunger, hate, and scorn,
We and our nation
are put before a world court
and bear silently, with patience, the bills but not the guilt!
We were only soldiers.

Mourning for fallen comrades, trench digging, homesickness, tearful portraits of families, the daily waltz of death, war as a bloody lottery, survival, and depression are rendered with litanous tones. Only a few of the poems showed potential power. Wolfdietrich Schnurre (b. 1920) was capable of sketching disillusionment with simple strokes: "I know photos in which our fathers winked, / in battle-gray dress and gay, with flowers on their guns . . . / We followed in their steps but trod upon corpses." The only poet of reputation in the volume was Günter Eich (b. 1907), and he took a drastic departure from his earlier nature lyricism in several poems. One of them, "Inventur," "Inventory," became a manifesto poem for the new style:

> This is my cap
> this my coat,
> here my shaving stuff
> in a cloth bag. . . .

The poem goes on not only to inventory his possessions, pitifully small, but also to suggest a slow orientation to the present, a salvaging operation. The inventory technique was to become, with greater and excrutiating elaborateness, a part of German prose and poetry.

After his experience with *Der Ruf*, Richter thought of collaborating with a weekly, *Die Epoche,* but this fell through. Then, in July of 1947, he attended a meeting whose topic of discussion was "The Occupation of the Poet in his Time," sponsored by Stahlberg Publishers. The meeting opened in a well-ordered tea-party atmosphere but then turned into a battle royal between those who supported the belletristic function of literature and those who felt that it was a horror to speak of aesthetics when the time demanded revolutionary engagement on the part of writers; the split was deep. Nevertheless, Richter thought that gatherings where writers read and discussed their work had real possibilities if the participants had certain outlooks in common. Consequently, Richter called a meeting of his own early the following September at the home of Ilse Schneider-Lengyel, an essayist and poetess, in the Bavarian town of Allgau, inviting a small group consisting mostly of contributors to *Der Ruf* and to the poetry anthology which he had edited. The bohemian élan of the group was at no time higher than when members recruited a rickety vehicle, reeking of ersatz gasoline, and piled into it with their shabby suitcases, arriving at their Bavarian retreat grimy and bone-weary and stumbling nude into the sea and capering as if on a vacation. The reading and discussion sessions lasted into the morning hours and the discussants' exhilaration was as boundless as the critical exchanges were unsparing. No masterpieces were pulled out of the rucksacks, and discussions tended to stress content over formal qualities—the "what" transcended the "how." As a matter of record, Wolfdietrich Schnurre gave the first reading, and it was a vignette called "Das Begräbnis des lieben Gottes" [The burial of the dear God] in which a conglomerate of onlookers, gravediggers, and a priest bury God, an occurrence which seems not even to have merited publicity nor have caused any concern: "Loved by no one, hated by no one, today, after long and divine endurance of pain, died: God." The content conveys a totality of apathy by and within the world while sardonic realism and low-brow colloquial dialogues mark the narrative method. The reading was symptomatic of the attempts to do away with pathos and sentimentality, yet it fell into a piteous tone.

The group could hardly wait for its next session and this took place a few weeks later, November 8 and 9, in the city of Ulm. By that time, one of the oldest members of the assemblage, Hans Georg Brenner (1903–62), a translator of Sartre, had knighted it the "Group 47." From the start it was clear that the initiator Hans Werner Richter (whose name means "judge" and has received its share of puns) regarded the meetings, in his own words, as a private matter—a circle of friends and newcomers invited or dropped at his pleasure and conforming to the rules of reading and discussion which he laid down. That the meetings rarely ever became private in the strictest sense is accounted for by the growing presence of outside publicists. Of course, as the attendance at meetings became swollen, there could no longer be assurances of all simply being friends, a euphemism at best. One of the purposes of the Ulm meeting was to discuss a satirical periodical appropriately called *Skorpion*, which would serve as the amplifier for opinions and writings of Group 47. Richter had assembled and printed a trial issue, at his own cost, during the previous summer. As it turned out, the issue slated for publication in 1948 never materialized because the American military government of Bavaria (called by many of the group an occupation dictatorship, *Besetzdiktatur*) thought the publication "nihilistic" and, anticipating its sting, put up obstacles to obtaining a publication license. Even with the removal of such obstacles, group members felt that the current economic situation would have made attempts at publication impracticable.

Although Richter's statement, during an interview, about the characteristics of the "new literature" applied to the contents of the projected *Skorpion*, it held equally true of the literary intent of the writings presented at meetings during the first several years:

> All signs attest to a new language which will be realistic. For the most part, the young generation has still not recovered from the enormous shock of the last years and has withdrawn into an imaginary, romantic world. One example of this is the growing number of lyricists. They still live in another era and their models are Rilke, George, Heyse, Alverdes, and others.

Richter never was to have much of an ear for poetry, but as for prose he insisted on a spontaneous and unambiguous style which prunes away tricks and decorativeness and avoids imitation of earlier German authors. He saw the need for creating a "magical realism," starting from the ABCs of prose and ignoring the criticism and ridicule of snobs. He found a perfect designation for this bare prose in Wolfgang Weyrauch's word *Kahlschlag*, a ruthless and pioneerlike clearing of language thickets. For years, a great deal of crudeness in the readings of the group was mere affectation growing out of the new style. Yet this style was hardly new; it resembled some of the work of the realists and naturalists like Max Kretzer, Arno Holz, and Johannes Schlaf, who explored the depths of misery in which industrial workers were caught in the 1880s and nineties and whose writings nearly have vanished into obscurity; it resembled also the expressionists' pathos revived by Wolfgang Borchert in 1947. More important, however, was the sure transition from the political journalism of *Der Ruf*—without loss of socialistic ideologies —to the diversity of literary genres (short stories, novels, dramas, poetry, essays). Interest centered mainly on the immediate present while, for the most part, any deep probing of the problematic past was avoided. Matter-of-factness and ridicule seemed to be surgical-literary methods. It was some time before writers of the group regained absolute trust in

the lyric instinct and sentiment. Some outside critics regarded the literary activities of the group as regressive rather
than progressive in matters of style and content, and only
infrequently did some experimentation break through to
suggest the possibilities of other directions. The charge of
literary provincialism was not entirely unfounded.

Quite rapidly the format of the meetings—and their rituals
—took shape. Richter originally wished to recruit a democratic élite in the realm of literature and journalism in order
to have, in widening circles, some mass effect; these objectives were to be gained without programmed meetings or a
dues-paying organization and without encouraging collective
thinking. The meetings were to give unpublished and published members of the younger generation an opportunity
to demonstrate their talents. It was understood that those
who were invited—by postcards—to meetings were anti-
Fascists, anti-militarists, politically liberal or leftist-inclined
but not toward the extreme of communistic Stalinism. Most
of those invited during the early years shared the common
experience of war as soldiers of lowly rank; officers were sus-
pected of having worked too hard for the cause. The invita-
tional process was to give the group internal flexibility, to
encourage talent, to discourage dilettantism and commercial
writing, and to attract new blood which would give the
group vitality and currency. Since the group had no publications organ, it offered instead a visible forum for scouts from
all media and an opportunity for fledgling authors, with
some toughness, to try their fortunes in what was to become
a literary stock exchange. One critic of the group estimated
that nine out of ten novitiates failed to gain approval for
entrance into the holy—or as some have dubbed it, unholy—
order. Richter admitted that criticism during the early stages
was somewhat uncivilized and too blunt; it was a reaction to
the repression of all criticism during the Hitler years. As a
result, novelists like Luise Rinser and Rudolf Krämer-Badoni
packed their bags in 1950 and left the group. Rinser became
a writer of best sellers bordering on soap operas, and Krämer-
Badoni a free-lance writer and a vocal, as well as bitter, anti—
Group 47 critic. Publicity, whether good or bad, through all

the media proved to be of invaluable assistance in giving group meetings an aura of newsworthy cultural events.

Even some of Richter's readings received harsh treatment: "In the early years listeners who did not wish the reading to continue turned their thumbs down. At that point, the leader of the meeting had to interrupt the reader and send him back to his seat. He fell through. It was completely immaterial if the reader was a friend, an acquaintance, someone of prominence, an unknown person, or the founder of Group 47." However, Richter pointed out that whoever "could take the sharpest and most devastating criticism without showing an emotional reaction, he could be invited again, certainly," and try anew. The ritual, I think, bore resemblances to that of the university student duels, popular though outlawed, which gave evidence of manliness through physical scars; the group-inflicted scars were psychic. How many new writers were discouraged from continuing is not known, but the number of works by known writers who were dissuaded from inflicting some of their work upon the public is a matter of record.

One device for educating and exhibiting authors who read from their work during group sessions was the "electric chair," a jocular or diabolic designation, depending upon whether one was in or out of it. Nearby would sit the group guardian, Richter, who sized up the mood of the audience or followed his own. At any time he might interrupt the reader in a curt, collective voice to say that the group had heard quite enough. If he was lucky, the reader would be allowed to finish his selection, on the average twenty to thirty minutes with exceptions made for the more prominent members of the group, and then discussion would ensue. In any case, the reader was expected to retain *Haltung,* poise or equanimity, and to listen silently to favorable or unfavorable criticism. Whatever indignation or elation he felt would have to be repressed. Stoic martyrdom or silent suffering had to be learned. From 1947 to 1968, more than two hundred authors submitted themselves to this Prussian ritual and more than a hundred critics and guests, mostly from the mass media, had ringside seats; the guests included persons from many European countries. Through 1955 the group met almost regularly twice a year and then once a year. Three meetings were held outside of Germany in Italy, Sweden, the United States, and one had to be cancelled in Czechoslovakia when the Russians arrived there first in 1968; since then full-scale meetings have been in abeyance.

During the first years, criticism was a rough-and-tumble affair as assorted voices rose from the floor. Gradually, however, a phalanx of professional and sophisticated critics — journalistic and academic — stepped into the jury box during the fifties: Walter Jens (1950), Joachim Kaiser (1953), Marcel Reich-Ranicki (1958), Walter Höllerer (1959), and Hans Mayer (1959) — there was no higher court of appeals for redress of instant judgment. The sureness of judgment and computerlike critical reaction of the phalanx is astonishing given the difficulty of following the oral reading of a text whether it is poetry or prose, whether the reading is distinct or mumbled, dramatic or nervously pedestrian. Does indeed the quality of the text unfold to the ear? The question had been debated and is debatable. Only a few poets of the first rank have been able to do justice to their own work by reading from it; certainly neither T. S. Eliot nor Robert Lowell could do the same. Recorded readings of Group 47 poets — ranging from the bellowing of Erich Fried to the subdued renderings of Johannes Bobrowski — also leave much to be desired. Prose and narrative are somewhat easier to manage because the exposition is easier and the language rarely ambiguous. It also seems to me that the out-loud reading of fiction generally tends to inhibit the reader, which may have some virtues. It also may account for the fact that for the most part it has the somewhat puritanical effect of not only purging eroticism, sexuality, coyness, and gross vulgarities from the texts but also discouraging psychologically delicate and emotional explorations. Nevertheless, reading, criticism, and discussion remained the ritual for novices and the stars of the group.

A saving grace of the group has been the ability of members, including Richter, to satirize the proceedings. However, the novelist and dramatist Martin Walser, who in

1955 was awarded one of the few group prizes, went beyond
satire in 1964 and called for a sweeping democratization of
the rituals and opening the doors to all comers by way of a
preliminary jury-screening; he felt that Group 47 had become a power-hungry literary monopoly. Of course, his suggestions went unheeded. A year later in his "Brief an einen
ganz jungen Autor" [Letter to a very young author] he gave
indirect evidence that his own recovery from group criticism
was never complete. Walser advised the eager and young
author to write to Richter, Jens, or Höllerer and to subtly
note that he has read all the writings of the addressee.
Further injunctions were listed: expect to be ignored as a
newcomer, demur at being among the first to read, affect
humility, anticipate the group's inattentiveness and door-
banging at your reading, be prepared for any eventuality,
count on the trained concentration of the critics who will
listen as might an off-duty detective who involuntarily overhears what is said. He had gone even further at a group
meeting in 1961, when tolerance ran low at two o'clock in
the morning, to characterize all critics as *Lumpenhunde*,
scoundrels. Walser's caricatures of the critics, however, do
capture some of their salient features. To wit, Höllerer
quickly carves up the reading into small specimens as if for
microscope analysis and discovers typical sentences which
are further dissected until they satisfy his "microscopic
view." He grumbles, may burst into sudden laughter which
frightens the novitiate, and as a "grower of cultures" he may
give the reader the impression that he is viewed as a new
form of bacteria or disease. Then Jens, as if he were ap-
proaching a spiny lobster, will handle the reading gingerly
and weigh and probe it. He is concerned with measuring
readings and assessing the reader's possible place in the
Valhalla of contemporary literature. When the work is
sweepingly labelled, then Kaiser slowly rises to the task and
with elegiac cadences, sighs, and empathic suffering will expose the reading for what it is, gently censuring writing
which he himself would have been capable of. In contrast,
Reich-Ranicki does not let a moment pass in silence and
with rapid-fire strokes repeats the executions visited upon the

reading by his fellow critics and applies ideas which had already been conceived before the reading even began. Reich-Ranicki, born in 1920 in Poland, resided in Berlin until 1938 and then in Poland where as a Jew he was shunted to the Warsaw Ghetto; he returned to West Germany in 1958. Somewhat ungallantly and exceeding the limits of satire and taste, Walser intimates that Reich-Ranicki has homesickness for the Eastern spiritual environment from which he came. Obviously, Reich-Ranicki did not belong to the exclusive club of the German homefaring soldiers. The same treatment is accorded Hans Mayer who went into exile in France and Switzerland during the Third Reich and later became a professor at the Leipzig University in East Germany until 1963 when he moved West; Mayer made his first guest-critic appearance at the 1959 group meeting. Walser calls Mayer's critical expressions ballistic hyperboles and "assuredly the most beautiful foreign language in the fatherland." If someone in the audience defends the reader, it gives the "provoked but eager-to-answer" critics an opportunity to go at it again. Sarcastically, Walser suggested that the author prepare a musical-text-for-listening: "It may not turn out to be bad literature." Intended is a sly dig at Kaiser who is a music critic as well.

What Jens said about the group also applies to its own corps of critics, namely, that instead of unity it is "the sum of disharmonies which characterizes Group 47." All the critics have an unimpeachable integrity and in their written reviews of books or performed dramas of writers identified with Group 47 it is hardly possible to detect favoritism or nepotism. In some cases their critiques of group members have been harsher than those of outside critics and their judgments differ more than they coincide. Their assumption is that if an author is worth writing about, he should be able to take it. However, I have the feeling that if the author's ideology is congenial, attempts are made to separate content from method and not to run the author's reputation into the ground. Of course, each of the critics has his own vocabulary and approach, despite the similarity of their social ideas and sympathies. A university professor who also has held visiting professorships in the United States and a lyrical poet as well, Höllerer develops the principle of a basic discrepancy between "the world" and "the I," effecting a counterplay, *Widerspiel,* so that the author's work becomes the "bridge" between the two as well as between "conscious-ness and vital feeling": "the bridge springs under your foot-steps." Jens is a professor of classical philology and a novel-ist, radio playwright, and adapter of Greek plays. His critical method, perhaps because of academic training, is analytical rather than prescriptive; of himself and others he demands meticulousness and elegance of style; he advises the writer to work intensely and well within a small compass, to use a pocket mirror rather than a giant telescope to reflect his observations, and to learn modernity from the unpoetically sparse diction of Kafka rather than the monumentality of word and lyric associations of Broch or the imitation-com-pendia of the so-called realists. By temperament he is moral-istic and pacifistic. One of his aims is to identify books with international potential.

Kaiser, like Höllerer, Mayer, and Jens, has doctoral cre-dentials and is a regular literary and music critic for the prestigious *Süddeutsche Zeitung;* he wields an academic style of precise analysis without journalistic cleverness or frills. It took Richter a while to become accustomed to Kaiser's cautious style, but I think that most members of the group approved of his high seriousness. He warned in a news report in 1957 that the group was engaging in fun sessions when it allowed too much time to the stars who read from published works which admitted no change rather than fulfilling the group's function of presenting young and un-known authors to the public. In contrast to his colleagues, Reich-Ranicki is a pyrotechnical phenomenon and probably one of the best instant critics I have seen anywhere. De-spite his avowed moralistic and educative intent and in-sistence that literature must foster a cultural democracy and have sociological relevance, he is the most widely read critic in the mass media. Some note facetiously that he has a sparse and thin broomstick style; he does quite brusquely sweep away what he disagrees with. He is the most polemical of the critics and many of his arguments are incisive and colorful within a logical and lawyerlike presentation. Peter Handke, the latest of the no-longer-young angry men, bitterly rejects Reich-Ranicki's measuring the newest literature by the criteria of naturalness or faithfulness to life, and he labels the critiques as no more than formulas and communiques. The most imposing of the group's critics is the literary historian Hans Mayer, a Marxist, much of whose somewhat cerebral criticism reaches only a special audience interested in socioliterary discussion. He is not bound, as are Kaiser and Reich-Ranicki, to act as a middleman between writer and public or to act as a simplifying interpreter. Among the more aggressive writers of the group, some have chosen to double as essayistic critics and like Helmut Heissenbüttel see it necessary to rid criticism of doctrinaire ideology if criticism and literature are to be effective in rehumanizing society.

Many writers have an inbuilt critical apparatus, which even the sharp group critics were only able to tamper with slightly given the limitations of the reading system and the oral critiques. At best these critiques were able to point to faults and merits by way of sweeping generalities or the dissection of "typical" sentences from the readings. Of course, the critics and audience could discourage, encourage, or kill with apathy any of the readers, but this was also true of published works. In an open society any programmatic intent by critics, if there were the unlikely possibility of critical unanimity, results at best in short-term trends. The changes in social, economic, and political climates, audience tastes, contact with other literatures, the individuality of writers, and conflicts among critics, all contribute to a renewing dynamics of literature. For the most part, Group 47 author-readers themselves pointed to new directions. During the initial postwar phase, one could easily discern a dominance of expressionistic modes, the realistic *Kahlschlag* prose, existential stylizations, the idea of art for man's rather than art's sake, the stress on social content, and other features arising out of the so-called *Trümmerliteratur*, the literature reflecting the ruins of war; the influence of Thornton Wilder and Hemingway was especially pronounced. One foreign visitor to the 1951 group session remarked that the younger authors were trying to catch a train which had departed twenty years earlier. During the early fifties, tentatively but surely, horizons broadened. The deep mistrust of words, slogans, and their values—such as love, honor, duty—which had been corrupted during the Third Reich, gave way to a more confident expression of emotions. With the aid of French, English, and American literature—as well as the discovery mainly of Joyce, Kafka, and Faulkner—it was possible to explore the literature of antirealism, the language of lyricism, surrealism, and to adopt aesthetic means without necessarily losing sight of social purpose. In the sixties, trends became even more diffuse, flowing mainly into two channels: politically active literature, more intense than ever since the end of the war, and avant-gardism which created hybrid forms of literature and aimed a massive assault upon every literary tradition.

In 1948 several German writers, some of whom had cast their lot with the Eastern sector in the hopes of a better political and social future, went to Moscow to receive the gospel of socialist realism. During a conference Alexander A. Fadejew told Anna Seghers and other delegates that Stalin regarded writers as "the engineers of the human soul." Fadejew saw it the task of the writer to educate the reader for the future and to view today's reality as a revolutionary development toward it. He extolled Balzac as the model of a realist who showed a capitalistic society in such hateful terms that the reader is caught up in the same emotion and understands that the future cannot be in the direction of such a system. Socialist literature has its humanistic or romantic aspects in that it gives preference to ideal relationships of ideal people, extols the virtues of work, and aims to change life through literature. Through the years, Walter Ulbricht, the late party boss of East Germany, continually exhorted the engineers of the human soul to assist the workers, farmers, and other working people in storming the heights of a socialist, nationalist culture and vanquishing capitalist ideologies and bourgeois habits. The problem of writing primarily for the revolutionary proletariat was formidable and the possibilities of creating anything resembling literature rather than propaganda was limited. Soon a number of writers who were unequal to the rigorous assignment left for the West while others unsuccessfully tried to mitigate bureaucratic policies; they nursed their disillusionments privately, rationalizing that the East, ideologically, was still better than the West. Some who objected to censorship were prohibited from publishing. Even distinguished Marxist critics such as Georg Lukács and Hans Mayer were harshly chastised for undialectical and revisionist attitudes toward socialist realism. In every conceivable way Group 47 tried to keep contact alive with East German writers by hosting them at meetings whenever the Ulbricht regime allowed a short leave of absence, holding small and impromptu discussion sessions with selected members from both sides, and encouraging open-letter exchanges on vital political issues. Although their social and political sympathies were similar, the physical gulf between them remained deep and the vocabulary of East German dogma grew more impenetrable and militant.

If the agreement on political matters between writers and government in East Germany was relatively greater than that in West Germany, it emphasized the ambivalent position of many Group 47 writers. *Der Ruf* subscribed to the myth of a revolutionary working class which could be led in a socialist direction, an idea which faded with the rapid economic strides and subsequent affluence of West Germany, yet the desire remained—and emerged with intensity in the sixties—to change the conservative political structure. Politics demands undivided attention and unrelenting activity as well as energies which writers struggling to make ends meet could not divert from their work. Perhaps the most damning analysis of the naïveté of the nonconformist who typified Group 47 during the fifties was made by the poet and critic Hans Egon Holthusen:

He himself wishes to be effective politically, he wants political influence, and that means he wishes power; yes, to a certain extent he already enjoys it in that he uses the so-called mass media and has at his disposal newspaper columns, air time, lecture halls, and the patience of book readers. At the same time he retreats from power. With a hysteric mixture of fear, hate, and desire he eavesdrops on power and is ever ready to denounce it as an enemy of the spirit and as immoral, not only power specifically but in general. He finds himself in the soulful condition of a *demi-vierge*, a half-virgin, known in erotic terminology as the most unappetizing thing in existence.

The last sentence is an example of the no-holds-barred polemical attacks and counterattacks between outside critics and Group 47; the acrimony is earnest but it also gives both parties much-desired publicity, a convertible currency. Holthusen points to the nonconformist's understandable fear and remembrance of the Third Reich, yet he proposes that power need not be evil if it is used in defense of civil and national freedoms and as a counterweight to the consolidating imperialism of Bolshevism. Holthusen posed such issues in 1960, and with many ramifications it became a crucial and on-going debate between pacifists who wanted a geographically neutral Germany and advocators of power-balance politics with the formation of political-military alliances. Holthusen pointed to Günter Eich's Büchner-Prize acceptance speech in 1959, in which Eich called for an active nonconformism and exhorted writers to employ criticism, opposition, resistance, and challenge to power, otherwise "we decorate the slaughterhouse with geraniums." Holthusen accuses the intellectuals of not really wanting to play active politics and even of ignoring Marx's injunction that social life is basically practical. Indeed, nonconformism and practicality rarely went hand in hand in the life of German intellectuals. In the twenties Bertolt Brecht exhorted the intellectual comrade to "join the Workers United Front, for you are a worker too." They dreamed of storming to victory waving huge red banners, inspired by the cinema of Eisenstein and Pudovkin, Gorky's socialist realism, Erwin Piscator's stagings and Brecht's plays, and Hans Eisler's songs; they proclaimed working-class solidarity but split the various movements wide open through tactical and factional differences. The German Communist party attacked the Social Democrats as the main pillars of the bourgeoisie and joined the Nazis in undermining the Weimar Republic in the expectation that out of the resulting chaos Communists would emerge triumphant. The general disillusionment of the Left was evident in the postwar attempt by writers for *Der Ruf* to chart a new socialist way. But except for the slow-developing trade-union movement there seemed to be no formulation of practical goals.

It must be said clearly that Richter kept programmatic politics out of the group's socioliterary discussions. Those group members who felt inhibited could initiate independent publications such as Hans Magnus Enzensberger's *Kursbuch*. Political protest letters and resolutions were signed by individuals and not by group acclamation, by voluntary and not coercive means; the protests were given weight by the reputation of the signers. The examples are numerous: declaration of indignation against the Soviet military rape of Hungary in 1956, the Anglo-French Suez venture, intentions of atomic armaments for the German army, the French war in Algeria, attempts by the government to encroach on the freedom of television presentations and the press, the American intervention in the Vietnam civil war, Arab threats against the existence of Israel in 1967; they charged some of the press with whipping up public hysteria which resulted in the police slaying of a student demonstrator, Benno Ohnesorg. Many Group 47 authors and critics took similar steps to protest the Soviet military intervention in Czechoslovakia. On the other hand, the left radical mass-circulation magazine *konkret* echoed the Soviet line and excoriated Czech attempts to emulate Western liberalism; it is ironic that *konkret* would deny the Czech socialists the very freedom it enjoys in a so-called bourgeois-capitalist reactionary society. Klaus R. Röhl, editor and publisher of *konkret*, had been a guest at Group 47 sessions, and a number of the group authors—including Peter Rühmkorf, Hubert Fichte, Alexander Kluge, Günter Herburger, Günter Grass, Heinrich Böll, Peter Handke, and Richter—were occasional contributors. There was little difference, however, between Röhl's

bitter ridicule—in print—of the group's liberal wing and the
attitude toward the group by reactionary government officials. Röhl elevates to political sainthood the revolutionary
conclave of Mao, Minh, Castro, Che Guevara, and he is a
cheerleader for terrorists, guerillas—from South America to
the Middle East; but he does not feel comfortable about
encouraging such movements in Germany, especially since
his ex-wife Ulrike Meinhof tried to annihilate his publication and later became implicated in criminal terrorist activities. Terror may be good for others but not for Röhl's
neighborhood and establishment. The phenomenon of a
radical publication achieving mass circulation is attributable
to its special formula: prolix nudity, low-brow erotica and
pornography, sensational and sadomasochistic photo journalism; occasional articles and polemics by name authors
supply a pseudocultural veneer. A reading of several issues is
likely to give any foreigner the moral impression that West
Germany is the sump hole of the world.

The political spectrum within the fluctuating periphery of
Group 47 ranges from the liberal to the ultraleftist, and their
political commitments vary accordingly. In general the separation between their essayistic-political writings and their
literary work does not prevent a mutual coloring, but this is
at a minimum when compared with the fiction of Malraux,
Koestler, or Silone. These writers of memorable political
novels were themselves caught up actively in the maelstrom
of their time and had been able to render the tone and dimensions of totalitarianism of the Left and the Right, as
well as the politically colorless masses who were pliable,
sullen, or acquiescent; the experiences of these novelists sat
deep in the marrow of their bones. Unlike them, the early
Group 47 writers could not make literature out of the tension between frustrated political hopes and realities; their
disenchantments, by comparison, were played out in a sand-
box; their concerns seemed self-centered and piteous while
their attacks on the early economic miracle and the conservative, political parliamentarianism (undiscriminatingly
called "restoration") as a cause for people's failure to re-
generate in a moral and political sense seemed peevish.

Moral regeneration rather than lip service to democracy seems to be an elusive process in German life, but many writers associated with Group 47 fought hard to set it in motion. The problem, however, is not an exclusively German one.

To come back for a moment to some of Holthusen's criticism of Group 47, it is hard to disprove that some writing, especially the polemical poetry, seems not to joyously praise total anarchy. True, there are streaks of political infantilism in the group. Holthusen in 1960 also threw cold water on facile comparisons between the German literary rebels, particularly the younger ones, and the American beatniks and the English angry young men, although all share tendentiousness. He notes that the German situation is more complicated because "all of us have to drag with us a political inheritance with which, in all honesty, we cannot appear before the eyes of others. The exhaust gas of a national plunge into hell still poisons the air, oppressive taboos clog the flow of open discussion—a form of self-imposed regulation of speech is not infrequent. How much dishonesty, how much concealed resentment and hidden hysteria on all sides." It is a perceptive and admonitory comment on a significant segment of German social, political, and literary thinking. Yet, I think that Holthusen overshoots the mark with his suggestion that unless writers become politicians, politics be left to the politicians who have proven themselves capable of handling power; he ignores the potential corruptiveness of power and the concomitant arrogance of office. The large body of German civil servants proved capable of serving any system—Fascist or democratic—with equal enthusiasm, as exemplified by some of its senior people, like the expounder of Nazi racism Dr. Hans Globke who was allowed to rise to high position in the Chancellor's Office in Bonn. The number of ex-Nazis in governmental service is even larger in East Germany, though nominally they have been retreaded by the Communist mill. All this has not enhanced the image of the politicians in the eyes of the Group 47 writers in particular. All serious literature is "engaged" literature, one way or another, and most Group 47 authors have increasingly concerned themselves with enlarging the opportunities for participating in the determination of who is to exercise political power and where it is to lead. The dangers to democracy are ever present from the extremes of the Right and the Left, overanxious threats of government actions against the press, provincial accents on patriotism, police powers, the dangerous swings of labor and the *petite bourgeoisie*. Group 47 writers cannot help but be sensitive to such societal affairs; they may exacerbate or meliorate, depress or encourage, aggressively or subtly express their values through the images created by literature; whatever their view or tone—loud or whispered, polemical or lyrical—it is amplified and made public through the mass media. Their literature is varied. Frequently it is rich descriptively and anemic ideologically, and even provocative in the rejection of ideology or in the portraying of a milieu without political thought; it is cantankerous, often evasive, exploratory mainly in a technical sense, illuminative and obfuscatory, oppositional and nonconformist in respect to the establishment, self-lacerating and self-assertive. The relation of ideology and aesthetic form has been much debated within Group 47 sessions, and the ideal relationship has not been persuasively demonstrated by any of its writers. In discussing their literature, one can only talk of approximations. The social and political aims declared through *Der Ruf* and periodically implied through discussions and polemics have not been achieved; neither a program nor an ideological and aesthetic rationale has ever been worked out; the question of mastering the past never was put in focus—it was overshadowed by concern for the present. In short, here are some reasons for a literature that speaks radically about frustrations and very little of hope. It would have taken a Dostoevsky to measure and delineate the amorphousness and normality of evil, the everyday inurement to evil by the mass of German society during the Third Reich, and the discontents and discomforts, morally and intellectually, of the present. The inheritance, of which Holthusen wrote, still disturbs but it has neither been totally confronted nor mastered in German postwar literature.

Economics, and often a consciousness of world image,

rather than culture as fostered through the arts, has dominated modern German life. The catastrophic unemployment picture during the early thirties contributed to the rise of the Nazis, while the recession of the mid-sixties coupled with the radicalization of students resulted in a backlash and a strong resurfacing of the neo-Fascist National Democratic Party. Whether this trend ebbed because the world expressed its alarm and the German public redressed its image or because economic measures deflated the situation, the message is somewhat depressing. Politics and economics have power value while culture gives the veneer of prestige despite its essential impotence. While some writers associated with Group 47 have achieved international visibility, and along with the reputation of the musical arts, have given Germany renewed cultural status, these same writers because of their sociopolitical views are barely tolerated by those who tend to gain most from the fostered image. To what extent their oppositional stance is, or will be, fruitful can only be tangentially indicated, but their work and thinking, their motifs and motives, do reveal the dynamics of the literature which they have created.

2

Fiction
The Normality of Schizophrenia

In an article which appeared in the September 1946 issue of *Der Ruf*, Hans Werner Richter reproached the older generation of German writers, mainly those who had ostensibly withdrawn themselves through foreign exile or inner migration, for wrapping themselves in a cloud of penitential incense and for their "self-satisfied professorial" attitude which disallowed the possibility that the young generation possessed any "spiritual and moral capacity." The silence of the younger generation stems from the feeling, he noted, "that the discrepancy between a threatened human existence and the tranquil problematics of the older generation, which is emerging from its twelve-year Olympian silence, is too great to be bridgeable"; the inherited picture of man has irrevocably been destroyed. Further, it would be paradoxical to attempt a continuity with 1933 "when the older generation left its continuable development track to capitulate to an irrational adventure"; the only possibility for a spiritual rebirth lies in an absolute and radical new beginning. Particularly in the literature which was to come from writers associated with Group 47 this plaint became fully orchestrated with innumerable variations; the older generation became the scapegoat for all sins. This also became a useful rationale for sweeping aside a whole host of problems and assuming that one could start with a clean slate or from "point zero," with few debts or liabilities. Richter offered attractive rallying points for young writers, including the seductive idea of an elite group. At first, it was guided by political thinkers (who may have been young in spirit but like Richter hovered near the age of forty), then its composition changed. Group 47 was cohesive partially because of the general exclusion of the older writers and critics; and its sense of alienation, iconoclasm, and high-spiritedness quickly communicated itself to the older writers. Thomas Mann groused that the reported behavior of participants at Group 47 meetings sounded unbelievably moblike and that they were a group of rowdies. It seems to me that much of the early Group 47 productions were barren until the literature burned or banished during the Third Reich and the availability of foreign literary riches provided a source for orientation.

There was no disagreement among the group members during the first several years that language inherited from the Third Reich and its "dictionary of monsters" had to be cleansed, almost to be denazified word for word, in order to achieve a new clarity, solidity, and sobriety. Yet the harsh, verbally aggressive, diffuse, and hyperbolic style of the writings for *Der Ruf* fell far short of being *Kahlschlag,* denuded prose or deforested language, because the defensively argumentative tone discouraged equilibrium of language. I would venture to disagree with much that has been written about postwar language, including the touted thesis that evil lurks in the German language itself, and to stress instead that language is the expressive medium through which intent and ideas are projected. The coincidence of a pure style and humaneness of thought, whether in prose or poetry, is of course an ideal. The deep postwar distrust of language— and words associated with the barbarities of the immediate past—at first led to certain prose-style artificialities typified by some of Wolfdietrich Schnurre's early fiction. The duration of the *Kahlschlag* was mercifully brief as it became stranded in neorealism of which Richter was one of the best representatives.

Like other participants, Richter too on occasions sat in the group's electric chair while reading from his works and received no greater amenities than anyone else; this is contrary to what one might expect when warned by Group 47 enemies that he is a group-boss, Mafia chieftain, Pope, chief judge, *maître de plaisir*. In any case, while the group could encourage, discourage, and publicize its authors, the public was the ultimate arbiter. Through five novels Richter made a name for himself during the fifties. Common to his novels were the reporting techniques, photographic realism, pointed and representational dialogue, all of which shunned aesthetic means or moralizing commentary and resembled documentary and social journalism. His first novel *Die Geschlagenen* [The defeated] (1949; *The Odds against Us*, 1950) recounts in biographical detail his experience during the Italian campaign and in American prison camps. The history of what became of a German concentration camp and its successive inhabitants from 1939 and into the postwar years—political prisoners, foreign laborers, assorted victims, ex-storm troopers, displaced persons—is given panoramic treatment, with no medals for anyone's behavior in the camp cauldron, in Richter's second novel *Sie fielen aus Gottes Hand* (1951; *They Fell from God's Hand*, 1956). While the first novel gained the Fontane-Prize of the city of Berlin and the approval of French critics for its pictorialization of the human condition, the second raised a bit of controversy in Germany. Side blows were aimed at Group 47. After considerable hesitation Thomas Mann joined others on a literary jury panel in awarding a substantial monetary prize to *They Fell*, with the citation that the author is "the voice of a person who does not abandon those who have been abandoned by God." Mann felt that the novel lacked artistic construction and that it was permeated by a disturbing moral equalization, a *Gleichmacherei*. The conservative German Academy for Language and Letters (*Deutsche Akademie für Sprache und Dichtung*) thought the novel to be without depth or art, "plain photo montage," and went beyond its author to attack Group 47 as reporters to whom art is an abomination, as traditionless tatterdermalion realists with no language except countryside jargon. Such attacks however did not prevent the academy later from crowning with distinction some writers who had first been discovered by Group 47 and brought to public attention through its forum. Some of the criticism simply verified what Richter had wanted to accomplish, namely, the introduction of plain truth through a plain style which would strip away the orgy of illusions of the past and lead to a sober and realistic appraisal of the present. Whether or not simplified truth is indeed truthful is another question. The literary historian Herbert Lehnert feels that Richter's work served an enlightening pedagogical function by showing a large cast of various Europeans and their fate during the war years without shirking the portrayals of the displaced and the foreign refugees unpopular in Germany at the time. Beyond that, one might note also the psychological satisfaction found by German readers in realistic fiction which showed no differentiation in the moral behavior of all concerned; the *Gleichmacherei*, which Mann shrewdly noted, became a favorite attitude imparted to fiction by many of Germany's novelists. It insured the realists, especially, a favorable public and allowed them to skirt the difficulty of reconciling emotionality and art, and at the same time to appear truthful.

Alfred Andersch (b. 1914), one of Richter's oldest co-workers and a consistent participant in Group 47 affairs, sensitively adapted the realistic style of reportage to literary-political fiction, a feat helped probably by his professional writing of radio features and plays since 1948. The theme of flight in his personal life and in his writings has been pointed to frequently, but his "flight" is rooted in existential decisions and a profound search for freedom and a self-determined life. He broke away from a home environment stifled by ultranationalism, joined the Communist party in Bavaria from 1931 to 1933 and withdrew from it though he had become a functionary, deserted from the German army in 1944 during its defeat in Italy, became a POW, then a journalist, radio editor, and an associate of Richter on *Der Ruf* and in Group 47. Since 1958, he has decided to free-lance and to live, with his large family, in a stone house lodged in a Swiss mountain retreat near Locarno. Rather than instinctive rebellion against authority and establishment—secular, religious, political—it was a probing discontent that shaped his decisions as well as fortunate escapes from potential disasters.

Large publishers often have both eyes on the public so

that Andersch's fledgling book *Die Kirschen der Freiheit* [The cherries of freedom] (1952), which dealt with the raw issue of military desertion ("flight from the flag" as it is called literally in German), first saw the light of day through a small publishing house. The work deserves a respectable place among the political and human confessions of modern writers who saw communism as the God that failed; it has importance as a document and as an interpretation of public events and private actions. There are many impressive autobiographical moments. In the streets of Munich during March 1933, he witnessed Hitler, "the canal rat," and a column of cohorts on parade and impotently reflected that this could have been "the precise time for an insurrection which would perhaps have given Germany another face"; but the international Communist central committee, for its own tactical reasons, did not give the signal for action by the about two thousand indoctrinated Bavarian Communists. For Andersch the party, and its revolutionary purpose, died lastly because it "denied the idea of free will, the freedom of human thought, the capacity of human beings to choose"; instead, it demanded submission to the terror of dogma. "We," wrote Andersch, "were the victims of a determinist philosophy." The revolutionary ideals died not because of opposition from the outside but because of calculated inertia within the international party, and this became the source of Andersch's disillusionment. For his known Communist affiliations, Andersch twice was thrown into the Dachau concentration camp and only through his mother's insistent intercession with the Gestapo, on the grounds that her husband was a war veteran crippled in the service of his country, was he released. The naked fear Andersch experienced and the scenes of cynical brutality visited upon other inmates are rapidly sketched in a section called "Verschüttetes Bier" [Spilt beer], which he incorporated later into a short story, "Drei Phasen," "Three Phases." The smooth transposition from the autobiographical to fictional narration tells much about his style which fuses clear reporting and intimate introspection. For a time after Dachau, he escaped from his surroundings by preoccupation with art and literature, and "emigration out of history. . . . I answered the total state with a total introversion." Art, he felt, should not be typified through guitar-playing muses or pinup girls who were the inspirations of writers in the belletristic and aesthetic modes; the muses are symbols and substitutes for reality. As a writer, Andersch feels uncomfortable with the philosophical approach or with symbolism and thinks it his task "to write about people because I must describe my own fear." Perhaps the "description of emotion" is one way of characterizing Andersch's principal technique.

The complexity of his emotions which led to his desertion from the German army is starkly reduced to the propositions that he did not wish to die senselessly in the face of imminent defeat, that the troops he was with followed a herd instinct and had an unusual and repulsive appetite for battle, and that the enemy across the indistinct lines was no enemy. He was impelled by the lust for freedom, that is, "a being alone with God or with nothingness." Though he left the Lutheran church, he wrote paradoxically, "though I do not even know with certainty that God exists, I have always prayed to him," and he wished to push aside anything which stood between God, or the idea of God, and himself. This was not a question of "fox hole religion" but an existential expression of freedom: one is never free while fighting a predetermined fate but only through living for that moment of freedom which comes when one allows oneself to fall out of the hands of fate. Passive resistance, timely action, and good or bad fortune are sequences played out in all of Andersch's fiction and are reflective of his own life. As in almost all political fiction, the author is his own source of experience and is its hero.

While he was working on his first novel, *Sansibar oder der letzte Grund* [Zanzibar or the ultimate reason] (1957; *Flight to Afar*, 1958), a Swiss publisher inquired about his fiction-writing plans; German publishers apparently lacked nerve which they regained after *Sansibar* went into innumerable editions. Andersch amply realized his intentions of writing a story with alternating shifts of perspective and simultaneous handling of characters; the result is so translucent that some

critics have snubbed the novel for the simplicity of its construction. Yet the simplicity results from an artistic integration of variably suited linguistic devices and themes and a
perfect synchronization of diverse actions. On the barest
story level, five characters interact for different reasons in
their quest for freedom in 1938 at a small German fishing
village which is two seafaring days from Sweden: Judith, a
young Jewish girl seeks clandestine passage to Sweden; Pastor Helander wishes a statue from his church to be sent to
safety; the roving Communist underground man Gregor is
about the desert the party for the same reasons that Andersch actually did—and to seek his *own* mission; Knudsen
is a fisherman and a disillusioned party member who would
flee except for the bond with his deranged and helpless wife
—he is hooked like a flaccid fish; and, there is his young apprentice who wanted to taste the adventure of freedom—because freedom, the ultimate reason, simply *exists*. The power
exerted by literature upon the imagination is illustrated in
two ways in the boy's mind: the stimulus to the life of freedom beyond the open seas and the clarification of life
through analogy.

> The girl is Jewish, thought the boy; he knew only about
> Jews what he had been told in school, but he suddenly
> understood that Jews were something similar to Negroes,
> that the girl here on board played exactly the same role
> as Nigger Jim did for Huckleberry Finn—she was some-
> one who had to be freed. The boy was almost a bit en-
> vious: one has to be a Negro or a Jew so that one could
> simply scram.

Ahab, Tom Sawyer, and Huckleberry Finn were no symbols
to him but reality. "Young Monk Reading," a woodcarving
obtained from a sculptor whose work since had been prohibited by "the others"—a phrase thematically used to refer
to those who in one way or another threatened the freedom
of the individual—became for the pastor a sacred object to
be preserved from persecution, a person reading as he wished.
And it is through his dialectics and studies that Gregor's

ultimate views are formed. Through some taut maneuverings amid dangerous situations in the fishing town, Gregor helps to launch a journey to freedom, although he decides to stay behind. The boy, not ready nor forced into freedom, returns with Knudsen, while the girl and the statue find an undisclosed destiny in Sweden.

Since *Zanzibar*, Andersch has written more expansively but the figures of alienation remain the same. *Die Rote* (1960; *The Red-Head*, 1961) features the wife of a West German capitalist who flees unbearable luxury and an adulterous affair, carries on with an Anglo-Irish spy in Italy, decides against doing away with her unborn child (by her German husband), and is last seen leading the simple life temporarily as a worker in a soap factory. In the novel *Efraim* (1967), a British reporter is assigned to cover Berlin during the Cuban missile crisis in 1962. He retraces some of his old life there as a child of a Jewish family and also tries to work out his problems as a writer, a cuckolded husband, and other psychic-sexual problems sufficient to burden a dozen people; he resolves nothing and remains in frightful isolation, a genteel bohemianism. Andersch's flight into the entertainment novel and labyrinthian plots has been successful but one misses the depth, the passion, the overwhelming sense impressions of his autobiography and of *Zanzibar*. "The real thing" and the earlier gut writing and the sensitive style have vanished into plot improbabilities and often he falls into belletristic artifices and linguistic experiments. Gregor's last thought in *Zanzibar* was that "everything must be tested anew" in the harsh light of day, and this ought to be a reminder to the novelist himself in order to avoid an impotent relationship to the substances of the world. Perhaps the conflicts he portrays are unresolvable, yet one may question the selfish and antisocial values adopted by some of his fictional characters in the name of freedom, that is freedom from responsibilities.

Of the original members of Group 47, in addition to Richter and Andersch—who had already published in the thirties—Walter Kolbenhoff (b. 1908) and Wolfdietrich Schnurre (b. 1920) had some literary resonance though no lasting fame; both wrote out of political conviction and with social indignation, and their fiction was anchored in past and contemporaneous problems. Although some old-timers came through resoundingly at group sessions—as did Günter Eich to win the group's first prize for his lyrical poetry that helped to break the tentative grip of *Kahlschlag* realism—the group needed massive infusions of new blood. Among the many newcomers in 1951 was Heinrich Böll (b. 1917) with his story—in precise and vibrant language—"Die schwarzen Schafe," "The Black Sheep," which showed that realism could be deepened by a sense of humor to portray plausible human dimensions; he was not afraid to display emotionality instead of being content merely to describe it as the realists would. Although Böll had begun to be known for his published stories, the acclaim and the group's monetary prize (funded by the American advertising firm MacCann) gave him a decisive lift, especially since he was out of work. From then on, the procession of literary prizes began while his public following made him the most widely read fiction writer of his generation—nationally and internationally, including the Communist countries (though he rejected the idea of writing wholesome "socialist realism which resolves all conflicts in discipline"). The reasons for his appeal inhere in his eminent storytelling ability—a commodity which will not go out of fashion—and his social concern for the underdog, the "little man," of whom he writes with a wry wit that is never condescending. One reporter noted that a dispute had taken place privately between Kolbenhoff and Böll as to who was the "truer proletariat." Böll generally felt that the writer had to know in his bones what poverty meant as well as "hunger, death, love, hate, happiness, God, and one's time." To be rich meant, from his point of view, usually to be bored and to yearn for the so-called elementals. Such social sympathies and antipathies course through his writings; at the same time, he is careful never to injure national pride. From the standpoint of politics, he has been called the chronicler and gadfly of the regime of Konrad Adenauer (1949–63), who was a fellow Rhinelander and Catholic. "There are people here," wrote Böll, "who manage

to believe simultaneously in God and in Adenauer, a spirit-
ual-historical phenomenon worth noting."

Although readers accepted Böll as an entertainer whose
moral messages were not unpleasantly cathartic, critics inside and outside the group provided their share of nettles. A
reporter from the periodical the *Spiegel* described Böll's entrance into Richter's "ambulatory literary salon," which met
in May 1951 at Bad Durkheim. Only after a second round of
voting did Böll win out over the Serbian Milo Dor (b.
1923), who had stayed in Vienna after having been a forced
laborer there during the war. Dor belonged to the circle of
young Austrian writers whose work had been sensitized by
French symbolism and surrealism, a trend which in a short
time was to affect Group 47 powerfully. A minority of the
group liked Dor's Kafkaesque or Gogolian story, "Salto Mor-
tale," and critic Jens saw the prize outcome as disgraceful,
while H. G. Brenner thought it to spell the end of the group.
The non–group critic Günter Blöcker at first called Böll "a
realist of secondary artistic rank." Influence upon Böll's
storytelling, as he clearly acknowledges, stems from Kleist
and Johann Peter Hebel, masters of early nineteenth-century pathos and lyricism, and it owes something to the new
matter-of-factness realism (*neue Sachlichkeit*) of the twenties; he blends these traditional narrative manners and bor-
rows occasionally from modern time-and-perspective shifts,
inner monologues and associations, and reporting styles in
some fourteen volumes of his stories and six novels. In all,
Böll is a conservative moralist in art, a liberal in religion, a
severe social critic and leftist in politics but at the same time
an enemy of ideology and a sceptical ironist in his humane
attitude. Like most writers of Group 47, he believed that
truthfulness could only be achieved by a clear and unadorned
style as well as sparse, focused, and undistracted narrative.
His wariness of a world in which he feels betrayed daily by
the state, the church, and other institutions describes the
nature of his engagement as a writer. Life and fictional
truth are constantly tested in relationship to institutions.

Böll's experience as an infantryman from 1939 to 1945,
mainly in eastern Europe, taught him that war means mon-

strous machinery, bloody boredom, and dehumanization. Above all, he thought that one ought to respect and listen to "the icy silence rising from the fields of Auschwitz and of Stalingrad." That Böll did not wish to plow these fields in order to reap a crop of stories is typical of writers who felt unequal to the task of going into the deepest hell of the immediate past. By juxtaposing Auschwitz and Stalingrad, he adopted to some extent the equalizing approach of *Der Ruf*: We all suffered and let there be no distinctions drawn among the dead. Böll concentrates on the living witnesses with their memory of the past and gives voice to the experience of people who endured the most during the postwar years. Böll thought that the soldier should shed all illusion and regard himself modestly only as a survivor. As a writer and survivor he felt it his responsibility to use art as a means of viewing society critically and from social and political perspectives.

Böll's fiction records with precision the life of the ruins, the conventions and pretensions of life, and the rise of the newly prosperous society behind whose façade lay vacuity. The astonishing range of his pictorial interests and narrative variations are clear in three of his novels which are landmarks in German postwar fiction. As in all his writings there is a confrontation between victims and victimizers in which the romanticism of defeat overwhelms the former who can claim moral victory as against the latter who inherit this earth. This is the way of the world. Realism and religious allegory merge in *Billiard um halb zehn* (1959; *Billiards at Half-past Nine*, 1962) as Böll divides people—sharply but not arbitrarily—into followers of the Host of the Lamb or the Host of the Buffalo (the beast). Within the family chronicle of three generations of the Fähmels—architects mainly—since the turn of the century, we find the same conflicts which tore the fabric of German society. During the events of a single day in 1958 the past emerges in the present and the victimizers—the evildoers of the Third Reich and the older generation—again are in the saddle. Protest is rendered futile in a society which is mainly concerned with prosperity rather than social humaneness. In such a world, concludes Böll, "Christianity has as yet not begun."

How brutally—and with what glee—the nonconformist, the lamb, can be led to the slaughter is the subject of Böll's *Ansichten eines Clowns* (1963; *The Clown*, 1965) in which an industrialist's son, Hans Schnier, refuses to play along with the establishment and declines to give "secular absolution" to the immoralists of the past; all his victories are verbal—and brilliantly acidic in the vein of Saul Bellow's introspective polemicists. His clown's mask hides the inner rage of the artist or writer, and he is reduced to impotence by those who commercialize religion. Hans's humane and moral inclinations—essentially grounded in religious feeling—are his undoing, and they represent Böll's view of bureaucracy and institutions which deny persons their political and religious individuality. During an interview with group critic Marcel Reich-Ranicki, Böll indicated that he objected to the apparatus and clerics of both communism and the church because they use their power to *stamp* people. Though one may be blasphemous against both (and *The Clown* is that), Böll notes that one cannot just rid one's self of either: "even in blasphemy lies a recognition of God; sometimes blasphemy is one's only recourse." Indeed, during and after the Hitler regime, few high churchmen in Germany gave evidence of their calling. Politically, Böll is aligned to most of the associates of Group 47 who believe that the world's hope lies in a form of socialist-communism purged of nationalistic and imperialistic tendencies.

Böll has frequently protested that the labels of old-fashioned or new-fashioned belong to the language of hair stylists rather than to literature. Yet, he has adopted the reportorial and documentary forms, popular in the sixties, in his novel *Gruppenbild mit Dame* (1971; *Group Portrait with Lady*, 1973). Fiction or invented truth is for Böll an imaginative completion of raw documentation; fiction and the documentary contain the language of life and through literary means one can document aspects of life. Through a facette-montage technique which enlists hundreds of minute observations gathered by an author who interviews people in all walks of life, we begin to see a near-total picture of Leni Gruyten at the end of the four-hundred-page novel. Like persons in documentary transcripts, she is neither a heroine nor an antiheroine; according to the sleuthing and sympathetic author she simply exists as a naïve, unpretentious, sentimental woman with "a proletarian and almost genial sensuality." She is openhearted without being promiscuous and allows herself to be exploited by causes merely because they are antiestablishment. In total nonconformism she resembles the clown Hans Schnier, but while he is doomed by his intellectuality she is saved by her near mindlessness; while Hans has no friends, Leni has the working class, mainly foreign workers hired for menial jobs, to give her comfort. Her financial support, though, comes from her obnoxious relatives who have corporate wealth. If she is a proletarian figure, she is *déclassé* and shrouded with a balmy romanticism that rises from romance magazines. At first the reader is coaxed into following the narrator's laborious piecing together of Leni's life, but after a while one may become somewhat embarrassed by the persistent peepholing and intrusion into the privacy of a pitiful creature who is allowed to hold onto few shreds of dignity. Even more unappetizing is the hint of sexotheological exoticisms underneath the genial proletarian exterior. If Böll wishes to drive home the point that Leni is capable of the most incredibly unselfish acts because her reflexes are not intellectualized, that she is a primal and instinctive creature, he succeeds at the expense of excluding any humanizing possibilities other than Rousseauistic metaphysics. His distrust of intellectualism and educative processes is not unjust although too severe. Leni presents a case of strange idealization.

Focusing on the city of Cologne, Böll has discordantly recreated in great breadth and depth the German political and social milieu of the past three decades, with particular attention to civilian life during the war. The slow, daily accumulation of miseries led to an anesthetized acceptance of evils from black-marketeering to the sight of forced marches of deathly exhausted foreign captives from the railroad station to the concentration camp: "It cannot be avoided that the

German public takes notice of these happenings," is the reporter-narrator's stark comment. Boris Lvović, a shy and intellectual Russian from this camp, is allowed to work in a small floral and wreath manufacturing shop in which Leni worked. And here reality is transmuted into fiction or perhaps unwittingly into a parody of the Romeo and Juliet story. From childhood on Leni observed the family tradition of offering coffee to anyone from beggars to customers and, the narrator suspects, even to the worst Nazi had the occasion presented itself. She offers coffee to Boris and the cup is promptly hit by the prosthesis of a war veteran who cannot tolerate such attentiveness to a "subhuman." Defiantly, Leni offers more favors than a second cup of coffee to Boris and during Allied air bombings their clandestine love affair is consummated in a mausoleum in the graveyard near the shop. As a result of the love act, Boris is given the dignity of becoming human while Leni becomes a mother, a complication which was to make her life extremely difficult after the war. With the increased tempo of the war on the various fronts and at home, business increases for the shop, and the ingenious owner—an ex-Communist and Nazi (for as long as the wind blew right)—resorts to stealing and re-using the wreaths and decorations. Literally hundreds of characters and their stories—some brilliantly told with great comic verve while others are sketched with cavalier negligence—appear and disappear like figures and ciphers on a relentlessly spinning roulette wheel.

Böll's view is encyclopedic and sometimes lapses into pedantry; his narrative technique resembles a somewhat awkward hybrid of journalism and fiction. One has the frustrated feeling that the substance of several potential depth novels are frittered away in the portraits of Leni and her group. He assumes the role of a restless reporter and he finds his muse everywhere as he tells us in a poem, "Meine Muse": on street corners, in a nun, as a factory worker, in the aged, in the housewife:

> My muse is a leper
> like myself

we kiss away the snow
from each other's lips
declare each other pure
My muse is a German woman
she gives no protection
only when I bathe in dragon blood
does she place her hand upon my heart
and so I remain vulnerable.

From the poem written in 1956 published in *Die Zeit*,
July 27, 1971

This is the attitude which may explain the atmosphere of his work and his vulnerable humanism. He will have nothing to do with the unreality that persists in melodramatic fiction which centers around regeneration of characters, vindictiveness, recrimination, retribution. He has compassion for the small fry caught in the web of life, and sometimes he falls innocently in love with some of them, as in his latest novel; he allows his scoundrels to rationalize their behavior and treats them with cold irony or contempt. Above all, he lets the reader judge situations for himself. Though he has gained headlines for espousing unpopular civil causes, his fiction is minimally political. He does not proselytize; if there is to be a conversion it must occur truly in the reader rather than in the fictional character who like his real counterpart is prone to give lip service to the expedient. There is almost no violence by those victimized—only the deranged Mother Fähmel will shoot at functionaries. The general passivity of his fictional characters and his refusal to work for reform through any of the established political parties has bothered some critics. Böll fears that a writer loses his critical function and conforms to society if he becomes a political agent and is subject to party thinking; writing is his best form of engagement. Because of his aloofness from practical politics and his publicistic essays he has come under the crossfire of the Left and the Right, who have simplified his role either as a "salon revolutionary" or as a supporter of radical activism. Böll's free-lance idealism has put him into an uncomfortable position. Similarly in his fiction, the rationally compromising man who might be willing to postpone the millennium for the sake of small political and social gains is absent; instead, we have a proliferation of Schniers stewing in sweet impotence and the Leni Gruytens who float on a cloud of incense. Böll's fictional world is ruled by a moral absolutism.

While in 1965 some prominent members of Group 47 like Günter Grass began a long campaign to put the Social Democratic Party (SPD, the democratic political Left) into power—though being critical of some of its policies—Böll was scornful of the unofficial association between Group 47 and the SPD. He felt that the party's stand on rearmament, its betrayal of the anti–atomic weapons movement, and the coalition with the conservative Christian Democratic Union (CDU) would lead to "absolute political promiscuity." In an article "Fear of Group 47?" he pointed out its credits and debits and sarcastically noted its harmless features as an independent, incorruptible, pluralistic association of people nonrepresentative of any one literary or political persuasion, which could therefore keep avenues of communication open with German writers on the other side of the wall; as a mobile academy, a group which remained a literary publicity instrument, with a growing tendency toward institutionalism (the bête noire in Böll's vocabulary) and less critical orientation; he noted its lack of solidarity and failure to strike en masse even when attacked. He saw the group as politically helpless, amorphous, and mythical in character, "And even in this it is like West German society, which need not have the slightest fear of the group." Nevertheless, he felt that the group's literary fame brought greater credit to Germany than did its political functionaries. Almost wistfully, Böll looked back to the years before 1955 when the group's sessions resembled workshops rather than the later public charades, Roman circuses with klieg lights, and talent auctions. Some say that this article was Böll's swan song in respect to Group 47.

In October of 1972 the Swedish Academy announced its award of the Nobel Prize for Literature to Heinrich Böll, stating that "It is not the smallest German miracle that after such years of destitution a new generation of writers, thinkers, and researchers was ready so soon to shoulder their country's and their own essential task in the spiritual life of their time." When the news reached the touring Böll in Athens, he promptly said that he would give part of the prize money to help jailed writers and their families. Again, his humane political reflexes were as active as when he participated in Group 47 affairs and as president of the West German PEN Club, an internationally oriented writers' organization. Many German journalists and literary critics thought that Günter Grass was just as deserving of the award as Böll and that they should have been recognized jointly. That point is well taken. The personalities and writings of Böll and Grass have brought immeasurable vitality to postwar cultural and literary life.

The intensity of an experience may make it emotionally impossible for a writer to convert fact into fiction. For instance, Ernst Wiechert (1887–1950) wrote *Der Totenwald* [The forest of the dead], in the form of a report published in 1945, which recounts his months in the Buchenwald concentration camp after he had condemned anti-Semitism and Hitler in several public speeches to university students in Munich. On the other hand, Ilse Aichinger (b. 1921) was able to interpret and filter into fiction her girlhood experience and impressions of the days during the German annexation of Austria when the regime prohibited her university studies in medicine. Published in 1948, her novel *Die Grössere Hoffnung* [The greater hope] (*Herod's Children*, 1964), is a stunning, lyrically articulated interplay of scenes and people, with the focus on a half-Jewish girl who is left behind by a mother who must flee and a father who has become a collaborator. The reality of slave labor factories, waifs playing in a run-down Jewish cemetery, deportations, shrill curfew warnings, is contrasted with the dreams of the characters to find a way out of hell through emigration or escape—and the silent, unspoken hope is death; the star of David is both the burden of this life and the symbol for a hope beyond. This was to be Aichinger's only novel, but with short stories in hand, which were to give her a reputation, she was among the growing number of Austrians to attend Group 47 meetings. Perhaps it was the influence of the Austrians—though few of their books had reached Germany—which made one of the discussants at the 1951 Bad Durkheim session exclaim, "At the next mention of Kafka I'll get the screaming meemies." It was reported that the name of the magus of Prague was mentioned twenty-one times, as were frequently Joyce, Pound, and Eliot. Hemingway's name seemed to begin disappearing along with prose realism. After Aichinger read, a friendly commentator confusedly caught himself referring to her as "Fräulein Kaf . . . Aichinger."

Listeners thought her story "Der Gefesselte," "The Bound Man," to be a vivid parable: a circus man finds himself bound by ropes and then slowly demonstrates to himself and audiences that even within the limitations of movement meaningful actions are possible; paradoxically, when the man is unbound, the problem of adjusting to real freedom becomes overwhelming. Aichinger's perspective, like Kafka's, is from the ironic view of an alienated yet compassionate observer. Bound, compartmentalized figures struggling to find their reason for being are constant themes in all her works, including radio plays; often the message seems to point to the need for purposeful direction, with an undercurrent of religious symbolism. Though the line between life and dream often becomes vague, Aichinger crosses the line between realistic and lyrical language at will. Like Günter Eich, to whom she was married in 1953, her concern is with language as a reflection of inhumane or humane modes of thinking and behavior as well as its destructive or sheltering capacity. Almost every writer of sensitivity wondered about the renewal of a language soiled during the Third Reich. One temporary solution was the attempted *Kahlschlag*, the other, mainly through poets, was the cautious reassertion of the humane imagination through the lyrical mode. Ilse Aichinger, in her novel, was among the first to state and to begin to resolve the problem:

Who of you is not a stranger? Jews, Germans, Americans, we are all alien here. We can all say "Good morning" or

"It is getting light". . . . and that is all we can say, almost all. Only brokenly do we speak our language. And you wish to unlearn German? I will not help you toward that end. But, I will help you to learn it anew, as a stranger learns a foreign language—cautiously, warily—as one kindles a light in a dark house and then continues on.

Despite the terrors and persecutions the young author had endured, there is a modest dignity and a tone unbelievably free from recriminations. Rarely have such tones—pure and vulnerable—been heard in fiction.

During the May 1952 meeting of Group 47 at Niendorf and with the reading of her story "Spiegelgeschichte" (which had appeared in the *Merkur* in January), translated as "Life Story in Reverse," Ilse Aichinger won the group's literary prize, funded by a group of German publishers. Listening to some of the highly polished writings, typified by the reading given by Wolfgang Weyrauch, Aichinger indignantly characterized the performances as "virtuosity without risk." She expressed the feelings of some listeners who for the past years had become impatient with the concentrated effort on polished style at the expense of content and that elusive "spirit" or inner significance. Her own story works outward from an inner core of meaning in a narratively risky respooling of the highpoints in the life of a girl, through a mirror-clear consciousness of her disembodied spirit, until the beginning of her birth fuses with her death; it is a vision real and haunting.

The triumph of Günter Eich's lyrical poetry at the group meeting seemed to be a forerunner of Ingeborg Bachmann's reception in 1953. In addition to the lyrical mode, the grotesque, the inner-confessional, and the surrealistic began to appear; yet, it seemed that the realistic war and postwar "asthma" literature still had a strong echo, judging from a report on the first meeting of the group outside of Germany in April 1954 at Cape Circeo, Italy. The meeting costs were met by the cultural division of the German foreign affairs office and indirectly indicated how little friction, as compared with later years, existed between writers and the government. Through the oppositional Social Democratic Party it was possible to voice political ideas and resentment against such policies as rearmament, and at the same time, there seemed to be an air of relaxation along with the successful economic stabilization after the currency reforms; all this may have contributed to the almost resigned or mixed feelings about the ability of literature and writers to influence decisively matters of state. And in this vacation atmosphere, the Dutch writer Adriaan Morriën (b. 1912) won the group's literary prize. He has been described as a literary globe-trotter with a genial sense of humor and a personal romantic charm expected by the public of poets; he was regarded as unique in this respect among the group and was completely casual in his relationships. In addition to being a short-story writer, Morriën was editor-in-chief of Amsterdam's *Litteraire Passepoort* and had been reading at group meetings since 1950, bringing along a contingent of writers from Holland. For a decade he was one of the group's best-liked colleagues and readers; however, his work found very little resonance outside the group.

At various early sessions, Morriën's readings were considered highlights. In 1951 his "Ein alter Brauch," "An old Custom," was approvingly received and described as a story mixture of fairytale mood, eroticism, and puberty psychology; in 1953 his story "Der Briefschreiber," "The Letter Writer," was praised as scintillating and as having true poetic content. At the Cape Circeo meeting he read the story "Zu grosse Gastlichkeit verjagt die Gäste," "Too much Hospitality Drives away the Guests" (published in his 1955 collection *Ein unordentlicher Mensch* [A disorderly man]) and won the group prize; it was also reprinted among other readings given at group sessions in *Almanach der Gruppe 47: 1947–1962*, 1962, edited by Richter in collaboration with Walter Mannzen. Hermann Kesten has called the story a humorous travel narrative and one of the best contributions in the *Almanach*. Although the humor of the story is largely confined to the title, the macabre views of people who insist on showing a visiting journalist their bomb-damaged city, the lady who runs the pension and overwhelms him with unwanted attention, and the depressing atmosphere of postwar times all come through clearly and realistically. Yet, whatever humor or realism informs the story may seem somewhat tasteless to the modern reader, as for example Morriën's description of the vain hostess who readies herself for a nocturnal dip in the quai: "Bent, panties still on, the hands in front of her breasts, as if fearing that they could fall to the ground, she ran across the low stones. . . ." The journalist, also a joyless character, decides to leave the city and its joyless people, but not before the author gives him an unproven parting thought, "The love for our fellow men is never greater than at the time we are preparing to leave them."

In 1957 Morriën was called gracefully naïve and was admired for being able to master "the playful elegance of the *petits rien* as no one else today in Germany." The winds shifted strongly in 1960 when Morriën sat in the electric chair and his reading was made short shrift of. A reviewer of the meeting wondered in print about the Dutch humorist, the only "foreigner" to win a group prize up to that time, and the undiscoverable reason for his having won it. I believe that it was the last reading given by Morriën at the group meetings. Whatever Morriën's literary merits, Richter's policy of inviting foreign authors was successful and Morriën became a continuous interpreter of postwar German literature in Dutch journals. He has several volumes of short stories to his credit and some of the stories were translated into German from the Dutch by Heinrich Böll. *Use of a Wall Mirror*, 1970, is the only translation into English of his selected and competent poetry.

During the eighth year of its existence, Group 47 held a meeting in Berlin in May of 1955 at the border of the divided German world. How divided the German writers were intellectually became clear during an informal get-together at a local bistro at which Böll, for instance, tried unsuccessfully to engage the East German writers Stephan Hermlin and Bodo Uhse in open literary discussion free from ideological jargon. At the Group 47 sessions journalists, reviewers, publishers' and radio network representatives, and assorted guests easily outnumbered the twelve authors who read from their works. Although many figures who had become known on the German literary scene attended as readers, critics, or guests, the reviewer Fritz J. Raddatz had some reservations: most often the criticism rendered *ad hoc* consisted of descriptive designation rather than a thorough analysis and evaluation; lethargy reigned pervasively, and the circle of friends had grown into a large family with too many cars parked outside its house. Of interest were discussions about the legitimacy of "theme" as an individualistic mode, "esoteric self-expression" through association-lyricism that brought together thought fragments in lines such as "An old man's smile is the human being"—an example of Helmut Heissenbüttel's "modernistic" poetry, and a realistic story by Reinhard Federmann about a wounded soldier, which could just as well have been written in 1947. The variety of readings and genres, including Wolfgang Weyrauch's superb radio play *Die japanischen Fischer* [The Japanese fishermen], seemed to make the audience a trifle soporific, and although some felt that Martin Walser (b. 1927) in his "Templones Ende," [Mr. Templone's end] did not measure up to the best in the German short story field, it was good enough for a prize. However, when Walser's story collection, which contained "Templones Ende," appeared the same year, reviewers generally hailed a new, talented writer. Aside from such biographical information as having been born near the Bodensee in Bavaria and having been employed in radio and television, the book jacket mentioned his doctoral studies which he capped at the age of twenty-four with a dissertation on Kafka. This information then led to obvious comparisons, but it was more the tone than specifics of technique that shows what Walser learned from Kafka. Walser's figures are largely abstract ciphers rather than persons in the round; we infer their psychological motivations rather than being told what they are, and we know explicitly what they think but not what they look like. Almost all of them, like Kafka's people, are fragile, unpretentious and helpless beings caught in the web of modern technology and living on the fringes of society.

In the short-story collection *Ein Flugzeug über dem Haus*

[An aeroplane above the house], the fatal and self-induced obsession that some imagined real-estate concern is after Mr. Templone's old house stands in contrast to most of the stories in which the establishment is about to rid itself of superannuated people, who then continue to exist on a small margin of pride. A brilliant re-creation of a puzzled mind anticipating the worst and laboriously examining a situation is the gist of a porter's reflection in "die Klagen über meine Methode häufen sich" [Complaints about my method are accumulating], showing the cameo clarity Walser can achieve if he wishes. Yet, Walser's tremendous energy burst out of the bounds of the short story and into novels which laconically satirize society and the emptiness of social ambitions among lawyers, doctors, politicians, entertainment people. In his first novel, *Ehen in Philippsburg* (1957; *Marriage in Philippsburg*, 1962), we follow the unsentimental education of Hans Beumann who comes to a big city, probably Stuttgart but also a model of any sophisticated city, and through no particular abilities of his own has his way cleared through social politicking by his marriage to an ungainly daughter of an industrialist; Anna had been his classmate some time ago. Hans is the naïve outsider who, as the critic Adriaan Morriën put it, goes through a personal and social defloration ritual. He becomes a conformist and learns to think and react as millions of others do. At one point when he finds a tear on his cheek, the surprise at being human—despite the vast dehumanization process and a world of fake emotions—is overwhelming. Walser's critical portrait of the professional classes is unsparing; its people view each other as chess pieces to be used "as if every possibility were the only one" to advance one's self. There is an ironic contrast between the happiness purveyors of the mass entertainment media and their own marital and extramarital lives, which they run into the ground. Perhaps it is just as well that Hans, although he has a scholarly background, is essentially a dumbbell, which, unlike Böll's "clown," lets him look forward to a bright future. Walser has a sharp and wicked pen and there seems to be little about the negative people he pictures in society that inspires optimism. When he read the opening chapter to the group in 1956, a reporter commented that Walser was the only writer at the session to have taken up a full-scale postwar theme.

The almost unrelieved malice which people bear one another in Philippsburg is continued into the moody and structurally complicated novel *Halbzeit* [Half-time] (1960) and its sequel *Das Einhorn* [The unicorn] (1966). These are the marathon and mammoth observations in fictive form of a salesman named Anselm Kristlein (literally, "little Christ") and the entwined commentaries of the author. Kristlein does not play out "the death of a salesman" but like Joyce's Leopold Bloom eventually returns to his marital bed. A reason which Walser gives for using a salesman is that no other profession makes one's superfluousness so insistently obvious, although the salesman can rationalize that his task of sales stimulation is more important than production. The totality of Kristlein's existence—even dreams "which are as untrue to us as we are to them"—is unfurled in a detailed Joycean monologue with periodic miniature essays. As a salesman he assumes many different roles: a romantic and conquering Ulysses, with flirtations and affairs; a front-line fighter who forces the customer to capitulate to his aggressive sales talk about oilburners or toothpaste; a planner of sales strategies to propagate products. His contacts are large and allow the reader an overview of an economically active society in which Kristlein and his bosses, customers, and friends are oblivious to economic and political forces which may eventually endanger their freedoms. "Half-time" in the life of Kristlein and Walser—both near age forty—and in the life of West Germany symbolizes the intermission period of a critical drama, a stock-taking time before a proliferating economy, including a rearmament industry, may careen out of control. Kristlein, who bears many burdens, becomes the reflector in which the precariousness of existence occasionally flares up. And in the novel we hear echoes of the atavistic time which ushered in the Third Reich as well as see the vestiges of the immediate past in the thoughts and actions of corporation executives who perform efficiently under any political system and for whatever purpose.

In respect to the salesman's superfluity, Walser is almost

inclined to draw parallels with the writer so that Kristlein awakens in bed in *Das Einhorn* to find himself a writer, amusedly saying, "Ach du Lieber Proust!" He has been commissioned to write a novel about love after the success of his novel *Halbzeit,* which gives us a clue to Walser's intended spoof—but also serious critique—of a writer's role, possible guilt feelings, and problems in a consumer society. Walser is extremely conscious of the public spotlight cast upon the writer and the powerful conditioning apparatus—sometimes Kafkaesque in its amorphous workings—which demands tribute from everyone. He sees no existential choice in man's life but makes the naturalistic assumption that the magnetism of one's environment either warps—as it did during the Hitler years—or encourages one's creative potential. Few writers of Walser's generation have interpreted man—even the lowest on society's ladder—as an incredibly complex being searching for equilibrium in an intricate industrialized society. Even fewer writers have attempted to explore the interior world of mind and emotion as thoroughly as Walser has in *Halbzeit,* for instance. Friedrich Sieburg, the most formidable anti–Group 47 critic, coyly noted that Walser's merciless flow of talkative, argumentative, gossipy language did not succeed in driving him mad, although it did suggest to him the picture of children trying to load an elephant on a handcart: "Walser can neither describe nor tell a story . . . but he has the power of language as no one else. . . . this man is a genius of the German language." Aside from the demands of a stream-of-consciousness method which makes it difficult for a professional reviewer to meet his deadline, conservative Sieburg did not seem to like Walser's populism, the lavish attention paid the little man, and the devastating criticism of West Germany. In-group critic Reich-Ranicki, who likes his storytelling to be natural and opts for a clear line between fiction and nonfiction, also took exception to Walser's writings. Not only has Walser defended his technique as a means of rendering the complexity of even the simplest observations and reactions, analysis, and penetration of environment as being truthful to the mind's flow and its improvisatory nature, but also he has engaged his critics in polemical battles. In his plays, particularly, his social and political criticisms have become plainer and more irascible.

In a laudatory foreword to *Bottroper Protokolle* (1968), consisting of interviews of working people in a small city in the industrial Ruhr and recorded by Erika Runge, Walser pointed to the economic deprivations of these people, their neglect by society at large—even by the liberal Social Democratic party, and the social snobbery accorded them in sociology textbooks. They are not heard in literature and in films. "All our literature is middle-class," said Walser, "even if it affects anti-middle-class attitudes. . . . It expresses middle-class existence." Workers appear only as oddities. Group critic Walter Jens had the same thing in mind when he wrote, "It has been customary for us to describe the human being only as if he were in the state of an eternal holiday eve." Rather than fake an understanding of working-class life which members of Group 47 did not appreciably have, most ignored it while some of them tangentially dealt with it through theoretical jargon derived from intellectualized politics. Although the literary output and activity of Dortmund Group 61, composed of writers who have working-class experience, cannot hope to compete with that of Group 47, it has fostered a continuing, modest research and group publication. One of its founders was Max von der Grün, a poet and novelist with experience in the Ruhr mines until a severe accident cut short his working days, who wrote a novel *Irrlicht und Feuer* [Will-o'-the-wisp and fire] (1963) which gained brief and agitated attention; it was also filmed for television.

After the last reading had taken place at the Group 47's twentieth meeting, held in the Bavarian village of Grossholzleute in 1958, Herr Richter swung a large cowbell and unexpectedly announced, "And now, we will award the prize." Not since 1955 when Walser received the accolade had a prize been given. Three quarters of the secret ballots were cast for the thirty-year-old Günter Grass, the first substantial recognition for him based on chapters 1 ("The

Wide Skirt") and 34 ("Growth in a Freight Car") read
from his forthcoming novel *Die Blechtrommel* (1959; *The
Tin Drum*, 1961). Heralding the noise which the novel was
to make internationally later were the immediate comments
of several group critics. Joachim Kaiser admiringly called
Grass "grim, like a predatory beast, full of wicked fantasy"
and described the narration as "betraying a wild energy of
expression, an irresistible sureness of gesture, and an uncanny
receptivity for bizarre-grotesque connections; often, diverse
stylistic means camouflage a wild attack before whose
strength Group 47 capitulated." Most participants agreed
that here was an unconventional and unmistakable talent,
expressing itself in poetry, sculpture, and art. Subsequent to
his first appearance at a group session in 1955, he has become one of its most loyal members and avoided any arrogance that could have been justified by sales of millions
of copies of his books throughout the world. Grass's family
background, like Richter's, is unpretentious and earthy; he
was born in a Danzig suburb in the rural area near the
mouth of the Vistula and grew up amid a number of different nationalities and gypsies. His father was a German
grocer and his Polish mother was descended from Kashu-
bians, Slavonic-Pomeranian peasantry. As a youngster he
mandatorily served in the Hitler Youth Movement (which
he compares with the present "Free German Youth" organization of East Germany), became a *Luftwaffe* aide,
later was wounded while an infantryman, and then became
an American POW. Upon his release in 1946, he found
various employment as a cook, a farm laborer, a potash
miner, became an apprentice to a stonecutter who bartered
tombstones on the black market, studied art at the academy
of Düsseldorf, and made side money as a jazz band drummer
and washboard accompanist. From 1953 on he chose to live
in Berlin—a city of tensions and political significance—with
his wife, a Swiss dancer for whom he quite naturally wrote
ballets, and slowly his writing career took shape as he drew
from his experiences. At their core is a decisive autobiographical realization: "When I was nineteen, I began to
have an inkling of the guilt our people had knowingly accumulated, of the burden of responsibility which my gen-

eration and the next would have to bear." It was not exactly
a popular or majority viewpoint in a postwar atmosphere of
social, intellectual, political euphoria and economic well-
being.

The Tin Drum, *Katz und Maus* (1961; *Cat and Mouse*,
1963), and *Hundejahre* (1963; *Dog Years*, 1965) are chron-
icles of the past extending into the fifties and are unlike
almost anything found in German literature. The Danzig
locale in these novels is as real and mythical as Faulkner's
Yoknapatawpha County, but the epic re-creation of scenes
and peoples is accomplished with a black and satiric humor.
No one has better expressed their scope than Grass himself:

> In literary form, I was concerned with the representation
> of the reality of an entire epoch, with its contradictions
> and the absurdities of middle-class narrowness, and its
> over-dimensional criminality. . . . Even the sexual realm
> . . . is part of this reality. . . . It is generally known that
> Catholicism in Poland, as in other countries where Ca-
> tholicism is dominant, has preserved residues of heathen
> origin, and that for example the cult of Mary far over-
> shadows a relationship to Christ and the Sermon on the
> Mount. The author wished to represent this playful,
> richly colorful, half-heathen and half-Christian world, and
> to put it into relationship with the epoch of National
> Socialism. . . .
>
> In the chapter, "Faith, Hope, Love," in *The Tin
> Drum*, the absolutely domineering ideology of National
> Socialism in its most aggressive form hits the Jewish
> minority and its religion. The barbarity of the SA [the
> Nazi storm troops] during the "Crystal Night" [of 1938
> when the signal was given to vandalize synagogues] finds
> its correspondence later in the aggression-lust of the
> roving youth bands. Only in this way, in respect to force
> given free rein, can one understand the destructive dis-
> mantling of Mary's altar in the Heart-of-Jesus Church.
> (*Münchner Merkur*, October 24, 1968, p. 9.)

The moralistic point is clear: once evil is unleashed, it
spreads into the fabric and fibers of society, without regard
to persons or institutions. Technically, Grass shied away

from the psychological realism which had dominated Group 47 fiction in the various attempts to master or overpower the past. Some group members such as Wolfgang Hildesheimer had proven the effectiveness of nonrealistic techniques but had not applied them to epic-historical contents. Grass chose a narration perspective which enforced an ironic distance between the narrative and the reader as well as writer. This buffer zone should discourage reader identification with any of the characters—who, with few exceptions, are grim stereotypes with exotic aberrations—and encourage a viewing of their wide-ranging political, social, and sexual behavior with ironic-critical detachment. Many readers of Grass's novels were of course unable to assume this view and subconsciously put themselves into the category of types presented; they felt affronted by what seemed to them accusations and pictorializations of their active or passive behavior, and their anger was vented in letters to the editors of newspapers and to the author. Echoing public criticism, the city of Bremen in 1959 refused to give Grass a prize which a literary panel had awarded him. Grass's work had the special capacity of raising that self-consciousness which some readers wished to avoid.

Like a true *picaro*, Oskar Matzerath in *The Tin Drum* retrospectively surveys his hectic and protean role-playing during the past thirty years from the tranquillity of an insane asylum; but he is ready at any time to step into the outside world and resume his mad drumming. At the age of three, Oskar had simply decided to remain a dwarf and, through his demonic infantilism, to manipulate the world for which he has contempt. Only in a chaotic society which has legitimized evil and violence can he operate to the fullest of his manic—and even artistic—imagination, playing whatever roles are needed to ingratiate himself with whatever powers are dominant at the moment. Unscrupulous, amoral, scatological, he exploits human weaknesses and impulses toward the forbidden. He is both an observer and a participant; he can be amused at the comic circumstances surrounding his Nazi father's death and experience pangs of remorse for his many betrayals of people in order to save his own skin when in danger. Yet Oskar, the "little demigod," can also undermine evil and show others the way to reason and sanity by producing counterbeats to evil. Grass is aware of world traditions in literature and allows that Oskar's ancestry may be traced to the adventurous *Simplicissimus* of Grimmelshausen's seventeenth-century picaresque novel of the Thirty Years War and in other respects to the *Moby-Dick* epic with Melville's "object mania."

Grass's next work, *Cat and Mouse*, represents the lull before the storm. His novella is stylistically incisive and in a melancholy key, as a high school boy, Joachim Mahlke, is harassed by his peers (the "cats") because of his monstrous Adam's apple (the "mouse"). In his anguish he turns to the worship of the protective Virgin Mary, with a fervor more idolatrous and paganistic than spiritual, but he cannot find refuge and must face a society for whose militaristic values he has contempt but whose standards he can more than meet through personal bravery. Mahlke's quixotic rebellions, though, lead to his death. (Unlike Mahlke, Grass along with most of his young contemporaries had been caught up in the war fever.) The novella, on the whole, unforgettably portrays what life was like in Nazi-dominated Danzig.

With *Dog Years*, a highly complicated novel structurally and psychologically, Grass's genius and raw anger found their most exuberant expression. Much militates against easy reading, especially the encyclopedic complexity of details and the extravagant baroque prose that often engulf the basic story—told by a fictional team of authors—concerning Walter Matern (a former Communist, ex-Nazi, and an opportunistic postwar anti-Fascist) and Eduard Amsel (a half-Jew, artist, entrepreneur). On one level, it is an elaborate —and sometimes ponderous—replay of the Cain and Abel story, but on a wider scale it is a fierce exposure of the "dog years"—the every-man-for-himself era, the "organized madness" which characterized life in the Third Reich—and the aftereffects. The novel's violence and bawdiness, its parodistic shredding of those intellectuals whose romantic-nationalistic balderdash extolled Hitler or those who turned

to an escapist "inner migration," and its merciless reconstruction of events that led to Hitlerism and perpetuated it,
all had the effect of an emetic that proved too strong for
much of the German public and critics. Its flaws are obvious
but its vitality exceeded that of any other novel to come out
of Group 47. The grotesqueries of Grass were deliberately
intended to rouse readers, "prisoners of their world," from
their lethargy. Klaus Wagenbach (b. 1930), who first attended a group session in 1959 and later published many of
the more off-beat works of group authors, predicted that
Grassian language with its power of pictorial associations
and black humor would have a profound effect on the
younger German literature. Undoubtedly there was such an
effect, but currents of social satire already existed before
Grass entered the picture.

Although Grass is profoundly skeptical about man, he
thought it imperative nevertheless to engage his energies
politically and literarily to help bring about the victory of
Willy Brandt's Social Democratic Party over the Christian
Democrats whose top leadership had included former Hitler
Party members. It was an uphill battle because the Christian
Democrats were identified with the economic recovery, "the
golden calf" around which, according to Grass, political
parties danced blasphemously and avoided such issues as
reunification. In speeches and letters since 1965, Grass has
gone on the warpath and shocked many an audience—including professional politicians and student radicals, who
looked askance at a writer's mounting the political platform.
From Group 47, he recruited the novelists Siegfried Lenz
and Paul Schallück and the composer Hans Werner Henze,
as well as the worker-novelist Max von der Grün of Group 61.
He was also not averse to taunting some prominent Group
47 writers for their aloofness from political engagement:

An election has passed over our country. Where were
those who only a few years ago still derived a certain radio
eloquence from their permanent political commitment?
Where, Alfred Andersch, did your eloquent indignation
sour the milk of the reactionaries? Where, Heinrich Böll,

did your lofty moral outlook put the Christian bigots to shame? O free and independent writer! What a beautiful fiction! (*Speak Out!*, 1968, p. 44, trans. Ralph Manheim)

Böll, like some other political theoreticians of Group 47 who would not compromise their "ideal," had attacked all political parties, including the SPD. Grass took a stand through what he felt was the best available, though not prefect, political means and castigated the corrupted communism which had developed a dictatorship of the bureaucracy east of the Berlin Wall, "the architectural wonder of our day," and denounced the West German democracy for permitting its parliaments to become subservient to lobbies. Grass insists on tolerance of differences within society, social justice and a socialistic democracy, an accommodation with the Warsaw Pact nations, and keeping hopes of German reunification alive. For Grass, it was especially gratifying to see his friend Willy Brandt, who had been vilified for being among the anti-Hilter émigrés in the thirties, become chancellor in 1969 and gain the Nobel Peace Prize.

Through his novel *örtlich betäubt* (1969; *Local Anaesthetic*, 1970), Grass seeks the cordinates of fiction and politics. In his previous novels the pervasive sickness of the middle classes and their failures were recorded retrospectively; and, like a persistent toothache, he finds the situation exacerbated in the sixties. Analogously, he feels that the situation requires "dental care," that is, the constant removal of tartar or "petrified hate" which prevents an understanding of the problems that caused student rebellions to materialize. Grass creates a diffuse moral allegory around the figure of Eberhard Starusch, who progressed from the teen-age leadership of a roving gang in the Hitler years to a sensible forty-year-old bachelor schoolteacher. Starusch seeks to divert the rage of one of his brightest students, Philipp Scherbaum, who wants to protest dramatically against public apathy generally and indifference to the war in Vietnam specifically:

These days you could crucify Christ and raise the cross on Kurfürstendamm . . . people will watch, they'll take pictures . . . but if they see somebody burning a dog,

burning a dog in Berlin, they'll hit him, and keep on
hitting him until not a quiver is left in him, and then they
will hit him some more.

Philipp is willing to immolate his favorite dachshund, but
his emotions evaporate in a running debate with his sympathetic—and humorously devious—teacher who counsels
moderation and search for a sensible position between political apathy and the gratification-seeking but ineffectual
Maoists. Grass also worked the dog-immolation episodes into
a play. His forte is caricature and ridicule through the power
of the grotesque; Grass has shown no inclination in any of
his fiction to draw a figure rich in personal dimensions. If
Starusch is the exemplar of reason, he is also most unat-
tractive as we see him in the dentist's chair, reviewing his
past through flash-on scenes on a television set—trick pro-
jections that gratuitously tear the novel into fragmentary tis-
sues. Starusch is satirized as a Casanova manqué but when
he grits his teeth in anticipation of "always new pains" he
bravely shoulders the lot of a man who espouses the unpopular idea of moderation. Grass's allegorizing is no doubt
ingenious but also wearyingly drawn-out: the best one can
hope for in this mad world is step-by-step progress through
prevention of disease whether dental or political.

  Grass's political, social, and global commentaries are so
prolific that one may well wonder at his omniscience.
Though he appears pugilistic, he also is very human in the
essayistic journalism displayed in his book *Aus dem Tagebuch
einer Schnecke* [From the diary of a snail] (1972). The
Tagebuch shows a fascinating and reflecting mind at work,
giving personal answers to the queries of the young as to
"how things were," "where things went wrong," "what were
you up to?" Grass defines the role of the writer as "one who
writes counter to elapsing time" and tide. The snail joins
Grass's metaphorical menagerie of rooster, cat, mouse, dog
and allows identification with the necessary patience of an
author as well as the steady snail's progress of democracy
with its antennas extended to the future. And the snail
references blossom into a mad catalog with entries from

ancient folklore to modern erotology. Grass read excerpts from a prepublication copy of the *Tagebuch* at a relatively small and informal gathering of Group 47, which met in 1972 after a lapse of five years. In his reading, Grass reminisced about the Brandt election campaign and its vituperative aspects, about his Kashubian forbears and his youth, he presented a fragmentary documentary of the forced emigration of Jews from Danzig and their subsequent fate, and he speculated on man's heritage of melancholia since Albrecht Dürer. Quietly Grass makes the points that human participation in seemingly small chicaneries and desire for preferential advantages led to great crimes in Germany's past. Not to be lost sight of, however, is the clear implication that moral issues and behavior, personal integrity, and the danger of institutional power and politics are problems and questions that deeply touch us in every society.

Some of Grass's colleagues have tired of his furious oscillations between politics and literature. Günter Herburger (b. 1932), one of the youngest writers to have joined Group 47 in 1964, has pointed out that Grass is free with tin-droning advice but will not take on political responsibilities. In a testy article, Herburger hopes that the oversized millionaire Grass will shrink back to normal and rejoin the fold: "He has . . . forgotten his class, the miserable small burgher of the cursing, crabby, desperate, exhausted, and one day murderous majority." Herburger, a short-story and film writer, had concerned himself with the potentially murderous majority, particularly in a story collection *Eine gleichmässige Landschaft* (1964; *A Monotonous Landscape*, 1968), exposing the disturbed psyches of an average range of people in German society; but he has been widely read for the pathological exoticisms of his characters rather than the message implicit in his stories. Whether we are talking about Grass, Herburger, or any other writer with social consciousness, there should be tolerance for the choice each makes in fulfilling his commitments to art and politics. It may be that Grass's dispersal of energies contributed to the artistic weakness of *Local Anaesthetic*; the anaesthesia was more than localized. Only his next novel will tell if he again can reach the peak exemplified by *The Tin Drum*. Grass is not unmindful of the problem, as evident in the self-analysis and the projection of self-skepticism that make Starusch a parodied character. Nevertheless, Grass's work has revived the power of fiction to stimulate, provoke, and to stir debate; he has used satire and the picaresque to create authenticity.

"And then came Uwe Johnson," was the heading of an article written by Helmut Heissenbüttel in reviewing the 1960 Group 47 meeting. He felt that Johnson showed the way toward a literature which could be spontaneous and deep at the same time. Actually, Johnson had made his appearance at the 1959 meeting shortly after he had left East Germany where, as a twenty-five-year-old free-lance writer, his means of independent expression had been repressed through censorship. At the meeting, Richter broke one of the group's unwritten rules and permitted a verbal duel between Hans Magnus Enzensberger and Johnson on the question of pure art and art with a message. Johnson noted that in creative work particularly, it is "a pedagogic mistake to leave out answers." Yet readers and critics have been frustrated precisely because "answers" seem to be absent in Johnson's writings and because he seems to straddle political issues. If the reader wants an either-or answer, he will not find it in Johnson's work; implicit answers, however, abound. As for his position on the divided Germanies and their deep estrangements—which are the central subjects of his major novels—he is quite clear: "It will, indeed, cause us to perish or to come to a good resolution." He is grateful for the hospitality of West Germany which has allowed him to pursue his vocation freely, yet he also suggests that it is necessary to prepare patiently and thoroughly for a future reconciliation. Given this position, it is understandable that his works are free from polemics that would rupture a relationship which he hopes will eventually be reestablished. Although Johnson obviously has fled from an oppressive political atmosphere, still the weight of his work tends toward nostalgia for his home countryside and its people. This helps to explain the dichotomy of the social and political-historic aspects of his fiction.

Johnson has learned much from Faulkner and the other moderns he admired; he translated some of their works from the English. Just as Faulkner proves difficult on first reading so Johnson's juxtaposition of shifting points of narrative view, monologue, dialogue, and reportage causes initial discomfort. Speaking about his first novel, *Mutmassungen über Jakob* (1959; *Speculations about Jakob,* 1963), which received instant acclaim without benefit of instant clarity, Johnson explained that his method of composition is based on rigorously thought-through schematics, a careful piecing together of information, telling a story and letting the reader draw his own conclusions. And so, Johnson's novel begins with the detailed statement that a twenty-eight-year-old East German railroad dispatcher Jakob Abs was scooped up by one locomotive as he was trying to avoid another in the fog while he was crossing the tracks on his way to work. Had Johnson simply said that Jakob was killed while crossing the tracks, he would have been unambiguous, but by mentioning that Jakob had just come from a visit to the West, seemed lost in the fog, was caught between two (symbolically East-West) trains, and so on, we are not sure whether this was an accident, suicide, planned political liquidation—or a combination of these. The natural question then, as Johnson puts it, is what memories does Jakob leave behind in the minds of people? It seems to me that through differing recollections, everything becomes speculation and the answer depends not upon the fact of Jakob's death but upon the individual who speculates about the fact, implying the doubtfulness of any of the answers or the relative correctness of all of them. Reality is made up of an individual's relationship to the world, which literature, as Johnson notes in the novel, preserves for us. Given all the facts about Jakob —his relation to friends, family, state propaganda of the East and West—I think that Johnson has portrayed essentially the progressive spiritual corrosion of a person. Jakob finds solace mainly in the solidity of objects and takes pride in his mastery of intricate scheduling of train movements even when such efficiency helped expedite Russian military troop transports to crush the Hungarian revolution of 1956. Jakob has become a man without illusions. He lived through the

early occupation of East Germany by the Russians and subsequently submitted to a political system which defines freedom as "accepting what is necessary," and he went briefly to
the West where he began to fear a repetition of history were
the economic structure to collapse. No other novelist has so
clearly caught the atmosphere and the problems which in
our time delineate both Germanys.

The techniques of information-gathering, reporting, description, and the surfacing of memories are again evident
in Johnson's social novel *Das dritte Buch über Achim* (1961;
The Third Book about Achim, 1967). In the novel a western
journalist named Karsch is drawn to East Germany by a
former girl friend, an actress whose career fades when she
withholds cooperation from the authorities. There he becomes involved in writing about a master bicycle racer,
Achim, whose exploits are twisted into heroic proportions to
reflect the glorious course of the state itself. Two other books
about Achim have been found politically unusable by the
authorities. In Karsch's attempt at a description of things,
decades of the past are minutely and often painfully reconstructed through memory reports. The story of Achim, who
is an enigma to himself as he resists and capitulates to the
state, is a brilliant complement to the Jakob story.

Johnson believes that a story, worked out in his mind long
before he commits it to paper, seeks its own form. *Zwei
Ansichten* (1965; *Two Views*, 1965) is a psychological novel
told in conventional narrative—from two alternating perspectives—about a nurse who is spiritually stifled in East
Germany and seeks freedom in the West. Her western friend
who helps her to escape becomes symbolic of luxurious de-
crepitude, and she loses her love for him as she assumes a
seriousness of purpose which will flourish in freedom. In
East German terminology, Johnson is an "objectivist," a politically unreliable person who sees both sides of an issue and
questions both; some western critics think that he fails to
apply the criteria of industrial and bureaucratic evils to the
East and appears to be naïve in his sympathies. Johnson
shrugs off such criticisms with the contention, "I am destroying beliefs which everyone has tried to establish in me."

Closer to home for American readers in Johnson's novel, the first in a series, *Jahrestage: Aus dem Leben von Gesine Cresspahl* [Anniversaries: from the life of Gesine Cresspahl] (1970). Johnson has spent some time in the United States, but the longest period consisted of his stay in New York, after the 1966 Group 47 meeting at Princeton, working on an anthology for Harcourt Brace Janovich publishers. During an interview, he commented that his profession as a writer required him to keep eyes and ears open and to rely on the materials of his experiences. *Jahrestage* is a topical novel which through a diary sequence (from August to December 1967) works horizontally in our time by putting selective and paraphrased news items from the States and from Germany side-by-side; it also works vertically by having the central character, Gesine, who appeared in his first novel, go back in her mind to childhood scenes, her mother's emigration to England in the thirties, and Gesine's experiences since arriving in New York in 1961 with her ten-year-old daughter. News montages from the *New York Times* not only report the realities but imply moral disfunctions: the Vietnam war, race problems, trivia, crimes, and political adventures throughout the world. Thousands of news items are pasted up: De Gaulle promises Quebec freedom, the backside of the moon is photographed, West Germans debate about lifting the statue of limitations on war criminals, Stalin's daughter settles in the U.S., and so on. Sometimes Gesine's interior monologues play on a news item recollected from the past: *"Do you believe in God?* . . . 1962 Ilse Koch [condemned to prison for sadistic crimes against concentration camp inmates] appeals to the European Commission on Human Rights. . . . *Do you want children, Heinrich Cresspahl?"* Gesine in various ways asks herself how one can maintain one's integrity in a world which has none, or where can one find a place morally uncontaminated. Although Dos Passos and Alfred Döblin were able to create literature despite adopted techniques of newsreel topicality, Johnson's similar techniques fail in this novel because he avoids human and scenic portraiture, context, and a substantial story line. One may marvel at all the devices which Johnson uses to create levels of reality, but one might with greater profit read the news summaries in *Facts on File* or a good textbook on contemporary affairs. I cannot see that the promised sequel of Gesine's interlinear memories will transcend this mono-chrome novel. Technique without the substance of emoted experience through characters becomes too cool an exercise of social indignation. That our disaster-oriented newspapers are daily catalogs of man's prejudices and assorted im-moralities is all too obvious and needs no speculations. In many respects Johnson's work is symptomatic of the erosion of the well-structured novel, which snobbishly has been left to those who write so-called culinary or entertainment fic-tion, and typifies some of the literature of the sixties in which the novelty of techniques overshadows storytelling.

Readings and reactions often took surprising turns at Group 47 sessions. Heissenbüttel heralded Uwe Johnson at the 1960 meeting but also made other observations as twenty-six authors read from their work. Neither the lyric poets nor the eleven authors who read from chapters of novels stirred listeners, but a sensation was caused by three authors, among them Jürgen Becker (b. 1932) and Dieter Wellershoff (b. 1925), who read "seldomly heard texts which consciously re-jected inner continuity and attempted to develop motion and composition out of language elements themselves." Such "texts" became more common as writing itself was used to imitate the process of vast depersonalization in a world in which the individual becomes a cipher. Even in the "report-ing" novel the author shrinks to minimal importance and gives the illusion of being a transmitting medium, a col-lector of information, but rarely a catalyst. As a result we have an abundance of depersonalized writings about de-personalized characters; in a robotic way, their thoughts lag behind action. The disintegration of personality at the root of novels by Gogol, Dostoevsky, and Kafka is carried to such extremes that the reader is able only to sense personality dissolution without having a firm picture of the individual. And the schizoid, emotionless performances of individuals, the lack of synchronization between their inner and outer world, and the disorientation of their sensibilities are simply

frightening. The justification, it seems, for breaking the barriers of plot and character and rearranging their narrative
relationship lies in the attempt to create a new totality of
experience for the reader. Although the differences among
writers are considerable, several Group 47 authors, aside
from Johnson, have on occasions been able to show the
dynamic possibilities of the drastic restructuring of the
novel, particularly Wellershoff, Hubert Fichte (b. 1935),
Heissenbüttel, Peter O. Chotjewitz (b. 1934), Alexander
Kluge (b. 1932), and Peter Handke (b. 1942).

Curiously enough, although Handke spoke out against the
endlessly descriptive prose to which Group 47 listeners were
subjected during the Princeton meeting in 1966, his own
three novels afford the same target for criticism; his de-
scriptiveness takes the place of analysis. The first and the last
pages of the novel *Die Hornissen* [The hornets] (1966)
describe the narrator's memory of his brother's fatal fall
through thin ice, or it may be the narrator's recollection of a
situation he had read about. The novel seems to be a slow-
motion re-creation of the narrator's or the recalled narrator's
state of mind as he seeks to distract himself with many details, possibly to avoid the one central event. Memories,
particularly of childhood—incidents and people—become
the subject matter of this themeless, formless novel and
vague narration. Yet, significant detail distinguishes literature from life, and when an author ignores this fundamental
premise and makes everything significant, he is likely to com-
pound the meanderings of a character's mind with such
prose passages as

> That is not the path. Was it therefore the path like the
> one to the sandpit? No, it was not the way to the sandpit;
> it was an unfamiliar path, which I had never seen before,
> a field-path which did not go through fields.

And Handke's minutiae accumulate, redundancies blossom,
tentativeness takes the place of certainties, prose becomes in-
dulgently lush or peculiarly anemic. Stretches of prose are
artistically fashioned and then dissipate into vagaries. Many
of the young German writers seem to be afflicted with what

might be called grasshopper prose, echoing the Ernest Hemingway style of *A Way You'll Never Be*:

> The grasshopper, you know, what we call the grasshopper in America, is really a locust. The true grasshopper is small and green and comparatively feeble. You must not, however, make a confusion with the seven-year locust or cicada which emits a peculiar sustained sound which at the moment I cannot recall. I try to recall it but I cannot. I can almost hear it and then it is quite gone.

While the Hemingway passage sounds like a bad translation from the German, Handke's sounds like a translation of exacerbating Hemingway prose. But in a fragment dated 1963 (in Handke's selected *Prosa, Gedichte, Theaterstücke, Hörspiel, Aufsätze*, 1969) called "Die Hornissen" and not included in the novel by that name there are scenes of Gothic horror—in the best Faulknerian vein—in which a distancing of consciousness from bodily existence has suggestive power.

The novel *Die Hornissen* was the target of a scathing review published in the *Spiegel* by Jakov Lind (b. 1927), who came to the group in 1962. Lind saw the language of the novel as rich in words which, however, said nothing. He linked these tendencies to Group 47 where yearly a formidable team of Germanist-scholar-critics insisted on judging a work by its style. Lind berated such literary Prussianism which drilled form and formality, successful sentence construction and metaphor, into the heads of sensible and sometimes brilliant young authors with the result that they wrote unreadable and boring fiction. Lind saw a general need for more "emotion—less head and more guts," and he conjectured that the grim lack of humor in the novel indicates that Handke's generation does not take our time seriously enough.

Handke took the reproach seriously and his belligerent reply characterizes the views that separate the newer from the older generation of writers within Group 47 as well as their differing bases of experience.

At the moment I am not very much inclined to give a programmatic explanation of my work. Jakov Lind speaks for himself. He will not halt the progress of literature. It bothers me only that he uses my book—as others do—in order to rid himself of his accumulated feelings of aggression against young writers. It is certain that Lind, and his ilk, committed as they are, will continue into eternity to use uncritically those literary forms of that society which they think they are criticizing. I myself am not committed when I write. I am not interested in so-called reality when I write. It bothers me. When I write, I am only interested in language; when I don't write, it becomes another matter. When I write, reality sidetracks me and makes everything unclean. During my literary work I also do not interest myself with criticism of society. I am simply not concerned with this. It would strike me as repulsive to twist criticism of societal order into a story or to aestheticize a poem. For one to work social commitment into a poem or to make literature of it instead of saying things right out, I find hideously phony. *That* is aestheticism, and that kind of literature makes my gorge rise. I write from within. ("Wenn ich schreibe," *Akzente*, October 1966, p. 467)

Whatever the effect of Lind's criticism, the eccentric prose was purged from Handke's next two novels, but other eccentricities appeared. In the crime novel *Der Hausierer* [The peddler] (1967), the main character, according to Handke, is a person who always figures in the story but who never belongs to it. The incidents are interspersed with outside comments, and Handke characterizes this technique as the "ordering of disorder," yet says, "morality is the least of my concerns." An amorphous internal-external view of a man escaping from a murder he has committed is given in Handke's *Die Angst des Tormanns beim Elfmeter* (1970; *The Goalie's Anxiety at the Penalty Kick*, 1972). Regression by a construction worker, Josef Block, to a time when he was a well-known soccer goalkeeper and progression toward capture, despite an attempt to lose himself in a small village, show a story format which absorbs elements of the *roman nouveau*. From the *roman nouveau* he has picked up the bloated inessential detail which, for example, pays more attention to the bed than the lovers on it, and he has couched the story in a realistic stream of consciousness. The Handke novels mentioned owe much to the inventiveness in Camus's *The Stranger* and *The Fall*, but they seem so flattened out by comparison that they approach tedium; style rather than emotion or guts dominates.

Another much-discussed novelist was Hubert Fichte, who polarized the critics outside and inside Group 47 with his beat-generation novel *Die Palette* [The palette] (1968), which contains more literate touches than those by Jack Kerouac and William S. Burroughs, his predecessors, but shares the seedy and depressing spectacle of a morally foot-loose group that lives on the margin—if not the sewage point —of society. His fellow group author and critic Reinhard Baumgart (b. 1929) wondered if literature ought not to be more than the sum of precise sentences and themeless reportage or inventory. Fichte gained first-hand information for his novel during three years spent at the Hamburg bar, the Palette, a hangout for perverts and pseudo-cultural drop-outs. Baumgart characterized Fichte's novel "realism as l'art pour l'art" and saw the exotic exhibitionistic show as designed to shock and provoke. Marcel Reich-Ranicki, on the other hand, uses one of his favorite criteria of praise—the novel "broadens our experience"—and he likes some of the short biographies of outcasts who have been pushed into the sump by a morally questionable society; but he also criticizes the uneven range of style. Undoubtedly the trends of the documentary, report-literature, and the stylistic experimentation in poetry have had a confusing impact on Fichte.

The search for new forms and new models to express reaction to the social, political, and technological ferment of the sixties caused the traditionally defined categories of fiction to split at the seams. Much of the work coming from Group 47 writers, which had been polished and sifted through various aesthetic and social conscious criteria, became even more intensely intellectualized and required strenuous attention by the reader who was confronted by hybrid forms, essay-poems, collages, multilayered linguistic and antinarrative configurations, and something which for want of a better designation was called "texts"—an assemblage of quotes, paraphrases, and commentary. Yet there was a countermovement to express life through a pure and direct style by means of prose miniatures which, like feuilleton stories, dignify commonplace happenings and commonplace people—as in Peter Bichsel's writings.

One of the successes scored at the Group 47 meeting at Sigtuna, Sweden, in 1964, was a two-page *Novel* and several prose miniature stories by the thirty-year-old Swiss schoolteacher Peter Bichsel. After the readings from the galleys of his first book, the group critics—accustomed to more intellectualized work—appeared delighted with Bichsel's accomplished reductionism of language and the poetical prose ground structure of his work. A year later, in Berlin, Bichsel was crowned with the group's prize for more of his laconic, compressed, and suggestive stories which, as group critic Christian Ferber noted, contained a small cosmos and seemed to be in response to Günter Eich's admonition in the early fifties, "*Alles, was geschieht, geht dich an,*" "Everything which happens concerns you." Indeed, Bichsel believes that a writer takes a daily inventory of his surroundings and his given language "which is never accidental. . . . it has its reasons . . . one can find truths by varying language and by observing it." But he is quick to add that language also is a form of self-portrayal and a means of manipulation: "literature is political in the sense that it holds a dialogue with men . . . and occupation with language in itself is always a form of one's occupation with humans." In that sense literature is political and social-critical work, although specific political problems require the more direct expression which he uses in period newspaper columns on politics.

Bichsel explains his fiction as discovery of what already exists; he has no sudden inspirations, no full-blown concept for an entire story, nor a capacity to fantasize. Instead his method is improvisatory. For weeks, to give one example, he was unaccountably pursued and fascinated by a sentence,

"The milkman wrote on a piece of paper: 'No butter left today, sorry.' " With expansion and variation this became the story "The Milkman," contained in *Eigentlich möchte Frau Blum den Milchmann kennenlernen* (1964; *And really Frau Blum would very much like to meet the Milkman,* 1968). Bichsel notes the Helvetians' love for the conjunctive method of narration—"what if . . ." Frau Blum were to wonder what the milkman was like as a person, what if the restive head of a family were to entertain the thought of escaping to "San Salvador," and so on. Except for the impersonality of their exchange of notes, Frau Blum and the milkman do not break through the anonymity of their relationship; modern life is caught here in a nutshell and *conjecture* becomes compensatory experience. Although the situations speak of commonplace reality, Bichsel is not interested in reality except for the relationships people have with it; the pervasive mood is melancholic resignation and solitariness. In his second work, *Die Jahreszeiten* [The seasons] (1967), the limited range of his technique and his materials become obvious and the narrations fail to muster the earlier charm and unpretentious tenderness. A recipe, even a tasty souffle, cannot be indefinitely repeated without losing its original novelty, which is the case, I am afraid, with Bichsel's miniatures. Perhaps, Bichsel's manner is too self-conscious, and instead of letting the reader discover essences, he reveals his own discovery of them and blurs the edges of fiction with his prose commentary. In his fiction-essay "Grammatik einer Abreise," "Grammar of a Departure" (in the periodical *Field: Contemporary Poetry and Poetics,* Spring 1972) the key sentence is, "I am packing my trunk," and Bichsel theorizes that here the grammatical present tense is an unstable tense in which a neurotic person tries to anchor herself; in the narration, her grammar of tenses, her spoken and unspoken thoughts, and her actions lack unity and thus identify her problems. Bichsel narrates and reflects about his narration, a recurrent device in postwar fiction used not only to create authenticity but also to destroy the illusionistic base of fiction; the newer writers are aiming for work free of illusions in content as well as device.

Like Bichsel, Jürgen Becker, who was born in 1932 in Cologne and lives in Rome, was catapulted to public attention when he received the Group 47 prize in 1967 for his readings from *Ränder* [Margins] (1968). He had read his realism-defying prose fiction to the group since 1960, described as "texts and typograms" in his *Phasen* (1960), and began to be taken seriously with his association prose-piece *Felder* [Fields] (1964), a round-up and survey of the author's levels of primary experience in the city of Cologne at one period in time. After the 1962 group session, Wolfdietrich Schnurre was sufficiently disturbed to ask in an article: Have the storytellers forgotten storytelling? He objected to the lack of relatedness to the human in the readings by authors, including Becker. Indeed, in Becker's works we feel and sense reality through a haze as his subjective consciousness allows itself free rein; reality becomes whatever consciousness decides to recall or give fleeting attention to. It is as if a photographer were trying unsuccessfully to focus clearly on objects. The prose plays impressionistic tricks as language, images, and objects dissolve in uncertainty or reappear briefly like thematic scraps. *Ränder* philosophically implies that we live on the margins of consciousness, that actions are illusory, that change or transformation is the only reality. While Günter Eich had taken inventory of objects in order to assure himself possessively that life has dimensions which allow one to function reasonably within them, Becker ironically denies them and creates a metaphysical ambience in which the inventoried elements become immaterial. In *Ränder*, his imagination superimposes the fixed points of a map upon the vague topography of life so that point resemblances become coincidental in recaptured or imagined trips:

> The time of the geographical map. There was Nevada, there was our destination, there we were, there Ostia and there with eyes closed. There we still are and we speak of that which slowly disappears and still remains recognizable by its margins; there, look again, there is, there was, we look up high and see our uplooking face, so we

begin anew again, if we are still there, after the forgetting, further, not here, where we still sit and look upward, and now, finally, we no longer see anything.

How much more memorably Rilke put his feeling about existence in a world-realm of transience and impermanence, and his defiance: "Let us stay between the teeth of Change." Despite the enervated tone, the discontinuities, change-ability, and dissolution of language in *Ränder*, paradoxically the work is highly structured and its disparate parts are yoked together by calculated design and composition. Technically the substance of language is brilliantly manipulated and the text surfaces have an intriguing cubistic effect. Like so much of current prose, Becker deliberately avoids a central mean-ing and concentrates on technique. His *Umgebungen* [Sur-roundings] (1970), is a pastiche of clichés, a form of anti-literary protest simulating life and empty communication among people, reminding one of Handke and Heissenbüttel. In his 1969 Büchner-prize acceptance speech, Heissenbüttel announced, "Actually, I have nothing to say," but like many of the present generation of writers, he nevertheless is un-willing to stay silent. The feeling of political and social im-potence has severely affected the works of many writers who are turning against the very medium which in the past has made protest effective; at the same time, they cannot bring themselves to discard their typewriters and join those "revolutionary" forces which they admire. Essentially, they are at war with themselves, with readers, and with institu-tions.

To predict that such trends will continue indefinitely or turn into absolute chaos would be hazardous. Remarkably enough, readers have been mesmerized by the Group 47 label and its bearers and have followed their output with unabated interest. In jeopardy, though, is the willingness to tell a story, typified by such works as Wolfgang Weyrauch's *Im Clinch* (1971), which begins, "I must tell a story, which is none." On the other hand, there is considerable life left in the younger ranks and in such "old timers" as Grass, Böll, and Ingeborg Bachmann. The "first lady" of Group 47, after a long pause, has again shown her strength as a creative artist with her novel *Malina* (1971), a poetic and psychologically rich exploration of a woman's distraught and contrasting love experiences, in which pathos rather than eros informs the daily aspects of life and contact with other humans. It is a tragic story and is weighted with the ineluctable sadness of an excessively contemplative personality. The discursive tone of the novel is almost elegiac as the central female character, up to the last, tries to be victorious in a dehumanized world by struggling against

> . . . corruptness and routine, against life and against death, against the casual coursing of time, all the threats emanating from the radio, all the headlines of newspapers exuding the plague, against the trickling perfidy from upper and lower-story apartments, against slow, inward consumption and being swallowed up from outside.

With Bachmann, language becomes a means and measure of one's experiential awareness, and as in her poetry it borders on mystery: "language is punishment; all things must enter it and within it they must die out." Without language we have no explainable sensation, and the uncanny genius of Bachmann consists of the integration of language and emotion.

In a perceptive critical comment, Wolfdietrich Schnurre has pointed to a deep-seated problem which has been resolved or unresolved, depending upon one's point of view, in the fiction of many of the Group 47 writers who have adopted satire or the grotesque as a way of expressing their attitudes toward the given world. He limits his criticism to Alexander Kluge, Jakov Lind, and Milo Dor, but it applies to others as well: "In order to work against the inhuman, authors themselves fall into the error of having to write inhumanely and letting their figures commit those murders and acts of violence which as authors they would wish to prevent." Political and social anger can turn into unmitigated literary sarcasm, and for the most part it has. Among those with some success in mitigating the danger in fiction are Grass and Jakov Lind. The divergent expressive-

ness and effects of fiction as against autobiography or factual
report become apparent in the writings of Lind, who made
his first appearance at the Group 47 meeting in 1962. Born
in Vienna in 1927 to a Jewish-Polish family, he found that
the city was but a "waiting room" until its cosmopolitanism
was killed by an act of "autocannibalism" instituted by the
Austrians and the Nazis from which, even in postwar days,
it was not to recover. From 1938 to 1943, he was in Holland
but then felt it safer to return, with forged papers, to Germany and live under the noses of the Nazis; incognito, he
shared the German experience to the full. With five years
of stock-taking in Israel after the war, he felt that he could
face "the rats of this plague-stricken continent [Europe]
again," revisiting Vienna ("a dead town, full of fat skele-
tons"), Holland, and finally settling in London. The jobs he
engaged in to survive remind one of the tales of a picaresque
hero, but intellectually he searched for an attitude which
would be consonant with his feelings. He could not tolerate
the mentality of the anarchist rebel, the Marxist-Leninist,
the Western democrat, the resigned eyes of the pious or the
Buddhist; instead he found asylum in hellish black humor
that produced the stunning short stories *Eine Seele aus
Holz* (1962; *Soul of Wood*, 1964), which instantly made
him a literary phenomenon. As the critic Günter Blöcker put
it, Lind's "prose is articulated horror, shock-writing." But
how distinguishable from fact is the title story in which Nazi
experimenters who poisonously injected thousands of victims
and then at the war's close fight over a surviving crippled
Jewish boy in order to claim him as evidence of their
humaneness and to avoid retribution? More metaphorical are
the stories "Journey through the Night" and "Hurray for
Freedom," grounded in solid detail, in which a cannibal
seems more reasonable than his victim and a normal-appear-
ing family turns out to be a group of cannibals. His novel
Landschaft in Beton (1963; *Landscape in Concrete*, 1966)
strains Lind's talent with the crowded allegorical, and macabre adventure of a German soldier—*Homo bachmannus*
with the body of a horse, the intelligence of a chimpanzee,
and the soul of a dove—who seeks a regiment to fight with.

That some of the episodes in Lind's fiction are grounded in observation, but blossom surrealistically, can be gathered from the first of his autobiographical volumes, *Counting My Steps*, published in 1969. "How can the picture in front of one's eyes be drawn with words? How can the intellect reflect itself in letters?" These questions asked by Lind have been variously answered by Group 47 writers, but the measurable success has been small and the nightmares have remained largely unmastered. Some scenes from much of the fictional realism of the fifties remain memorable and memorialize tragedy, as in the works of Richter, Böll, and others, particularly the somehow neglected novel *Polonaise Allerheiligen* (1959; *Camp of All Saints*, 1962) by Tadeusz Nowakowski (b. 1920), whose reading of chapter 11 (about the explosive rage within a concentration camp) chilled the spines of Group 47 listeners. Although Nowakowski is a minor writer, he proved the adequacy of fiction to present the picture in front of one's eyes, or in one's mind's eye, and exploited the relationship of raw material to the purposes of fiction. For the most part we must look elsewhere for the submerged past.

One day, early in the morning, he knocked on my office door, came in, stood at attention and begged permission to speak with me. He looked very worried. I said, "well then, Blau, what depresses you?" He said that it was his eighty-year-old father who had arrived in camp that morning with a transport. Could I do something about it? I said, "Well, Blau, you must understand that it is impossible. . . . " Quickly he said yes he understood, naturally. But could he not request permission of me to take his father to the "hospital" (where victims were shot) instead of to the gas chamber. And could he not first take his father into the kitchen to get him a bite to eat. I said, "Yes, do what you think is best, Blau. Officially I don't know about it, but unofficially you can tell the Kapo that I said it's all right."

In the afternoon when I returned to my office, he was there again waiting for me. He had tears in his eyes. He stood at attention and said, "Herr Hauptsturmführer, I only want to thank you. I gave my father something to eat and took him straightaway to the hospital—it's already all over. Thank you so much." I said "Well, Blau, there is no reason to thank me. But, naturally, if you *want* to thank me, you may do so."

And, later what happened to Blau and his wife?

"I don't know." And again, "I don't know."

This is documentary narration, not fiction. Yet, it does what much of traditionally structured fiction seems to lack or the "new" literature since 1945 should have been doing; it balances fact and drama, allows the documentary character to hide from himself but not from the reader through his verbal subterfuges or confession, and gives multiple levels of relationships—interviewer-subject and the subject and his past victims. In 1967 Franz Stangl, the commandant of the Treblinka II extermination camp—where 300,000 Jewish persons were murdered during 1942–43—was discovered in Brazil and given a life sentence three years later in Germany. The English reporter Gitta Sereny took tape-recorded interviews. Later when Stangl died, he said, "God knows me, and my conscience does not condemn me." Indeed, his conscience was narcotized. Drink-sotted personnel of the camps who regarded shootings as sport and female inmates who danced naked on tables Stangl regarded with disgust; he sought aesthetic satisfaction in beautiful landscaping, in taking orderly inventory of mounds of belongings legally stolen from the victims, and in obediently enforcing rules and regulations. After office hours he found escape from reality in the comfort of his family. He accustomed himself to the liquidations of humans by regarding them simply as "goods" or nonhumans; the only thing which haunted him was the stench of decaying blue-black bodies spilling from pits. Rationalizations abound as he claimed to be influenced by Cardinal Archbishop of Vienna Theodor Innitzer's call to Austrian Catholics not to resist the Nazis; repeatedly, he pleads personal survival as an excuse for his behavior. Journalists have called Stangl the exemplar of the banal, a frighteningly normal "Biedermann." They could not be more wrong. Normalization of murder is neither normal nor banal; repetition and large numerical figures dull the senses of the Stangls and the readers of their accounts, but it also deepens the mystery of evil and makes it all the more necessary to confront and analyze its protean monstrousness. Despite the fact that the Stangl account (narrated and published by Sereny in 1971 in *Die Zeit* and the London *Daily Telegraph Magazine*) has a quiet yet shattering effect, I think that only the novel can create the deeper subjective and emotional life of people and their time. The opportunity Group 47 novelists had to reflect the momentous personal and historical experiences that the postwar generation had lived through was rarely seized and most often avoided as too painful or too personal. Polished techniques of realism, naturalism, surrealism, the grotesque, and satire were exhausted during the fifties; newer forms of reportage with sparsely applied novelistic details proliferated from the late fifties on as a means of finding a fresh approach to story-telling. But progressively the novels seemed researched and the raw data seemed lost in the limbo of recent history; the most telling effect of the documentary has been upon the drama.

Of late, many Group 47 authors have put together fiction or "text" which defies genre description, so fluid are the boundaries of the prose, and the subject matter quite often is a collage of gray, everyday trivia as reflective of common experience. Somehow, much of the present fiction has an air of indecisiveness which grew out of the taboos and principles that dominated Group 47 writings since its origin. Lind, in his autobiography, described his manic feeling of walking about in the Nazi Germany of the early forties, undetected and as it were invisible: "To be schizophrenic is to be normal; unreality is reality." An analogous feeling might be ascribed to the postwar novelists who adopted one of two perspectives in their works namely, seeing life either as the normality of unreality or as the unreality of normality.

3

Poetry
Acts of Memory and Provocation

Shortly after the war, poetry anthologies seemed to favor daisy-plucking lyricism and the matter-of-fact and piteous poetry of the ruins, *Trümmerlyrik*, to which some early members of Group 47 were partial. To be sure, the range in between was moderately represented. While theoretical debates thrive on literature, rarely does poetry thrive on debate. The impasse was broken when the intellectual and technical maturity of the younger poets was demonstrated. In his sensitive reflections on contemporary literature, with a focus on Group 47 of which he was part, Walter Jens, retrospectively fixes a key landmark:

> (. . . social criticism can be practiced only with the help of artificial voltages: today, whoever writes as a critical or socialistic realist in the style of Balzac, he indeed remains a hundred years behind in respect to content and misses the present.) In short, neorealism is dead, and no genius can reawaken to life the postwar programmes. In 1952 the pendulum veered very far, and for a long time, toward the other extreme. I believe that I can tell the second when the turnabout occurred: it was in Niendorf on the Baltic during the early spring of 1952 at a meeting of Group 47. The *verists*, craftsmanlike and good storytellers, read from their novels. Then, suddenly it happened. A man by the name of Paul Celan (no one had heard the name before) began to speak his poems, songlike and ethereal; Ingeborg Bachmann, who came from Klagenfurt [Austria], as a debutante, whispered hesitatingly and

hoarsely several poems; Ilse Aichinger recited, with Vien-
nese quiescence, her *Spiegelgeschichte* [literally "mirror
story"].

At that point, seven years after the end of the war, a
young German literature of modernity unfolded itself
visibly and then developed tendencies of the past into
further milestones. (*Deutsche Literatur der Gegenwart*,
1961)

Jens did not exaggerate the importance of Group 47 as a
forum for writers and as a reflector of change. With considered judgment Victor Lange calls Celan's *Sprachgitter*
(1959; *Speech-Grille*, 1971) perhaps the most important
body of German postwar poetry; indeed, Celan was a poet's
poet. However, particularly in the early fifties, it was the
former "cubist expressionist" poet Gottfried Benn who
exerted the greatest influence on poets. His *Probleme der
Lyrik* (1951) became an *ars poetica* whose view of the poet
as a mandarin-craftsman attracted followers. His illusory goal
was the "absolute poem" free of didactic social and political
commitment, transcending history and addressing itself to
no particular audience. Actually the idea was as old as Edgar
Allan Poe's philosophy of composition which extolled the
supreme nobility of a poem written solely for the sake of a
poem; the poet should be exclusively concerned with achievement of an "effect," a principle which was adopted by
Baudelaire and the French symbolists. Not only did the
symbolist poem reappear in the postwar days, but other species which had been taboo during the Third Reich were re-
discovered and recovered. Much of postwar German poetry
had in common a strong intellectualization of content and
aesthetics of form whether it was the private metaphysics of
Benn, or the public value judgments in the plain speech and
razor-sharp comments of Brecht, or the brilliant emotive
poem-skeletonizings of Celan, who venerated the "word" as
a humanizing and humanistic link with traditions. Creative
impulses simply blossomed in every conceivable poetic form:
neo-Dadaism, neosurrealism, satire, analytical poetry, and
poetry of linguistic virtuosity—all were directed to the purgation of what might appear to be in the least sentimental or

imprecise. Günter Grass's poems with their fantasy, grotesque wit, and uniquely serious idiom were among the favorite of Group 47 listeners who might be regaled with such verses as "Die Seeschlacht," "The Sea Battle":

An American aircraft carrier
and a Gothic cathedral
sank
in the middle of the Pacific
simultaneously.
To the end
the young curate played on the organ.
Now airplanes and angels hang in the air
and have no place to land.

Poems of sophistication and polish were written by Krolow who, like the more experimentally inclined Helmut Heissenbüttel and Hans Magnus Enzensberger, regarded poetry as a superior amusement, a game of wit and meaningful stratagems. The relative impotence of poetry to effect social and political changes led Enzensberger to reject, in the late sixties, the output of such Group 47 colleagues as Walter Jens and Grass and to recommend to them, as well as to the European leftist "dilettantes and nothing-saying protestors," the taking up of arms against the power of the state as did the South American *Tupamaros*; fortunately he has not taken his own advice. The restlessness of the poetic temperament was also expressed through political, visual, and concrete poetry. And, in a surge of counterculture convulsions of verbally dissipative revolution, pop poetry coincides with certain suicidal or anarchic intent in other art forms to bring about the end of art. We have seen such cycles before, and up to now art has managed to survive and provocatively to enrich life. Amid such profusion of poetic tendencies and expressions there remains a core of poetry which since 1945 speaks with permanent power, and many of its voices belong to poets who were, in one way or another, among Group 47.

Günter Eich (b. 1907), a charter member of Group 47 and the father of the German radio play, has become one of the most respected poets within and outside of the group through a body of about two hundred short poems and scores of radio plays over a period of thirty years. Much was expected of Eich at the group's meeting in 1950 at the monastery of Inzigkofen, and a groundswell of enthusiasm for the nine unpublished poems which he read—described as possessing the author's uniquely individual tone and melody, a pure language with contours and colorations—led to the award of a prize, the group's first such badge of distinction. As a poet, Eich does not allow himself to be hurried, so that the poems were not published until five years later in a collection called *Botschaften des Regens* [Messages of the rain]. Quite as notable as the prize was Eich's break with the neorealistic, prescriptive criteria of the group.

Symbolic perhaps was the cloister atmosphere at Inzigkofen, for it seems that Eich had developed a position at once hermetic as well as open to the experience of what we call "world," a paradox already evident in his academic studies of Oriental cultures and jurisprudence. In his symbolistic nature poems from 1925 to 1935 birds sing sweetly, the blue autumn knocks on window panes, and lights are lit in the mineworks of the stars—lovely tones and harmonies without basic configurations except for generalized commentary on cosmic and prosaic themes; the poetizing was very conscious and decorative, with awe for the power and mystery of nature. The oppressiveness of events in Germany after 1935 were answered by Eich with silence. After a long period of soldiering and then release from an American POW camp, he found his voice in several poems which expressed a wry outlook:

With sad silence the stillness of the camp disappears.
My own sigh fills no ear.
Greeting of the world wafts over
through the smell of latrine and chlorine.
                    "Frühling in der goldenen Meil"

Eich had adopted a new, personal rationale for writing poetry: "to orient myself within reality." Quite literally he took inventory of his possessions in order to face the postwar world.

Slowly, however, and programmatically Eich formulated an aesthetics of poetry which gave strength to his work in the fifties. In a nutshell, much of Eich's poetry became a surrealistic topography in which the actualities of life and the intuitions of metaphysics fuse. The sense of "time" and "actuality" causes Eich discomfort because even the moment during which one expresses this sense or feeling it fades from present to past and becomes absurd. Eich has difficulties similar to those of a deaf, mute, and blind person; only a successful verse seems to him like the solidity a blind man knows when he taps his stick and finds objects. For Eich orientation is everything: poems are trigonometric points or buoys which mark passages in unknown territory. For Eich, world is language in which "work" and "thing" coincide to form an original text; we can only sense the original text, and through a successful translation of it into poetry it is possible to achieve the highest degree of reality. Poetic apprehension comes first and whatever psychological, sociological, political meanings may be drawn from a poem, they are secondary: "The poem is my sole necessity."

In some of the poems read to the group, Eich's theories of "translation" from a sensed "original text" are put to practice. Notable is the poem "Schuttablage" [Refuse heap] which resembles the disordered world out of which the poet assembles meaning. Things are the buoys of the poem: thistles, mattress springs, cup, flames, helmet, water birds—in seeming disarray as is a refuse heap. Charity, hope, faith, soul are the abstractions inscribed on a mended cup. Abstractions in the poem fuse with objects to open up a greater reality. Time passes relentlessly and fragments everything; human efforts to mend things result in bitter jests, and for the big questions—the questions of Job—there are no answers, except sometimes through such biblical symbology as the burning thistles or bush. A profound pessimism hangs on Eich's lines, rendering everything questionable and yet worthy of questioning in order to define existence at the very moment it is cannibalized by time.

The coincidence of the timeless and the timely is caught

in one of Eich's most popular poems, "Der Mann in der blauen Jacke," [The man in the blue jacket]. Reality is represented through a farmer who shoulders a spade, which resembles a rifle, and in a quick succession of images he is linked to the farmer of biblical Canaan and his contemporaries in Burma and California. The poet-narrator must resist the temptation of envying the imagined familial life of the farmer, for his happiness is confined to a home within "secured" windows. Indeed, the spade can turn into a rifle and then the primitive implement for tilling becomes an instrument for killing. The fear of accepting happiness runs through many of Eich's poems as the poet warns that we must pay for all such conditional gifts, and the only coin we have is of copper with which we pay Death's ferryman. Anticipatory fear and its mitigation become the pathos of such aphoristic lines as, "Whoever is well acquainted with horror / may await its visitation with equanimity."

Eich is a collector of words and arranges them in teasing patterns, as in his latest collection, *Anlässe und Steingärten* (1966), a title which suggests that Eich compares his poems with Japanese gardens. His words are highly visual, but often the absence of coherent metaphor and image strips words down to private hieroglyphics which defy the associative power of readers. An increasing and deliberate sparseness of language is noticeable as Eich — within a decade — moved from lyrical to antilyrical poetry, to juxtapositions of the concrete and the abstract, and then surged against an invisible barrier beyond which thought and feeling are no longer suggestible through cryptic representation or mere naming of objects. Eich's poetry of statement or declaration frequently leaves the reader high and dry. We sense a meaning and then it eludes our grasp. There is no vestige of romanticism in his "Ode an die Natur" [Ode to nature]: "We have our suspicions / against trout, winter / and accelerated descent." Or, we sense something amusing without finding the point of the joke, as in "Timetable":

> These airplanes
> between Boston and Düsseldorf.
> To make decisions

> is a matter for hippopotamuses.
> I prefer
> to put lettuce
> on a sandwich
> and the privilege of being wrong.

Eich's poetry could no longer stand the strain of the impossible demands of the poet's own theories. Instead, Eich found a new outlet in 1967–68 with the publication of short prose essays *Maulwürfe*, or moles who burrow underground and surface lightninglike. Eich does not disguise his hope that the "moles" will prove unsettling for readers, but the only thing unsettling is Eich's frequent lapses into the banal or forced cleverness: "Sin: The temptations of the flesh are not unfamiliar to me. I admit to succumbing every day (except Fridays when we have fish). . . ." Or, "Truth has acne and pustules; lies, however, do not." No one denies that the world is unsettled and instable, and poets of Eich's stature are tempted to respond in kind, with negligible gains; yet, absurdity rarely is effectively countered by absurdity.

In several speeches Eich has made no bones about the intended function of his poetry as hostility to regimentation, especially of the political variety ("the police sticks of West and East Germany"), and as opposition to robotism and the accretion of state power. Just as Eich resists the cyberneticists' definition that "man is a message," he will accept no less than unrestricted freedom of thought and expression for poets and the preservation of individuality. If Eich's tones are dark and laconic, they are attributable to his feeling that poets ought to hold a seminar for survivors (his strongest political poem is "Seminar für Hinterbliebene") of the world's past and present miseries which should never be forgotten. Yet these sociopolitical sentiments, which came through strongly in some of Eich's radio plays, are largely sublimated in his poetry. During the early years of Group 47 he heeded the call to descend from the ivory tower; in the sixties he went back up and from its top directed occasional potshots into the hectic street scene below.

Few poets have risen as meteorically as Ingeborg Bachmann (b. 1926), gaining the tacitly acknowledged title of
first lady of Group 47 although some ungallant souls also regarded her as its prima donna. At the May 1952 meeting
at Niendorf on the Baltic Sea, the dangers of instant criticism became obvious as interpretations of poetry readings
shot wide of the mark and discussions turned into incon-
clusive polemics. Some thought her poetry to be brittle, but
most were impressed with the intensely lyrical and restrained
attitude of the twenty-six-year-old Austrian poetess as she
read some unpublished selections, among them "Dunkles zu
sagen" [To speak darkly], a manneristic parade piece con-
joining the feeling of a modern poet with that of Orpheus:
in the throes of metamorphosis "we both lament" dissolution into nature. Bachmann plays on the words *Saite* and
Seite (the strings of the lyre and the word *side*):

> Like Orpheus I play
> the tune of death upon the lyre-strings of life
>
> . . . .
> But like Orpheus I know
> life this side of death.

Of primary interest is the previewing of her manneristic
method, the mutability theme, her sense of isolation, the
personification of the inanimate, her strong image patterns,
and the dark subjective mood so prevalent in her poetry.

Later that year she read at another meeting of the group,
but it was in 1953 that she gained its prize, $500 donated by
Rowohlt Publishers and a radio network. As numerous as
the microphones were figures from the publishing world,
magazine editors, reporters, heads of radio studios, literary
agents, and other representatives of the literary marketplace
so that it was an auspicious time for the "young, pretty
woman" to read. No other poet made any burnt offerings at
the sessions, and she made the most of the spotlight and attentive critical focus, eliciting praise for "an astonishing
talent" and "a moving power of language." Through the
available publicity apparatus at the Mainz meeting from

which the encomiums emanated, Bachmann's career was launched, and she was able to sustain it with two slim volumes of poetry in 1953 and 1965, libretti for the composer Hans Werner Henze, and then turning from poetry she wrote radio plays, short stories, and finally a novel in 1971, garnering on the way several prizes of distinction and visiting professorships, including a term at Harvard.

Among Group 47 writers, Bachmann strikes me as having one of the most disciplined minds, subtle and probing, formulating a modern-day gnosticism but often giving way to ecstatic desperation when touching on the subjects of love and language; her existential pathos often becomes the sheer sentimentality she tries to avoid. Her first path was academic —studies of law and philosophy—resulting in a doctoral dissertation on the critical reception of Martin Heidegger's existentialist philosophy. In modern fields of inquiry one finds the greatest morass of verbiage and confusion of thought among philosophers so that the precision of Ludwig Wittgenstein, to whose writing Bachmann fortunately was attracted, wrought a long-overdue revolution. Deliberately seeking isolation, Wittgenstein, a former pupil of Bertrand Russell, taught school in a remote village in Austria and worked out a series of aphorisms in a book called *Tractatus Logico-Philosophicus* (1921), with profound impact upon philosophy and poetics through its inquiry into the necessary relations between "words and things" in language. Judging from Bachmann's essay on the philosopher, she climbed the ladder of his aphorisms and then threw it away as he suggested in *Tractatus*, and turned to poetry. Wittgenstein noted that philosophy is not a theory but an activity of linguistic analysis and logic which clarifies thought yet has a purely tautological character—it can only mirror the world; philosophy, therefore, can neither probe reality nor tell us anything new about it. For the philosopher Wittgenstein, the *"limits of my language* mean the limits of my world" (*Tractatus*, 5.6) and it follows that "whereof one cannot speak, thereof one must be silent" (*Tractatus*, 7). The nondidactic poet goes beyond the denial or assertion of facts, which is the essential business of language, and seeks to elucidate feelings through nonlogical metaphor and to change the "limits" of the world. Bachmann made the transition from the logic of philosophy to the existential pathos of man, a bound creature "not completely capable of saying what he suffers," but, said Bachmann in her essay on *Music and Poetry*, one must respect this anguished human voice for we all live "on this darkling planet" threatened by ever-growing madness.

The remarkable rapidity with which Bachmann's poetry gained individuality may be attributed in part to her realization that "the facts of literature are accompanied by theory." She was encouraged by the example of Hugo von Hoffmansthal, who felt that when routinely used abstract words fall apart "in one's mouth like mouldy mushrooms" one must abandon comfortable simplifications. The poet must seek some unifying principles amid daily fragmentation and seek orientation through art as to one's actual and potential place in fateful time, using the vantage point of a historical present. Essential to her theory is the idea that the poet is in conflict with language and that out of this conflict should develop a new manner of style, *Gangart*, which houses a new spirit and moral drive and seeks perception rather than aesthetic satisfaction: within given boundaries, the poet must establish the signification of language and renew language through ritual.

By associating ritual with language, Bachmann revives the oldest function of both, that is, to allow man to participate in the re-creation of the universe, the drama of man's fall, the longing for Eden. "Everything is a question of language," writes Bachmann, and the poet as *Mitwisser der Schöpfung* has co-knowledge of creation and must engage in a constantly renewing empathy. In her poetry volumes *Die Gestundete Zeit* [Borrowed time] (1953) and *Anrufung des grossen Bären* [Appeal to the Great Bear] (1956), Bachmann opens her senses to ancient and modern experiential processes through which psychological symbols (Sun-god, Earth-mother) became universal archetypes and accepted mental patterns. Specifically, she found in the zodiacal system, which has maintained a hold on the popular imagination since Babylonian times, an interplay of fact and intuition, science and magic, and mythopoetic accretions. Some of her poetics are strikingly similar to Aristotle's *De Caelo* in which the stars and constellations are viewed not merely as bodies arranged in order but are possessed of soul and life and activity comparable with that of animals and plants. Bachmann was fascinated by the zodiacal pictorialization of the interpenetrative relationships of everything within time—animals, humans and heroes, gods, objects— as well as the zodiac's service as a mathematical measuring device of time.

It would be wrong to read astrological symbolism into every poem that Bachmann has written, but on the other hand an interpretation of many of her poems without recourse to a table of constellations with signs, names, meanings, attributes, and color significations is to ignore the coherence of the imagery. In her poetry there are striking resemblances to the facts and metaphors of the astrological system as the sun annually enters the signs of the zodiac, ascends eastward from dawn to its apex at noon, pitiless and splendid, and descends westward below the horizon into dark night. The figures of wolf, lupines, dogs, fish, sea snakes, dragons and monsters, crabs and dancing scorpions, bear, and others of the constellation lead their double life—cosmic and related to the borrowed time of man. Stars and moon have their symbolic functions as omens—the moon with its oldest significations hovers over such disasters as shipwrecks —and are not to be taken as romantic paraphernalia.

In the title poem, "Die Gestundete Zeit," *Zeit* simultaneously means the measured time of the zodiac—its mathematical and prophetic function—and the idea of borrowed time—a duration of time before humans must pay their destined debt. Within the poem a prophetic warning is heard, "soon you must tie your shoes" (a colloquializing of the biblical "gird your loins"), and later the urgency of time elapsed and not to be denied, "Do not look back. / Tie your shoes," as the end of human time "becomes visible on the horizon," the line between the ascent and descent of the sun. Characteristic are the tautological lines which inexorably repeat facts while the names of constellations and stars actualize mythic-cosmic-human relationships. Who is the loved one sinking in the "sand" of time and ready to part from this life "after every embrace"? She seems to be the partner in the eternal replay of the Orpheus-Eurydice drama and at the same time the girl with the "flowing hair" (*Coma Berenices*, the constellation named after the ancient princess who sacrificed her hair to the gods in order to save her husband), assuming one of the many thematic motifs in Bachmann's poetry.

Once one understands Bachmann's numinous interchange between constellations and man within the context of time and hears the mythological and biblical tones, one appreciates her art. The poem "Anrufung des grossen Bären," "Appeal to the Great Bear" (with echo meanings of "invocation" and "conjuration") illustrates her orientation as a drama ensues between poet and the bear in its stellar and literal figuration.

> Great Bear, come down, shaggy night,
> cloudfur beast with the old eyes,
> star eyes,
> through the underbrush break shimmering
> your paws with their claws,
> star claws,
> wakefully we guard our hearths,
> though in your ban, and we mistrust
> your tired flanks and the sharp
> half-exposed teeth,
> old bear.

> A pine-cone: your world.
> You: its scales.
> I prod them, tumble them
> from the pines in the Beginning
> to the pines at the End,
> snort at them, test them in my maw
> and seize them with my paws.

Be fearful or be not fearful!
Pay into the jingling purse and give
the blind man a good word
so that he keeps the bear in tow.
And spice the lambs well.

Could be that this bear
tears itself loose, threatens no longer
and chases all cones that from the pines
have dropped, the great, winged ones
which plunged from paradise.

With a display of foolhardy daring and a sense of fear, man challenges the cosmos anthropomorphically only to be again thrown back upon his own, as was Job after God's rhetorical question, "Canst thou guide the bear with her train?" (Job, 38, xxxii). With trepidation, the poet summons the great bear and is warned that just as the bear of the woods toys with cones so the bear of the stars, a concretized primal force, toys with the planetary world until the inevitable apocalypse. The pines are the trees of paradise, the winged fallen cones are angels or symbolically Adam's fall; the blind Tiresias is the prophet priest who propitiates God, gods, constellations, or forces through sacrificial lambs and he is the circusman who thinks he has the bear in tow. If one also sees the "star eyes" as the planets or "the eyes of the Lord" (mentioned in Zechariah, 4, x), one indulges in a luxury allowed by the allusive yet tight structure of the poem. Again, neither man's hope nor despair counts in the workings of a universe in which the bear can change from *Ursa Major* to its original nameless potential force; the world is independent of man's will. Bachmann's existential allegory of the bear is as brilliant as Camus's interpretation of the Sisyphus myth.

Statements of fact and the figurative have the same syntax in Bachmann's poetry, and one readily accepts their reversibility particularly within the elegiac sense of time which is so prevalent as to be obsessive.

And what does your heart already attest?
Between yesterday and tomorrow swings your heart,
soundless and strange,
and what it tolls,
is its fall out of time.

"Fall ab, Herz" [Fall off, heart]

In Bachmann's poems the fall of Icarus-Adam-angel-man-pine cone is identical:

... he approaches the shears of the sun
in the fog, and when it blinds him,
the fog embraces him in his fall.

"Die Brücken"

Sometimes such concepts, personifications, metaphors, and realities combine kaleidoscopically to yield a message, "Botschaft":

From the corpse-warm vestibule of heaven steps the sun.
Not the immortals are there,
but the fallen, we perceive.

No light touches decay. Our godhead,
History, has reserved us a grave
from which there is no arising.

In the poem "Nachtflug" [Nightflight], associatively the bombardier too is a plower who tills the heavens with motors and he is no less destructive than the Plough-star created by the gods of Babylonian legend to kill Gilgamesh. When the air is rent asunder by the man-made comets, "Sun and earth have not disappeared, / but wander like stars and are unrecognizable." The point-of-view alternately shifts from the pilot above, who concentrates on the cold mechanics of his job, to the people affected by the devastation below. The moral horror of the pilot's dissociation from the effects of his pin-pointings is as coolly rendered as the attempt to pick up everyday routine by people who are in a state of shock— yet, above them also hovers the question, "Whose hands were clean?" One may interpret celestial conjunctions of the

zodiac, but who may interpret the man-made plane's lingering silver cloud-strip? "Who dares to remember the night?"
Facts, symbols, rhetorical questions are unfamiliarly juxta-
posed in a familiar context (a bombing incident) and define
Bachmann's *Gangart*, her poetic stance.

As in "Nachtflug," several other poems touch on the past
and contemporary events in a generalized way.

> Where Germany's sky blackens the earth,
> its decapitated angel seeks a grave for hate
> and hands you the dish of its heart.
>
> . . . .
>
> Seven years later,
> in a house of death,
> yesterday's executioners
> drain the golden cup.
>
> "Früher Mittag" [Early noon]

No one seems to have learned:

> The war is no longer declared
> but continued. The outrageous
> has become commonplace.
>
> "Alle Tage" [All the days]

For the most part, Bachmann was haunted by the flux and
decay of things and the lack of cosmic causality; cyclic
stellar conjunctions either will preside over the millennium
or the destruction of the world through deluge or fire—
"Ahead of the hurricane the sun flees westward, / two thousand years are up and nothing will remain for us" ("Grosse
Landschaft bei Wien," [Great landscape near Vienna]).

Bachmann is at her best when she gives us her own "Cur-
riculum Vitae," passionate lyric confessions, which must be
respected for their sincerity, power, and openness of heart.
They range through manneristic conceits, the elegiac, the
psychological loving-is-dying theme, and the unreservedly
erotic which reminds one of Sylvia Plath's tragic poetry. If
she despairs of finding reciprocity in love or torments herself
with impossible questions in that extraordinary poem
"Erklär mir, Liebe" [Tell me, Love], she also can achieve a

Wittgensteinian calm, "Nothing is more beautiful under the sun than to be under the sun" ("An die Sonne" [Hymn to the sun]), or to live wakefully within the demands of one's calling ("Die Brücken" [Bridges]). Though rejecting clichés from every quarter ("Reklame" [Advertising]), she has no recourse but to fall back on those which are true and not disprovable. If a number of familiar poets and their turns of phrase are heard in her lines (for instance, Rilke: "Herr: es ist Zeit. Der Sommer war sehr gross"; Bachmann: "Die grosse Fracht des Sommers ist verladen"), she was slowly finding her own idiom. Of the poet, poetry, and audiences she wrote: "Poetry: like bread? This bread would have to make a crunching sound between teeth and re-awaken hunger before it stills it. And this poetry becomes sharp with perception and bitter with longing. . . . We sleep, yes, are sleepers for fear of taking stock of ourselves and our world."

With her two volumes of poetry she showed intimations of greatness, but in declining to continue, possibly out of fear of being submerged as were other poets she pointed to, she did not rise to the challenge implicit in the verses she quoted from Petrarch: "I cannot stay silent, / though I fear that my language may not match what is in my heart." She displays no particular Heimweh or nostalgia for any of the many places and countries she has lived in, except for Italy, and gives the impression of carrying her isolation from place to place. Rome, for all intents, has become her home. Her perception and withdrawal are particularly well portrayed in two stanzas of her longest poem "Von einem Land, einem Fluss und den Seen" [About a land, a river and the seas]:

> Of what concern to us are moon and stars,
> to us, whose stars darken and kindle!
> When the most beautiful of countries fades
> it is we who draw it inward as a dream.
>
> Where is decree, where order? Where appear
> to us leaf and tree and stone completely graspable?
> In the language of beauty they are present,
> in pure being. . . .

Bachmann's reassertion of the lyric tradition came in the face of Group 47 opposition to a mode which it felt would lead to the abyss of sentimentality.

Paul Celan (1920–70) is perhaps the one author who read at a Group 47 meeting only once and still had several poems included in the selective fifteen-year cross-section in *Almanach der Gruppe 47*, a collection of readings published in 1962 and edited by Hans Werner Richter. It was belated recognition of an opportunity missed to foresee and honor one of the most distinguished contemporary careers in poetry. Few of Celan's poems cause immediate reader understanding; often their frame of reference is invisible and must be searched out. The group's tendency toward instant criticism favors works that lend themselves to immediate gratification; otherwise they enflame useless debates about "pure poetry" (a term which wrongly covers everything from symbolic and linguistically difficult poetry to sound-without-sense) as against engaged poetry, a debate which ensued after Celan's readings in May, 1952, at Niendorf. In retrospect, one of the group's most perceptive analysts, Rolf Schroers, noted that criticism during meetings was a matter of temperament allied to political tensions and preconceived critical views, and so it was that Paul Celan with his "visionary" articulation and undeniable pathos had the estranging experience of running into moods and criticism more attuned to less demanding imagination and language.

Among the many literary works to which Celan was drawn by affinity and which help to clarify his poetic and existential mood is Shakespeare's *King Lear*. Celan's tone is reflected in the Duke of Albany's words which ring down the curtain on the tragedy: "The weight of this sad time we must obey, / Speak what we feel, not what we ought to say"; and, Lear's last words which verge on madness and absurdity: "And my poor fool is hang'd! No, no, no life! / Why should a dog, a horse, a rat have life, / And thou no breath at all?" In Shakespeare's language the incommunicability of grief and thought has been made communicable. It seems to me that Celan in his own ways has hit upon similar solutions to communicate the incommunicable with powerful, reiterative words and allusive fragments which gain meaning as one follows them through his ten volumes of poetry. "We live under dark skies," wrote Celan in 1955, "and—there are few humans. Therefore there are so few poems. The hopes which I still have are not great; I attempt to retain what has remained." Specifically, "Reachable, near and not lost amid the losses, remained one thing: language." Retention, clarification, and objectification of feeling through poetry engaged Celan for two decades, and here I can only hint at the evolution—or more accurately the radicalization and frequent antilyricism—of his work, pushing symbolist poetry to the limits of its potential. Reductionism of language to the brink of silence was the road which many Group 47 poets followed.

Celan, born in 1920 in Czernowitz (a city in the Rumanian province of Bukowina), was the son of a construction technician; his parents were Austrian Jews. He began studies in France but returned for Romance language work at the University of Czernowitz until 1941 when the city began to be occupied by German and Hungarian troops. From the ghetto his parents were deported to a German extermination camp, but Celan escaped and survived in a Rumanian forced-labor camp. After the war, he left Russian-annexed territory, with no glowing memories, and worked as a translator and publisher's reader in Bucharest and in 1947 saw the publication of his first volume, *Agora,* which contained some poems in German, written under the pseudonym Paul Celan (Antschel was the family name). Following a short stay in Vienna he settled permanently in Paris, renewing his studies and specializing in Germanistics and linguistics. In 1950 he became a lecturer at the École Normale in German language and literature and married the graphic artist Gisèle Lestrang. He sat in Group 47's electric chair in 1952, garnered the 1958 city of Bremen literary prize and the prestigious Georg Büchner prize two years later, giving acceptance talks which offer the few keys to his personal poetry, though he warns that keys to the "house," like words, must be changeable and changed. Generally, he steered clear of explication: "It is part of the nature of the poem that it tolerates the co-knowledge of him who 'delivers' it only as long as it is necessary to come into being." Celan was not being merely ingenuous but he began more and more to believe that a poem has a life of its own, takes its shape in the hands of its creator, and then becomes transfixed at a critical moment to achieve *stasis*.

Among critics who considered Celan to have been the most representative of contemporary lyricists writing in German, Kurt Leonhard suggested that "he is the only one to continue, in his own and in modern ways, the great transmission of the free-rhythmic hymns and elegies begun with Klopstock and carried over from Hölderlin to the late Rilke." Others feel that much of Celan's poetry consists of metalanguage, that is, language about language, or metapoetry, namely, declarative and suggestive constructs and symbols, which result from certain linguistic theories. Validation can be found for both views. In Celan's poetry one senses the strenuous effort to retain control over the expressed emotion through the dialectics of antithesis, synthesis, and paradox. He has an overwhelming sense of time (the evanescent now which crystallizes the past or the idea of time as yet not arrived), place (where poetry "singes" the ground beneath the poet), and people (that is, the search for relatedness). Of the accents he thought could be placed on words and ideas —the "acute," "gravis" or the historical, the "circumflex" or the stress on the eternal—he chose the acute or the emphasis on the now in which everything converges. The poetry which transformed his experiences has a linguistic virtuosity and learnedness that remind one of such superacademicians as Joyce and Beckett. New coining of words, insertions of phrases and loan words from Latin, Russian, French, Spanish, Hebrew, Yiddish, and Middle High German, macaronic mixtures, Slavic use of prefixes, etymological punning to get at root meanings, recombinations, and other linguistic constructs have kept exegesists busy; with the aid of computers, we now have a concordance and a path-breaking linguistic study by Horst Peter Neumann.

In Celan's earliest poetry one senses an attempt to find his

métier as he discarded poems that were either too traditional
in structure, as "Der Pfeil der Artemis" [The arrow of
Artemis], or incongruous in harboring both imagistic-sym-
bolic and realistic descriptions, as "Schwarze Flocken"
[Black snowflakes], in which the grief over a murdered father
becomes poetic slush. Theodor Adorno in his oft-quoted remark that poetry would not be possible after Auschwitz posed
the problem of whether poetry—or fiction—through aesthetic devices would be able to pictorialize unspeakable horror without giving potential pleasure to the reader who witnesses the naked relationship between victim and victimizer.
Nelly Sachs's epitaph poems and Celan's much-anthologized
"Todesfuge," "Death Fugue" of 1945, are among the few
poems which somewhat allay fears of the unintentionally
perverse possibilities of art. Though one can admire Celan's
fugue construction, the poem does not allow unalloyed en-
joyment because it strips away any pretension that aesthetics
may not be incompatible with brutality and that the denial
by a man of another's dignity may not conflict with love for
one's own family. The juxtaposition of a concentration camp
commander's sentimentalization of his wife—a golden-haired
Margarete—while coolly supervising a grave for the ashen-
haired Sulamith to the tune of music requires no overt
comment by the poet; it induces shame in the reader whose
sensibilities are not dead and it presents a single, graspable—
yet endemic and symbolic—experience. The miscued symbol
of "black snowflake" has now turned into the appropriate
one of "black milk" which the victims must drink night,
noon, and morning, until the bitter end, while a handful of
simple, declarative phrases are arranged and rearranged into
a stark memorial mound, unadorned and unmarred by punctuation. Of the poem, the German critic Harald Weinrich
has said that it "sits upon all our necks."

Celan rapidly distanced himself from what might be
called the mellifluous horror of the "Death Fugue." In the
volumes *Mohn und Gedächtnis* [Poppy and memory]
(1952) and *Von Schwelle zu Schwelle* [Threshold to thresh-
old] (1955) Celan's poems sound his main themes and concerns: the martyrology of the "word," lament for the dead,

existence and personal experience, a secular or nontheological confrontation with God. Although Celan drives language to the limits of intelligibility, he is careful to avoid an absolute mystique: thought about word and language is as socially oriented as with Joyce. Celan also regards the Word as it was in the beginning and still remains—the conscience or consciencelessness of man; the "contorted" or crippled or "upright" words, whichever suits the poet's state and verbalizes his frustrations or hopes; the martyr words of the martyred dead, which lived on to haunt Celan; a word *becomes* its object—flower, stone, corpse—and it can seem as forlorn as the specific person it represents. Words can assume extraordinary weight as *never, no-one, time*; whether the word is lifeless or full of life, sacred or profane, maimed, silent or vocal, it has meaning and with care may be loosened from one's "heart wall." The word may reflect states of being, disparateness of "Dis- / parates"—the torn-ness of humans or *Men-schen*; punctuation becomes a guide to meaning. In these terms one may understand Celan's remarks that poetry is a visual form of language with the characteristics of dialogue—"sometimes desperate dialogue"; words have a goal: the reader and a reality which are addressable and against which a poem can hurl itself.

One might choose the poem "Schibboleth" to stand for the many which show far-ranging associative use of "the word." In Judges xii, 1–6, is the biblical story of a civil war in which 42,000 Israelites were slain when they mispronounced the password *Schibboleth*. Along with the disaster at the fords of the ancient Jordan river, the poet asks that the reader also "think of the dark / twinredness / in Vienna and Madrid." If one brings memory of recent history to fill in the meaning of the places named, one recalls the late thirties when these cities were engulfed by a similar blood-red fate, German annexation and civil war, which meant the decimation of Jews and Spanish anti-Fascists, as well as the blackout of freedom. It is a memorial poem and a call to participatory remembrance:

> Set your flag at halfmast,
> memory.

At halfmast
for today and ever.

. . . . . .

I lead you across
to the voices
of Estremadura.

He wants us to hear the voices of the dead at the battle of
Estremadura, Spain, as they perished with the cry, "*No
pasarán,*" "they shall not pass," which also were the words of
French soldiers at Verdun. The selected weight of words in
this sparsely worded poem creates new dimensions of
rhetoric.

Celan's insistence upon memory as a function of poetic
activity encompasses his political, personal, and social consciousness, summing up the process with the phrase "Mohn
und Gedächtnis." The juice of poppies is the narcotic of
forgetfulness, sleep, out of which must rise memory to attain
a concrete reality. Love does this in the poem "Corona":

. . . we love one another like poppy and memory,
we sleep like wine in the sea shells

. . . .

We stand entwined at the window, they see us from the
    street

. . . .

It is time that it be time.
It is time.

It is time, he feels, that memory flourish though it does
not heal; on the contrary, bitterness and lament remain and
become increasingly pointed in language and reference. At
the end of the "memory" volume he expresses the wish that
he be counted among the bitter almonds one bites into, and
literally he continues to carry his lamenting word from
threshold to threshold (the title of his subsequent volume of
poetry).

In the volume *Sprachgitter* (1959; *Speech-Grille and
Selected Poems,* trans. Joachim Neugröschel, 1971), barriers
or screens stand between poet and word or person and person. Voices and words keep turning up in various contexts:

> Voices, from which your heart
> retreats into the heart of your mother.
> Voices from the gallows-tree. . . .

and

> Jacob's Voice:
> The tears.
> The tears in the brother's eye.
> One tear clung, grew.
> We live within it.
> Breathe, so that
> it may free itself.

These short poems are indicative of the way Celan finds breathing space and release that allows a renewal of strength to bear the sense of isolation as all searches for relatedness throw the poet back upon his own resources. He rejects no avenue or representation of experience and finds truth in the paradoxical epigrams of the mystics, without, however, succumbing to blind faith. The power of conviction through contradiction and paradox in Angelus Silesius's seventeenth-century poems, *Cherubinischer Wandersmann, The Cherubinic Wanderer*, reaches through the commonplace what-ought-to-be-said to individualistic assertions:

> God is nothing at all;
> and if he be something
> it is only within me,
> he having chosen me.

And, in another epigram, Silesius said,

> The rose which here and now
> thine outer eyes behold,
> For all eternity
> hath also blossomed in God.

Such representations occur in several Celan poems, among them "Tenebrae" (Matthew, xxvii, 45 f., "there was *darkness* over all the land. . . . 'My God, my God, why hast thou forsaken me?'"):

Near we are, Lord,
near and graspable.

Already grasped, Lord, clawed into one another, as if
the body of each of us
were your body, Lord.

Pray, Lord
pray to us
we are near.

The lines pose an inversion of relationships, a secularization
of the religious.

In Celan's volume *Die Niemandsrose* [The no-one's rose]
(1963) the mystic rose also becomes mundane (the "ghetto
rose") and blossoms into many meanings. The technique is
fascinating but a few examples will have to suffice. Though
using the tone and parallelistic style of a psalm, Celan turns
prayer insideout and grafts his own interpretation onto the
rose mysticism typified by Silesius and the theosophic speculations of Kabbalism; his poem "Psalm" also expresses the
lament and hope of the dead and the living.

No one kneads us again out of earth and loam,
no one eulogizes our dust.
No one.

Praise be to you, No-one.
For your sake shall
we blossom
Towards
you.

Nothing
were we, are we, will we
remain, blossoming:
the No-one's—, the
No-one's rose. . . .

A poem, according to Celan, exists on the border of itself,
speaks of what no longer is but draws back into what still
persists: "This poetry . . . this eternal, unending 'saying' is

of pure mortality and nought." Man's creative striving, a creative nought, finds its complement in the concept of God, No-one (*Niemand*), the name of the ineffable who, according to some Kabbalists, lives in the depth of his nothingness, infinite and *without* end, *en-Sof* in Hebrew (Celan poetically connects the *en, without,* to its appearance in the German word Mensch*en, humans*).

During his Büchner-prize talk in 1960, Celan pointed out that some of his "topography" would be unfamiliar to the German reader, a topography or early homelife in which Martin Buber's stories of the Chassidim (a Polish-Jewish mystical group founded during the eighteenth century) played a role. Traditions and prayers observed by his parents come back to punctuate many of his memory poems which —like the Kaddish prayer for the dead—are marked by a feeling of respect and intend to give honor, most obviously in such poems as "Hawdalah," "Benedicta," "Radix, Matrix," "Du sei wie du immer." But unlike Buber's emphasis on the "I and Thou" relationship between man and God, Celan's search for relatedness also leads to other conceptual and physical contacts; at the root and matrix—the source or mother womb—he finds ambivalence and multiplicity, the essences of interpretive and symbolic poetry. Even the most common words in Celan's poetry become metaphors and part of a noninformational, emotional and associative language, an experience per se, which requires the utmost "attentiveness that is the natural prayer of the soul," a phrase by Malebranche quoted by Celan. How attentive one must be is evident in "Corona," seen by some exclusively as an erotic love lyric. We note the line, "My eye descended to the sex [*Geschlecht*] of the beloved"; yet the word *Geschlecht* also means race or generations of family cut to the roots, as in the poem "Radix, Matrix":

. . . generation [*Geschlecht*] which was murdered, which standing black in the heavens:
rod and testes—?

(Root,
root of Abraham. Root of Jesse. No-one's
root—o / ours.)

In the poem "Soviel Gestirne" [So many stars], we find the lines:

there, consumed by fire, stood
nipple-proud [*zitzenprächtig*] time

. . . .

I know, I know and you know, we knew,
we knew not, we
indeed were there and not there,
and at times, when
only that Nothing stood between us, found
we ourselves together.

Through memory, time despite all its tenses becomes dimensionless and allows renewal with the lost. Aside from the obvious wordplay, time is characterized as feminine and maternal—a recurrent personal motif—but the word *Zitze* additionally refers to the Hebrew word for fringe (as one of the four fringes on a prayer shawl, which signify the corners of the earth, worn by the orthodox as a constant reminder from afar of the laws from Sinai).

The titles of Celan's last volumes of poetry consist of disparate words yoked into metaphysical metaphors (speechgrille, No-one's rose, breath-turning, thread-suns, lightforce) which name and define the most unexpected relationships; among men these are emotional and between man and nature they are intellectualized. Celan felt that the greater the kaleidoscopic possibilities of expression the more necessary it was to be precise, not to obscure the perceived, not to "poetize" but instead to find "the lost," as he phrased it in *Schneepart* [Snowbreaker] (a volume published in 1971, one year after his suicide in Paris where he drowned in the Seine) and to find "Kargheit, Klarheit," the paradox of clarity through word-stinginess. As Celan explained, the poet in a search of his identity meets himself through detours, *Um-Wege*, in his own poetry and sets himself free. If some of Celan's later poetry is too condensed, too miserly with words and turned inward, it is probably because Celan increasingly feared that aesthetic elaboration in a poem falsifies human experience. More often than not Celan's disciplined chariness resulted in a poetry of conviction which eschewed religious and political doctrines yet subscribed to a religious and political humanism. The deep faith he had in the power of the poet to face man-made darkness is evident in the poems he dedicated to Ossip Mandelstamm (a victim of Stalin's purges in 1938), whose poetry he translated from the Russian. (The name itself afforded Celan sources of puns and metaphor: *Mandel* or almond, *Stamm* or family tree.) The envoy of a poem in Celan's *Niemandsrose* reads:

> But,
> but he uprears himself, the tree. He,
> also he
> stands opposed to
> *the pest.*

Of modern German poets, Karl Krolow (b. 1915) is the most widely read, and his popularity owes little to his association with Group 47, an association which at best was peripheral since there seem to have been few bonding elements. He contributed a poem to the short-lived periodical *Der Ruf* and read from his work at group sessions during the years 1952 and 1954. The group critics characterized his poetry as embodying lyrical realism and harboring flawless pictorial richness. Largely, these are the hallmarks of his poetry, and while his forms changed within some ten volumes from traditional nature lyricism to later reductionism, though mild by comparison with Celan, the mellifluous tone remained as did the basic ideas that self-knowledge comes through understanding of nature and that experience is visual rather than metaphysical.

Krolow's blend of aesthetic and moral observations without glaringly abrasive social criticism puts him close to the public pulse and, aside from popular recognition, has gained for him membership in three literary academies (Darmstadt, Mainz, Bavaria), the Georg Büchner prize, and visiting professorships. As a gifted theoretician of contemporary German poetry, he wrote *Aspekte zeitgenössischer deutscher Lyrik* (1963), showing his predilections. He explained his own premises for the writing of poetry in an essay called

"Intellektuelle Heiterkeit" [Intellectual cheerfulness], which appeared in an anthology *Mein Gedicht ist Mein Messer* [My poem is my knife] (1955). For Krolow, the writing of poetry is a calculated procedure, fairly brief, which takes place preferably at a time distant from the factual experience for which the poet acts as a mirror or filter; distance allows for objectified observation and avoids capitulation to emotion. The poem should not be hermetic but porous, experimentally open to all impressions and never occupied with itself, implying Krolow's dissatisfaction with poets who agonize over the inadequacy of language or who take poetry as theoretic substance for their poetry. Metaphors of the greatest possible precision and evocativeness ("Night is like the school-chalk into which one bit when a child") activate poems instead of chance inspiration or language experiments. In sum, Krolow sets for himself the goals of elegance without mundane snobbism, polish, and intellectual cheerfulness which often becomes wry observation.

From Wilhelm Lehmann and Oskar Loerke, Krolow learned how to "deindividualize" poetry and to shear it of mawkish sentiment and bucolic ornamentation, to utilize the infinite possibility of imagery association between the life of nature and the activity of man, to focus on a time-centered now as if with an "aperspective" lens. He was impressed particularly with Loerke's "experience of being" (*Daseinserfahrung*) as central to poetry, and which is rendered by intelligible metaphors, without ciphers or the need for learned apparatus. Constant in all of Krolow's poetry is an immediacy of sensation. For instance, eleven years separate the following lines taken from two of Krolow's poems:

> The ashes of my voice
> I strewed into the river
> so that they flow downstream
> like tracks of rust.

"Notturno," 1948

> Landscape seen after the eye-measure
> of two libations:

She moves about you with whip and flute
"The Fairy Queen," 1959

Although the imagery throughout the years holds new surprises and freshness, the tone of the poems remains almost undeviatingly urbane, and the nature-life associations display the same techniques.

Krolow, however, takes important technical departures from his admired predecessors, the nature lyricists, by expanding his lines to almost prose length in many poems from 1948 to 1959 and then gradually contracting them by deliberately thinning out imagery, abandoning rhyme for acoustic and visual reasons and perhaps greater word simplicity. Moreover he sought to avoid the ossifying tendency of century-long traditions of nature poetry by adopting principles discerned while translating Spanish and French poetry, particularly the possibilities of surrealism. As Krolow diagnosed nature poetry, he found that even the best suffered from excess "weightiness of meaning," to the detriment of free movement and variability, as well as overstuffed content. The remedies he wished to apply would create a poem lighter in words and movement, with "geometric clarity, algebraic sureness," surprise, and sudden illumination of meaning. Toward these ends he dedicated the poem "Der Augenblick des Fensters," literally, the instant wink of a window:

> Someone shakes light
> out of the window.
> Roses of the air
> blossom,
> and in the street
> children at play lift
> their eyes
> Doves stealthily nibble
> of its sweetness.
> Girls grow beautiful
> and men tender
> in this light.

But before they can tell each other,
the window is closed again
by someone.

If only the momentary light of that unnamed love pouring out of the window had graced the poet, we might have had a poem worthy of all the theorizing. As it is, the operation was successful but the poem died. and the autopsy is repeatedly performed by twelve-year-old German school children with the guidance of lesson plans. Few of Krolow's allegorical vignettes are successful, and his strength lies in descriptive and observational poetry, the conceits and liquidity of his nature poems, and still-life renderings as in "Tote Jahreszeit" [Dead season].

A criticism most often levelled against Krolow is that he followed rather than led poetic trends. The charge is too facile, and it may be that the changeable moods of the times and his own cautious approach rather than fads determined his directions. When he made his debut during the war with an empyrean volume gaily entitled *Hochgelobtes Gutes Leben* [The high-praised good life] (1943) one may have wondered justly about his sense of reality. Germany's defeat in war and concomitant misery changed his mood as reflected in the poem "An den Frieden," a hymn to peace, published in 1946 in the fourth issue of *Der Ruf*, which ends with a plea that peace, the consoler of those writhing in the abyss, may revive mankind amid the bone-strewn meadows. Neither man nor nature from then on remained untainted by demonicism in his poetry. A patina of skepticism began to cover most of his poems; retrospectively he said, "The sharpness of a knife shows itself / by cutting through illusion," "everything is optical illusion." To wit, occasionally his poems speak of peace as "prescribed indifference," of politics—"one hand grows out of the earth indifferently separated from the other hand," of political man as a robot, and of soldiers with their "flat, machine-gun eyes." Some of Krolow's topical poems such as "Koreanische Elegie" [Korean elegy], have power; others are resigned, lamenting, or poignant poems on inescapable death, as well as erotic poems about love and its evanescence (some were written in 1956 and 1964 but not published until 1970). Of "Historie" he wrote,

> Men carried a flag through the square.
> Then centaurs broke out of the underbrush
> and trampled the cloth
> and history could begin.
> Melancholy States
> fell apart on street corners.
> Orators stood ready
> with bulldogs,
> and the younger women
> rouged their faces for the strongest.
> Ceaselessly in the air
> voices quarreled, although
> the mythologic creatures long since
> had withdrawn.
> Still there remains the hand
> which closes about one's throat.

His view of history and of man darkened, and the same feeling pervades Krolow's volume *Nichts weiter als Leben* [Nothing but life] (1970) with its personal epitaph, "It is time to ready one's self." In that collection the poem "Nur weiss" [Only white] is typical of Krolow's newly compressed imagery and stark reduction of the nature poem:

> Only white. The pictures
> no longer play a role.
> The day is
> a white spot when
> eyes ache.
> One lives with bare words—
> coldness which warps
> objects. The snowfingers
> of surviving plants
> point into the air, in which
> the energy of winter
> sleeps, sounds of glass

rubbing against glass
which breaks soundlessly.

Krolow does not take nature symbolism as far as did Eich,
Celan, and Bachmann because of his constraint that poetry
should not exceed the limits of instant comprehension.
Although the range of content and the achievement of
chiselled form in Krolow's poetry is impressive, what is not
discernible is the intellectual center of the poet; subject and
themes are fogged by moodiness or diminished by ironic
elegance, which rob the poetry of the significance it might
otherwise have had. Still, one is grateful for poems through
which one vicariously experiences the poet's journey into
"the inner moment," the coincidence of nature and human
life on a plane which might be described as a "soulscape."
For English readers, Michael Bullock's translated samples
of Krolow's poems, *Foreign Bodies* (1969), should be welcome.

Helmut Heissenbüttel (b. 1921) made his debut at the
May 1955 session of Group 47, during which his poems met
with mixed criticism. Despite the toneless recital of poems,
some participants thought them to be expressive, bold, concentrated, and unmotivated pictures. Others felt that the
series of thought fragments or pure association lyrics were
pretentious and esoteric models of self-expression and defi-
nitely not everyone's bag. Actually, the poems had an air
of incompleteness about them as if Heissenbüttel had just
poured them out of his literary test tube; a full assessment
was premature.

Among autobiographical items cryptically mentioned by
Heissenbüttel in an early questionnaire were, "No vocation.
Married. Amputation of the left arm (1941 Russia)." The
experiences of the heavily wounded German soldier at the
Russian front may have molded his view of a senseless world
in which the written word becomes the one mode of intellectual assertion, but there is no overt translation of autobiography into literature except for some doomsday prose
in his work during the sixties. A long period of academic

studies ensued after his release from the army, including architecture, at first, and then serious concern with Germanistics and art history. In 1955 he did free-lance work for the noted Stuttgart radio network and two years later became its Radio-Essay editor when Alfred Andersch left.

During Heissenbüttel's almost continuous presence at the Group 47 meetings, he stood out as the most intelligible representative of the new avant-garde and, in many respects, laid the groundwork for acceptance of the abstractionist prose of Jürgen Becker, Peter Bichsel, and Peter Handke. Through his wide-ranging studies in comparative literature and art, as well as films, he felt the impact of the moderns: Joyce, Faulkner, Gertrude Stein, Cummings, Beckett, Wallace Stevens, Queneau, Tardieu, Dufrêsne, Arp, Klee, Picasso, Schwitters, Max Bense, Eugene Gomringer, Franz Mon, Bazon Brock, H. G. Helms, and the philosophy of Wittgenstein. Recognizable then are Heissenbüttel's explorations in dadaism, abstractionism, concrete poetry (with its emphasis on the single word rather than syntactic connections), the *nouveau roman*, and other forms of modernism. The geometrizing of art by Mondrian and Kandinsky and the subsequent techniques of constructivism to manipulate forms in order to design a new reality distinct from nature (and even antagonistic to it, as in the case of Mondrian) led in the late forties to the idea of "concrete" art, a concept adopted by poets. In art the various forms of constructivism require a reduction of representable objects to geometric-mathematical planes, lines, and points. The idea was to isolate the representation from its natural surrounding and throw absolute emphasis on the object represented, achieving a new purity of style in art and language and forcing the viewer or reader to see things in a new and aperspective way. The dangers to communicability were obvious to Heissenbüttel in putting art theory into prose or poetic practice; but since he mistrusted the traditional "speech reproducing" literature and traditional contextual grammar, he was willing to gamble on the possibilities of a literature whose language was rigorous and ascetic and still open to the fantasy of the intellect. A cue for modern poets lies in Eugen Gomringer's assertion that with the constellation of poetry something new is placed into the universe, which is a reality unto itself and no longer poetry *about* something; poetry, he implied, should be implicit and not explicit.

It is impossible to shed subjectivity totally even in objective poetry, as one may gather from Heissenbüttel's remark that "as a writer I search for methods which can express my experience in the world and my irritation" (*Frankfurt Lectures on Poetry*, 1963). Yet, one way toward objectivity is through mathematical formulation, as in Heissenbüttel's poem "das Sagbare sage" [say the sayable]: "not to complete the noncompletable" or not to say the unsayable, but to extend the possibilities of a language which defines the boundaries of one's world. Writing, thus, is directed toward the "engagement of perception." Heissenbüttel, unlike Celan, does not coin new words; he uses the simplest and most unmistakable form of a word as a building block in the arrangement of his poetry or prose. At times, he reproduces the liquidity of Gertrude Stein's style, but he falls far short of her accomplishments. His skeletonized word-algebra erases the line between poetry and prose and most often withdraws commentary and sentimentality from his writing to render a pure "happening," past or present, and to demonstrate the "happenable" as might a chemical scientist. He is fascinated by the thesaurus techniques of word compilers whose listings show the individuality of words as well as similarities and contrasts.

Kombinationen (1954) and *Topographien* (1956) are books which represent Heissenbüttel's hesitant and unsure explorations in new forms, coldly precise and unlyrical. His footing became surer in the series of "text" books, *Textbuch 1, 2, 3, 4, 5, 6* (1960–67), which incorporate a residue of what he felt to be the best of the earlier works and which aim for the conjunction of individual experience and reality. The designation "text" refers to the possibility of *recapitulating* experience through combinations of words and the selection of details and facts as distinct from *invention*. The dilemma, however, is that selectivity itself becomes a form of invention.

One of his most popular prose pieces, first read at the

1955 Group 47 session, is about a Sunday painter, "Der Wassermaler":

> He painted on water. This was his invention.
> He painted on water, that is, he did not as earlier painters let water color run over paper. He did not paint pictures for hanging. Above all, he painted no pictures. . . .
>
> He painted on water. All sorts of water. On rain puddles on sea surfaces on the mirror surfaces of overflowing pots. . . . He painted on smooth water. He painted on turbulent water. On clear and muddy water. . . . In painting he used various methods. Mostly he had several kinds of sticks. Besides he used boards rubber-plates hairbrushes combs fly swatters also paintbrushes. . . .

The enumeration of details seems as endless as the possibilities for endless enumeration of details. Yet, amid the details one is able to discern a state of mind and attempts to develop patterns both in the behavior of the painter and in the variation of simple sentences.

Aside from the enumeration technique, Heissenbüttel fashions large collages of quotations, employs cinemascopic scenes, imitates grammatical constructs, logical propositions, and geometrical corollaries ("If I were not only I but we I would be you he she it. Because I am I and not we I am I and can only talk about myself," "Grammatical Reduction," *Textbuch* 2); he collects catalogs of all sorts (i.e., qualification, "sometimes perhaps momentarily sometimes but not always. . . .", *Textbuch* 3). His visual or op poetry in *Textbuch* 4 is tame and hardly bears mention alongside more imaginative efforts by predecessors and contemporaries. Much of the content of *Textbuch* 5 is written in digital computer language which is based on the simplest arithmetical procedures. Typical is the passage from "schematische Entwicklung der Tradition" [schematic development of tradition]: "In the name of those who are here no more and are more because those who are here no more and are more have a name and in this name we are here." In this thirty-three-word asyntactical sentence, seventeen different words are strung together mainly through the conjunction "and" as well as the verb "are." If tradition is additive and its implication funereal, Heissenbüttel has graphically demonstrated and parodied the essence of tradition. Any idea or abstraction may be delineated in this digital manner, which also allows permutations and combinations as demonstrated in the poem "die Zukunft des Sozialismus" [the future of socialism]. I am quoting only the first lines of the four stanzas and then the second lines: "no one owns anything. . . . no one possesses nothing. . . . all own all. . . . all own nothing"; "no one exploits. . . . no one exploits any one. . . . all exploit all. . . . all exploit no one." All possible situations are represented here and no one thesis is espoused to the exclusion of others; the mind resists monolithic thought and encourages its explorative capacity. If the subject matter often does not run deep, it seems to be by choice because Heissenbüttel's bravura prose piece "Deutschland 1944" in *Textbuch 6* proves that he can bare with candor and power a cancerous state of public and private mind, namely the war psychosis of those who "wore the soldier uniform of history" and their successors who provide excuses which no one can believe; in all, Heissenbüttel notes, "we plant corn and lilies in the ashes and ivy, gathering wood-anemones in the shadow of our swords." The bad dream is still existent and awakening would mean the facing of monstrosities.

With proper game plans, however, one can delay confronting reality (i.e., experience, the possibility of experience, the relativity and complexity of experience, *Textbuch 2*, p. 17). Heissenbüttel well knows the score: "Every game has its rules. Does the ball in play know the rules? . . . Can one play ping-pong with marbles?" Obviously the rules and the objects of play are relative to the player's intent; he controls the game. Words or marbles exist independent of a player, but only if the poet-player puts them to use do they have a function other than intellectual gymnastics. Without a medium there is no message, but without some "message" the medium becomes unimportant. This is all too often true of Heissenbüttel's mechanics and massive concern with techniques, which come close to preciosity or pedantry.

Heissenbüttel has attracted followers and imitators. Among the latter is Peter Handke, who manages however to convert influence into something that becomes his own. Handke is obsessed with the search for identity and seeks it through writings to which he constantly applies new labels. *Die Innenwelt der Aussenwelt der Innenwelt* [The inner world of the outer world of the inner world] (1969) is a collection of prose poems or "texts" like Heissenbüttel's, but Handke attempts to give them an individual stamp by calling them *Satzspiele*, descriptive sentence-play which shows the reversible simultaneity of inner and outer consciousness of the author. The book had sufficient appeal to warrant an edition of 80,000 copies. Actually he is no more successful here than in his theater speak-ins in defining anything except through negation and assertion: I am neither a militarist nor a defender of inert peace, neither a black pessimist nor a blue-eyed utopian—"What I AM: / that *I* am!" (This was the assertion he inverted, and discarded, for his play *Kaspar*.) And what that may mean is not evident in the solipsistic refusal to be categorized. The volume ends on the word "quiet":

> "Ru.........hig."
> "Ru................hig."
> "Ru........................hig."

But even within silence there is sound. He knows that the meditative mind and the attentive ear are sensitive to every impression. Handke had taken the following quotes from Jean Paul as his text: "and in this quivering minute, the month-pointer of my watch crackled"; "your outer and your inner world jointly sound and use you as their shellfish." Yet, Handke's recorded impressions barely rise above the banalities they reflect nor do they advance the techniques formulated by avant-garde poets; in fact, he merely imitates the acoustical poems of Eugen Gomringer. His *Satzspiele* are earnest and sometimes clever but offer insubstantial proof for his thesis that "every sentence contains a story," a fallacy to which Heissenbüttel gave impetus. A sentence or statement such as a newspaper headline may contain the nucleus of a story and chart its beginning, however, it cannot pretend to be more than that.

When Hans Magnus Enzensberger (b. 1929) first read at the fall 1956 meeting of Group 47, many welcomed his "new, strong, and unpretentious prose." Two years later he was placed among the "star trio" of the group's lyricists along with Bachmann and Walter Höllerer. A portraiture-accolade by group critic Joachim Kaiser put the seal of approval on the "itinerant, lyrical ne'er-do-well" Enzensberger:

> One day a young man came to the Group and he wore red and green socks. He spoke only seldom but always with a gay and open enjoyment of antibanal parlando. His name sounded like a Carl Sternheim invention: Hans Magnus Enzensberger. Today [1962] he is married, wife and child require subsistence, and the color of socks is matched. Aside from all this, neither because of success or talent, has he permitted himself to be corrupted.

Yet, if an author of whom much is expected lets the group down during his reading, he can be made to feel quite uncomfortable. Enzensberger's intended theater piece *Die Schildkröte* [The turtle] was unmercifully set upon during the fall 1961 session and rejected as a yawn-producing flight into pure infantilism. The group rarely permitted its members to rest on their laurels.

Of Germany's "angry young men," Enzensberger is most deserving of the title, which he began to earn in the fifties. Proud of his Bavarian origins, he propounds his ideas as stubbornly as men who herald from that province. Enzensberger got a full taste of the Third Reich when he grew up in Nuremberg and served in the Volkssturm. After the war, he studied literature and philosophy at Erlangen, Freiburg, and the Sorbonne, gaining a doctorate with a dissertation on Clemens Brentano's poetry. For a brief period he taught, worked as radio "essayist" in Stuttgart, and after 1957 began to see the world first-hand, including North and South

America. For a while he resided in Italy with the Norwegian wife of his first marriage but a burst of wanderlust in the sixties again took him to the Americas, to Greece, Turkey, India (the last three countries saw him as lecturer for the Goethe Institute), twice to Russia (where he married the niece of Alexander Fadejew, a poet who committed suicide in 1958), and for the present Enzensberger resides in West Berlin, a neighbor of Richter and Johnson. One of his spectacular public eruptions occurred in January 1968 when he curtly terminated a visiting professorship at Wesleyan University, Connecticut, and announced his intentions of going to Cuba. In a blistering letter published in the *New York Review of Books*, Enzensberger protested against what he felt to be the world-dominating aim of American politics. Some of his American friends were stunned by what seemed to be a gratuitous and unreasonable gesture against them, though they shared his political beliefs. Even before, critics had pointed to Enzensberger's inability to distinguish between fact and fiction.

Indeed, Enzensberger's sharp, witty, and often facile rhetoric are at the mercy of hair-trigger impulse, and the blunderbuss shots are indiscriminate of targets. Yet, no one writing in German today has more effectively mastered satire in the service of the sociological essay and poetry as forms of polemical protest. To clarify his critical position in 1962, he described its ground rules: "It has no intention of subjugation or aggression. Criticism as I attempt it does not seek to make short shrift of its objects nor to liquidate them but to subject them to a second look: revision and not revolution is its objective." Perhaps his voice has become more politically strident since then, but basically he regards it his task to expose the condescensions of the consumer industries and the distortions practiced by the mass media. Their tolerant humoring of whims and the manipulation of the consumer, Enzensberger views as chicanery and cynicism, which have subsidized barbaric cultural tastes and fostered delusions of freedom. The German worker and the middle-class burgher, Enzensberger exclaims, "live in a condition closer to idiocy than ever before." His illustrations range from the publicized news of a hotel for dogs, at the same time when housing shortages afflict the big cities, to the indictment of tourism as a flight from reality and as a ploy in the game of social pretension. Obviously the polemicist Enzensberger wants a revision of social and cultural perspectives. Just how effective Enzensberger can be in drawing blood with his moralistic polemics was evident in the long and detailed response by the noted *Frankfurter Allgemeine Zeitung* to his "superficial, hate-filled, and libelous" analysis.

Enzensberger has spoken of his pride in Group 47: "Three days of the year the clique to which I have the honor of belonging is the central cafe of a literature without a capital. These are strenuous days . . . because literature is a strenuous matter." Despite his scorn for academies, commissions, or soul-saving societies, his uncompromising social criticism has gained for him numerous literary prizes. A union of German critics (Verband der deutschen Kritiker) in 1962 applauded his "time-hating" poems, their "somnambulistic clarity," and their ability to free readers from misery. Sometimes, in addition to his frequent writings for the news magazine the *Spiegel*, he has used the platform of a prize-giving society to gain even wider publicity for his views. Among the points of his Georg Büchner prize acceptance speech in 1963, a speech which was called "uncomfortable," were the condemnation of nationalism as a frail reed and a warning about the possibility of a resurgence of fascism not only in Germany but anywhere. These and similar outspoken sentiments against flag waving were rewarded with a Kultur prize by the city of Nuremberg in 1967; Enzensberger promptly consigned the prize money to "people brought to court in West Germany because of their political convictions." His action produced a row in the Bundestag and some went so far as to call him a destroyer of the German soul and a professional disrupter. The sensitive question of the Berlin wall he dismisses with the observation that the wall was not erected in 1962 but on June 22, 1941, when the German armies invaded Russia. Criticism from the right as well as from the left, he greets with equal contempt: "The moralistic rearmaments of the left can get lost. I am no idealist. I prefer confessions to argumentations. Doubt is dearer to me than sentiments. Revolutionary prattle, I detest." Lately he has even begun to doubt the efficacy of doubt, but he will not fall into goose step with the dogmatists of the radical Left though he often is identified with them as editor since 1965 of the publication *Kursbuch*.

In his doctoral dissertation Enzensberger developed the principle of *Entstellung*, a poetic regeneration of conventional or trite language through individualized speech. Most poets attempt to do this anyway so that the validation of the theory lies in its specific application. In Enzensberger's case, *Entstellung* (literally "displacement") is utilitarian because he regards poems as objects to a means; they are intended to have a function as do posters, leaflets, weapons, or hats. Three slim volumes of Enzensberger's poetry illustrate his versatility within the boundaries of his theories: *verteidigung der wölfe* [in defense of the wolves] (1957), *landessprache* [language of the land] (1960), *blindenschrift* [braille] (1964). Not only does Enzensberger fashion a poem into a utilitarian object but he also wants interaction with the reader:

> my wisdom is sedge grass
> cut your finger on it
> and paint a red ideogram
> on my shoulder
>
> ki wit ki wit
>
> my shoulder is a speedy ship
> lie on the sunny deck
> and rock yourself toward an island
> of grass of smoke
> ki wit
>
> my voice is a soft trap
> do not let yourself be captured
> my sedge grass is a silken dagger
> do not listen
> ki wit ki wit ki wit
>
> "lock lied" [bird snare]

Although poems about poems generally hold no appeal for me, Enzensberger's language here is fresh, spontaneous, and the serrated warning about his intent is imaginative and honest—the poet wishes to disturb the reader's complacency.

A resigned uncertainty breathes through much of Enzensberger's poetry as a felt emotion is rendered through examples rather than absolute definition or description. Love means many things, and for lack of something more precise, Enzensberger in one poem gives examples which could stand for many more; he says, "call it love":

> deafeningly
> april crashes through glassy foliage
> . . . fur coats of the ladies burst open
> . . . the thieves praise the evening
> . . . the evening is beautiful

Through laconic language, eccentric line and image arrangement, and the trite phrase, which mirrors the triteness of a situation, the poet expresses his emotionless stance. It is as if sentiment embarrasses him and he seeks ways of avoiding traditional constructions. Many Group 47 poets share this approach.

Sarcasm often takes the place of anger in Enzensberger's poems:

read no odes, my son, read timetables:
they are more accurate . . .
be wakeful, do not sing
the day will come when they will nail blacklists on the door
and brandmark the naysayer's breast. . . .
"ins lesebuch für die oberstufe," "for a college textbook"

Alternating his tone, he castigates the naïve ("candide"), the indifferent, the neutral, and blindly accepting persons and suggests that they invite being devoured by wolves, vultures, commissars, popes, generals:

should the vulture feed on forget-me-nots? . . .
who sews the blood-red stripes on the pants of the general?

who carves the capon for the usurer? . . .
who yearns for the lie

look in the mirror. . . .
lambs are your sisters. . . .

praised be the robbers: you
extended them an invitation to rape. . . .
you do not change the world.
"verteidigung der wölfe gegen die lämmer," "a defense of
                    the wolves against the lambs"

In his longest and most violent poem, "Schaum" [Froth],
read to the group in 1959 and published a year later in his
second volume of poems, he says, "I do not wish to change
you! forgive me god! / that leaves me cold! that has no
purpose!" Yet, though Enzensberger doubts the likelihood
of change, he rarely eases up his scourging. The scourgings
in the volume *landessprache* and the characterization of
Germany as a bomb made of flesh has led some to think of
the poems as defamatory of country and fellow citizens.
Although Enzensberger sees limitless corruption around
him, one should also measure the depths of his feelings in
poems such as "landnahme," "taking of the land":

> my land, I do not spare you,
> I hold you mortal
> in this mortal light.
>
> we are close, reciprocally radiant
> with each other's fair summer,
> my land, light like shadow of an olive tree . . .
> my infinite land
> . . . flowering against the bloody rubble
> of the time still remaining to us.

Enzensberger's aim of converting worn-out, colloquial,
everyday language into poetry was most successfully realized
in his third volume of poems, *blindenschrift*, where sensibility overrides the poet's previous search for shock effects.

The noncapitalizations and minimal punctuations no longer seem affectations—as they were in Stefan George's aesthetic canon—and the lyrical quality often reveals a new-found musicality and linguistic clarity. The moralistic polemics have been subdued and patience seemed to have entered the picture. Since Camus's adoption of the mythological Sisyphus figure as a patron saint for creative artists, Enzensberger has identified himself with the labor of rolling boulders uphill only to see them roll down again. But, as in his own "Sisyphus" poem, though he may be close to feeling hopeless about the possibility of changing the world, he manages to recover and "to increase anger in the world by one grain . . . / and roll anger up the mountains."

A funereal atmosphere enfolded the participants of the October 26–28, 1962 meeting in Berlin and dampened a celebration of the fifteen-year existence of the group. The year before, on August 13, the East German government signified and sealed its state borders by constructing a wall through the heart of Berlin and reports of shooting incidents created tensions. It was a time of national and international crises as well. On the first day of the meeting news broke of police searches, spearheaded by a former Nazi, the night before of editorial offices and homes of the *Spiegel* staffers. The weekly news magazine had printed a sharply critical article about the defensive strategies and capabilities of the West German army against potential attack from the East, drawing on nonclassified sources but managing to anger the military whose power of semijudicial actions was pursued through defense minister Franz-Joseph Strauss. For some people, the night raids, arrests, and prosecution for treason were so reminiscent of the Third Reich that it brought quick apprehension to the public mind. (Eventually the editors were cleared and Strauss lost his portfolio, easing a scandal whose warning did some political good.) As if such events were not enough, the Cuban missile crisis was escalating as Soviet ships steamed toward an American naval blockade.

One reporter from a Berlin newspaper watched the proceedings of Group 47 with incredulity as the sessions began and politics was neatly severed from literature; political discussions were relegated to coffee breaks while seventy-three writers, critics, editors, publishers' representatives, and guests from all over the continent immersed themselves in the business of literature during the meetings. Released to the press, however, was a letter signed by thirty-six attendees condemning the abuse of power by the defense ministry and protesting the arrest of *Spiegel* publisher Rudolf Augstein, who had been expected at the meeting. The assembly was startled briefly by two sonic booms caused by Soviet fighter planes overhead but otherwise was attentive to a wide stylistic range of readings by new and old participants, including Grass who created his own boom with a chapter from his novel *Hundejahre* (*Dog Years*). As the meetings progressed, the group sensed a literary contest shaping up between the reading of Peter Weiss's story of marital tensions and Johannes Bobrowski's latest poetry, characterized immediately by one listener as humane, quiet, and naturerelated. By a majority vote, as customary, Bobrowski (1917–65) was awarded the group's laurels, a $3,000 award contributed by fourteen publishers; yet, Bobrowski who had been given too short a leave by East German authorities was not on hand to receive the plaudits. Neither the fact that Bobrowski was one of the few "safe" writers allowed by the East German bureaucracy to step over the border nor the prize was exploited politically by Group 47 because it would have cut off any further avenues of valuable contact and would have wasted the message that literature without dogma transcends all borders. History, however, has a way of turning a poet's words into unintentional irony as Bobrowski read a powerful poem, "Die Wolgastädte [Cities of the Volga], opening with the words, "Der Mauerstrich" (the stretch of wall) and going on to limn a bloody siege by Tartars.

For Group 47 the Berlin meeting afforded participants the second opportunity of hearing Bobrowski read his poetry. Two years earlier at the Rathaus in Aschaffenburg, Bobrowski had read nine substantial poems without causing a stir of recognition possibly because amid a glut of readings by twenty-six authors, including Grass and Johnson, the several poetry renditions simply were deluged by fiction. In the meantime, Bobrowski's poetry which had only appeared in small samplings in East German periodicals saw publication in an anthology of "poetry written on the other side," *Deutsche Lyrik auf der anderen Seite* (1960) and *Sarmatische Zeit* (1961), both published first in West Germany.

A reading of the published poetry made it easier to get the drift, tone, and style of Bobrowski's work, preparing the way for acceptance of the spoken poetry. In either case, one is caught up in the songlike surface of Bobrowski's free rhythmic verse which works through sound rather than accent, his uncanny ear for absolute tonal pitch and melodic variations, poetry fashioned out of sorrow so that everything his words touch turns into melancholy and pain, as Horst Bienek so aptly put it. Yet Bobrowski was worried that his poems might be conveniently ribboned as artistic products by some West German critics, and their content neglected. Indeed, at first his poems were characterized as "engaged esotericism," but the keys which he provided eventually opened the hermetic gates. The language of poetry for Bobrowski has the triadic function of *remembrance* (the mytho-historic and immediate past), *communication* (bringing the past meaningfully into the present), and the causation of *effective change* (a vision of the future). Remembrance through memory can expatiate and expiate past guilt by setting humane feelings into motion; forgetting or burying the guilt of the past is a crime. Communication implies the multiple aspects of creating openness among people and searching for relatedness, companionship, communality, neighborliness—a totality of feeling which Bobrowski called *Nachbarschaft*. Catharsis in the present is a constructive necessity which opens the way to a hopeful future. Foremost then, Bobrowski saw it the task of contemporary literature not only to "state" the guilt in which Germans enmeshed themselves in relationships with their Eastern neighbors but also to awaken more sensitive inclinations toward Lithuanians, Poles, Russians, and others. Bobrowski understood that historical resentments made such themes unpopular and that simplistic propagandization of views would achieve nothing. Perhaps it was naïve of Bobrowski to hope that ideas and feelings so internalized in poetry could be effective in swaying the emotions of readers not already sympathetic or receptive to the intent of the poet. If poetry had the power of social persuasion perhaps matters might be different. Bobrowski's personal answer to realistic pessimism was his persevering optimism: "Perhaps literature works slowly. . . . I am against the big words, the superdimensional demands. . . . The so-called undigested past must be invoked again and again until it is digested; it must be done only because one has hope." Bobrowski's programmatic statements may be applied with precision to a fair portion of his output.

In a biographical note, he recollected his prisoner-of-war days: "Near Lake Ilmen in 1941, I began to write about the Russian landscape, but as a foreigner—a German." What results is a rendering in quick strokes of an alien landscape:

> Wilderness.
> Against the wind.
> Frozen. Into the sand
> the river had sunk.
> Charred branches:
> the village before the clearing. Then
> we saw the lake . . .

"Der Ilmensee 1941"

What became typical in Bobrowski's poems was the strong, expressive opening line—short and explosive substantives—setting the tone for the rest of the lines. A number of early poems chart the silent landscape of the Russian steppes and the villages but slowly a dimension of historical time is gained. The present opens up to the past, real and imagined, as the contours of the lost lands of Samartia (the region between the Vistula River and the Caspian Sea) and other shadowlands become dimly discernible and ancient deities, evil spirits, and heroes flit ghostlike into the picture. Then, as if the poet were presiding over their creation, villages, towns, and cities are minutely localized and their names become part of the euphonious poetry—Ostra Brama, Trakai, Vilna, Novgorad. Almost imperceptibly, people begin to enliven the stillness as they are invoked out of the childhood memories of the poet who himself was born in East Prussia, in a village in the Memel area inhabited by a conflux of Poles, Lithuanians, Russians, Germans, and Jews "subject to a long story of misfortune in which my people are implicated with guilt since the days of the Order of Teutonic Knights: perhaps never to be erased or expiated but worthy of hope and honest attempt in German poetry."

Peasants, fishermen, shepherds are seen in their ancient pursuits calmly enduring whatever comes; particularly powerful is Bobrowski's dramatic poem about the wives of the Nehrung fishermen. Few contemporary poets have been able or willing to enfold with the integrity of compassion the lonely figures of the persecuted as witnessed in such poems as "Die Spur im Sand" [The spoor in the sand]. The poet invokes through memory the figure of "Aaron," a victim of the Nazi ovens, who becomes as real in the present as a Chagall painting (Bobrowski admired the painter) and gently brings the seeds of hope for all men; the poet empathizes and expiates for his guilty "brother" and himself; Aaron's indelible traces, figuratively in the dust, lead into the future. Bobrowski's triadic functions and tenses take on dynamic statement and emotion:

> The pale old man
> in the threadbare kaftan.
> The prayer-sidelocks, ancient. Aaron,
> I knew your house then.
> You carry away the ashes
> in your shoe.
>
> My brother drove you
> from the door. I went
> after you. How the frock
> swirled round your feet! Only a spoor
> remained visible to me in the sand.

Then I saw you
sometimes at evening
you appeared, whispering,
from the fireclearing.
With white hands
you scattered the seeds of snow
over the barn roof.

Because the God of your fathers
will yet brighten
the years for us, Aaron,
the spoor still lies
in the dust of the streets
for me to find you.

And I go.
And your distance,
your expectation I bear,
upon my shoulders.

Perhaps only the coincidences of Bobrowski's background
as an East German of Polish-Jewish extraction with Lutheran affiliation, a non-Marxist in a Marxist land, fitted him
for the mediating role he elected and account for themes
he chose as a poet. He was modern without being modernistic in his poetic expression and traditional in his religiosity
without being at all orthodox. His view of history was poetically idiosyncratic and permeated by an idealistic logic.
In his poem "Gestorbene Sprache" [Dead language], Bobrowski imagines the language of nature and man of older
times as still dwelling in one's ear. If one but listens, one
hears echoes of old pagan and Christian traditions in the
poem "Absage" [Refusal]. The opening word *fire* (as opposed by the seeding power of snow, two of his favored
symbols) leads to associations with the Slavonic thunder
and sun-god Perkin, before whose image an oak-wood fire
was lit continually, and the waters upon which memory
flows is an image associated with the fisherman, "the stam-
merer," Christ. In those times of old, "there I was," says the

poet, "the new has never begun," imputing a static quality to history. Like the biblical Adam, the poet in the present says,

> I am a man,
> one flesh with his wife [Genesis, ii, 24],
> who raises his children
> and foresees a time without fear.

The last verse looks optimistically to the future. Perhaps, the strange title of the poem, *Absage*, means that one ought to face the past and *refuse* to continue its barbarisms. Bobrowski has pointed to the static quality of history, that there has been nothing new since times of old, and that real progress toward a future and change can be wrought only through a vision of love. Bobrowski's recurrent moral emphasis is on a thorough humanization of man through *Nachbarkeit*.

When Bobrowski was awarded literary prizes by Austria and Group 47, the East Berlin Akademie der Künste followed suit, but although the East Germans realized that an obscure reader in a publishing house had become a continental figure (the Swiss also honored the poet), their critics did not quite know what to do with him, as illustrated by two posthumous eulogies. Alfred Kurella, a political-literary functionary, saw Bobrowski's work as cut short and fragmentary, a tentative groping without falling into the pitfall of "western symbolism" (defined as "a pale thought decoratively dressed in multiplicity of meanings"). According to Kurella, Bobrowski portrayed real trees, leaves, vultures, gypsy women, historical events but is to be criticized for flirting with complicated rather than firm narrative techniques. In a radio talk, the formidable critic and fellow poet Stephen Hermlin faintly praised Bobrowski as a genial and serious person who did not exclude the possibility of the errors of his own opinions and who "gathered power for the fight against fascism and chauvinism." If these tightwire views are distortions by omission, the same may be said of West German editions of Bobrowski's poetry that fail to include one of his longest, angriest, and artistically emotive poems, "Pruzzische Elegy," "Pruzzian Elegy." German lexicons refer to the Pruzzians as a germanized Baltic-Lithuanian people who died out in the fifteenth century. What is neglected is the fact that the crusading Junkers through their cult of virtue and the sword helped these "pagans" to die out. Bobrowski sees the Pruzzians as

> People of the black woods,
> of swollen, surging rivers . . .
> of the night hunt. . . .
> People
> of Pirkun and Pikoll. . . .
> like no other, no other of death!

They were sacrificed to the fires of extermination but remembered through lingering song and legend and names of hillsides, rivers, roads. Ironically, the conquering Prussians inherited the name of their victims. By extension, the same martial spirit sought its twentieth-century victims. Names and naming with biblical and secular allusions in Bobrowski's poetry have sacral and memorial functions.

Almost consistently, Bobrowski's poetry has been placed in the tradition of German nature lyricism, and critics have taken much too literally Bobrowski's acknowledgment of the nineteenth-century poet Friedrich Klopstock as his master. Although there are likenesses in the buoyancy of their verses, in the view that poetry is moral beauty, in their assent to life, their humility and their love of the world ("With deepest awe I view all of creation," wrote Klopstock in one of his odes to Spring), Bobrowski never permits himself Klopstockian rapture over "the grape which brings joy to the heart." Where he differs from other so-called nature lyricists is in his ability to capture a sense of the totality of creation *and* the singular relationships of man, creatures, the land, the elements—all within a single frame of experience. His poems consist largely of memory and landscape which are almost always integrated with "the effective activity of man." He feels that the poet must do more than exercise his emotions by momentary identifications with birds in flight, for instance, or exercise his gift of describing or naming things in nature:

> it is
> a game, I am dubious;
> it may not end
> justly.

Man must reach beyond such games and learn to assume moral responsibilities without waiting for God—to wait would be futile because God is not "in the flesh" ("Immer zu benennen," "Always to be named," in *Schattenland, Ströme* [1962; *Shadow Land*, 1969]).

Just as subjective affinity rather than imitation marks Bobrowski's relation to Klopstock, so it is with the poems he devoted or dedicated to an international panoply of figures: Villon, Góngora, Joseph Conrad (his great-uncle), Dylan Thomas, Gertrud Kolmar, Else Lasker-Schüler, Nelly Sachs, Adam Mickiewicz. An indomitable human spirit shone in the lives of these people, which is admired in Bobrowski's biographical poems. It may be a purely speculative reconstruction but it seems to me that overwhelmed by the vast destruction caused by the German armies in their eastern campaigns, Bobrowski during his Russian captivity from 1941 to 1949 assumed for himself a personal task of expiation:

> High over the sea, the silent Novgorod.
> I contemplate well and my heart
> contracts,—and yet,
> a peacefulness beckons within the devastation.
>
> "Anruf" [Summons], 1943

It meant choosing a quiet way of living in East Germany among a small circle of friends, closing his eyes and ears to an array of injustices in Soviet-dominated areas, and finding self-sufficiency and outlet through his writings. Yet, there is integrity in his theory of what the new poetry should be: more incantation and conjuration, the elimination of the didactic and topical explication; "We plant flowers on chaos and with a verse of David and Deborah we again pull ourselves into daylight." Choosing to avoid propagandization through poetry and refusing to be exploited politically, Bobrowski was in a neutral limbo from which he was brought to public light by the force of publicity resulting from the prize awarded by Group 47. The price of survival under the conditions he set for himself was political silence, and he paid it even when fellow writers (as in the case of his older friend, poetry mentor Peter Huchel who first published Bobrowski in 1955 in the periodical *Sinn und Form*) fell victim to Communist party displeasure. Some western critics would like to read Bobrowski's protest into poems published two years after his death (by appendectomy complications), namely the collection *Wetterzeichen* [Storm signal] (1967). One of the poems is called "Das Wort Mensch" [The word *man*], and ends with the lines "Where love does not exist, / do not utter the word." While the exhortation generalizes a humane feeling, it does not have the force of direct accusation against specific contemporary persecutions. In some respects this typifies the tragedy of a resigned inner emigration and the instinctive urge of the poet to transcend it through indirection, condemning poetry to impotence. While Bobrowski's poetic language was intended as a bonding element among people, an idealistic reaching out and communing, the political languages of the East and West tragically have served the opposite ends. The conflict between poetry and politics in our time is evident in Bobrowski's experience. He chose, in a muted voice, to pit moral vision against political expediency.

After Germany's annexation of Austria in 1938, the seventeen-year-old Erich Fried emigrated to England and made London his permanent home. Adaptable to occasions, he was a factory worker, librarian, chemist, glassblower, and fire warden, but after the war he turned to free-lance writing, editing a periodical called *Blick in die Welt*, and in 1952 serving as radio columnist and commentator for British Broadcasting Corporation programs directed to the German Soviet zone. At a time when German authors and readers needed to reestablish contact with the outside literary world, Fried set about indefatigably to translate modern English drama and poetry, including the works of Dylan Thomas and T. S. Eliot; he received the Schiller memorial prize in 1965 for his efforts. As part of an ambitious project, he recently completed the translation of fourteen Shakespeare plays, using the deservedly famous Schlegel versions as guides but utilizing his own talent at wordplay to reflect more accurately Shakespeare's art; some of the newly translated plays were successfully tested on stage.

The majority of his poems written between 1947 and 1963 were collected in a volume called *Reich der Steine* [Realm of stones], which moved away from his earliest love and political poems and through which, as he noted, "I became immersed in experiments with sound and association, anticipating some of the techniques of recent German 'konkrete' poetry," as well as poems "operating with word associations" within longer poems of complex structures. If indeed these were meant to be experimental they should have been kept in the author's files; their word and soundplay is somewhat pretty and the effects somewhat effete. The techniques which he developed, however, served a more vigorous purpose in the poems after 1963 when his political and social ax began striking at contemporaneous targets. Coincident with this turn was his enthusiastic involvement with Group 47's literary marathons as a reader and as a vocal critic.

The 1963 meeting by all accounts proved to be a dull affair, but for Fried it was a chance to read his poetry alongside that of Hans Magnus Enzensberger and Helmut Heissenbüttel, with whom he had some political and artistic aims in common. A reviewer of the meeting noticed Fried's sententiousness, wit, adeptness at definitions and wordplay but lamented the fact that most of it was lost in the oral reading. Much of that loss was rectified when the poems he read were published in *Warngedichte* [Poems of warning] (1964). Fried was beginning to sharpen his comments. One "Definition" illustrates his colloquial reduction of existentialist philosophy:

> A dog
> that dies
> and knows
> that it dies
> like a dog
>
> and that can say
> that it knows
> that it dies
> like a dog
> is man.

Sentimentality becomes anathema to Fried and he combats it with the sarcasm we find in the first stanza of "Kampf ohne Engel" [Battle without the angel]:

> Now are the bows of high edifices tensed
> toward the next war
> and the bow of lips of girls
> tensed for farewell
> and violin bows are tensed
> for a false song. . . .

Typical are the parallelistic comparisons which are part of Fried's mannerisms. Often he makes a point by a brutal juxtaposition of the abstract and the concrete, creating a modern exemplum, characterized by "Das verschleierte Bild" [The veiled picture]:

> They love freedom
> as they
> love
> their wives
> in the dark
>
> They grope
> and dare
> not direct their gaze
> into her
> open lap.

He expresses displeasure with mass-man who allows others to think for him, feel for him, and make political decisions for him because soon those surrogate figures also will take our lives ("Die Abnehmer"). Guilt, he felt, is incurred by inaction and "the consequences of my fear / are the causes of my fears" ("Bedenken"). A tone of pessimism more strongly began to permeate his poems as in "Antwort," possibly in "Answer" to the softer strains of his earlier poetry cycles:

> To the stones
> someone said:
> be human.
>
> The stones then said:
> we are not as yet
> hard enough.

At Sigtuna, Sweden, in 1964 Fried read a prose piece which was a cross between a novella and an essay, sparking a discussion of the application of narrative techniques to raw materials, a problem with which the group had been wrestling continuously. The following year he read an act from a play which the group, almost in unison, asked him to discard, a suggestion which left Fried unmoved. At the April 1966 Princeton meeting, Fried recited poetry resonantly and stentoriously, with what the American observer Joseph Bauke called a mischievous grin and "with the air of a lion ready to pounce on any critic"; but apparently he did not have to fear opposition because no one had anything to complain about. Through the years the political and social criticism voiced in his poetry became more strident and topical. Suiting action to the word, in 1968 he resigned his BBC post because he could not see the justification for following an anti-Communist line in view of what he felt was a thorough Russian purge of Stalinism. It did not take long for this assumption to turn sour but the message seemed lost upon Fried. On certain issues like the Berlin wall he had to tread carefully in order not to alienate many members of the group so that he resorted to neutralized irony in his poem "Prüfung von Freunden in Friba-Frabi," or the testing of friends in Friba (West Berlin) and Frabi (East Berlin). Inhabitants of both parts of the divided city test their guests or visitors by their reaction to the wall and judge their sympathy by the quantity of tears shed. Fried caustically suggests that strangers bring along onion juice, "then one can cry so beautifully."

Fried's topical poetry owes much to the example of Brecht and speaks with clarity, conviction, and barely controlled anger. In an introduction to his selected poems translated into English by Georg Rapp, *On Pain of Seeing*, 1969, Fried states his aim of avoiding obtuseness and cynicism so that "trying to communicate my attempts of coping with the world can . . . make its infinitesimal contribution to changing this world." One of his main targets is the role of the United States in Vietnam, one-sidedly ignoring the role of other foreign powers and North Vietnamese guilt in that nightmare. Just how effective Fried can be is demonstrated in "Gezieltes Spielzeug," "Toy on Target," a wry commentary on U.S. dropping of toys on a village where children had been killed earlier by bombings:

> If the aeroplane
> had dropped the toys
> a fortnight ago
> and only now the bombs
>
> my two children
> thanks to your kindness
> would have had something to play with
> for those two weeks.

(Trans. Georg Rapp)

His unsparing criticism and guerrilla "wordfare" has also been directed against Germans who prettify the past. In anticipation of attacks levelled against him, Fried gives deadpan advice, which of course, he does not follow: "In the house of the hanged man do not mention the rope because that is where his hangman now enjoys his retirement." In this prose poem, "A Question of Tact," each word is on a separate line to pictorialize a dangling rope. There is no modern German poem which like Fried's "Verwandlung" [Transformation] transfixes the explicitness of degradation; one finds such reminder photos in the museum of the former concentration camp in Dachau. With macabre realism, the poem describes the transformation of persons in their girlhood to corpses hosed down and ready for transport from gas chamber to crematoria. And with a gesture of love and reverence the poet kisses the blueish colored bodies. Fried counts himself among those who suffered persecution, and occasionally he characterizes his personal feeling in lines such as, "Nothing but the pain / of having survived / his pain" ("Vorahnung des Endsiegs" [Premonitions of final victory]). He reacts strongly to condescension and belated gestures to redress wrongs which were caused by religious intolerance as embodied in a news release from the Vatican:

> After nineteen hundred years
> it was proclaimed in Rome
> that Israel does not bear collective guilt
> for the death of Christ
>
> Now it's the turn of the
> dead Jews to declare: We were never killed
> by Christian hands.

"Fortschritt" [Progress]

Cleverness as well as one-sided argumentation mark poems in which Fried began more strongly to espouse the political line of the new Left; in their negative dialectics, the poems combine relentless catechism with the joking style of the limerick. Before letting a news item cool, he has his prose-poem commentary ready and there is no mistaking his editorial bias, as might have been possible in poetry written before his latest political turn. Fried assumes the prerogative of changing with the times but does not reject poems written under earlier political persuasion, as did W. H. Auden; instead, he has published *Befreiung von der Flucht* (1968), counter-poems on Vietnam, the Middle East, and on a range of other topics and attitudes which seem less pessimistic but also more pacifistic. In five years, he will probably have to write countercounter-poems, but the prospects do not seem to bother him and he appears to be concerned primarily with instant reaction to news material through his propaganda barrages. As a debunker Fried has few peers, although often at the sacrifice of poetry to pop journalism. Following the lead of those who have fashioned the antinovel, and the antihero, Fried tends to write antipoems. Pity the poor nightingale in the hands of Fried:

> Whoever let burst
> Philomela's heart
> with eternal love-pain,
> he lies
> he lies
>
> What means the sweet song
> of the nightingale
> It means
> scram
> scram
>
> In these trees
> only I
> only I
> am
> the male

"Philomel' mit Melodey" [Philomela with melody]

It is a pale carbon of John Crowe Ransom's parody. Fried is quick to demolish what he feels are political or aesthetic lies and prefers the protest or activist poem in reaching his goal. He has had his quarrels with Group 47 colleagues when any, like Enzensberger, display equivocal attitudes in respect to political dedication; yet, like other firebrands in the group, he is aloof from and distrustful of any organization.

Some of Fried's poems have served as models for younger writers who feel that a culture revolution and a radical democratization can be achieved through "battle texts" or agitation-propaganda, *Agitprop*. In a volume by that name, Fried is well represented among thirty writers, as are Group 47 authors Nicolas Born (b. 1937), F. C. Delius (b. 1943), and Guntram Vesper (b. 1941). Their political commentary is voiced through the mechanics of poetry, supposedly lyrical, and the commentary as well as mechanics are of the plainest variety. Almost all of them feel that it is necessary to use crude and unmistakable language in order to appeal to the masses. Yet, they seem to be unaware of a monumental condescension in assuming that vitriolic and excremental language are the best means of reaching the so-called masses. Ironically, the very crudity of Nazi agitprop which sensitive writers wished to purge after 1945 is being revived partially, although the political objectives are different. The lesson that barbarous language encourages stereotypes and mental laziness and discourages honest analysis has to be learned all over again; hate and hatefulness quickly become bedfellows and righteousness may turn into horror. Fried's poems, at least, have a sharpness of wit and the element of sympathy; the others are sadly deficient in these qualities.

For poetry with aims to bite deeply into the sensitivities of readers, one turns to the sassy and provocative lyrics of Wolf Biermann (b. 1936), who lives in East Berlin and has managed to enrage officialdoms and conservatives in both Germanys. The abandon with which he attacks the shibboleths of East and West have gained him a wide audience on both sides of the Wall—of which he grimly writes:

> . . . for a joke he [the poet François Villon, were
> he alive] makes a harp
> Out of the Wall's barbed wire
> The guards accompany the tune
> And keep time while they fire.
>> From *Die Drahtharfe* (1965; *The Wire
>> Harp*, 1968, trans. Eric Bentley)

On several occasions, he was invited to Group 47 meetings but could not get East German visiting permits for the occasions. He is the heir of the political balladry of Heine, Frank Wedekind, and Brecht in the fight against oppression, whatever the source. Fiercely individualistic and skeptical of collective thinking, he criticizes impartially without fear of consequences:

Each part of the wide world has its own
Part of the German po-po.
The biggest part's West Germany.
With reason good, I know

And so with German industry
To save embarrassment
West Germans polish and perfume
The West German excrement.

. . . .

The DDR, my fatherland,
However, is very clean
And a return to Nazi ways
Is nowhere to be seen.

With the hard broom of Stalin we
So rubbed our bodies down
The backside now is scratched all red
That formerly was brown.

(Trans. Eric Bentley)

Such needling has prompted the progressive East German government to prohibit his public performances. In 1969 Biermann won West Berlin's Fontane prize, awarded by a jury which included Group 47 critic Walter Jens, and promptly let it be known that he was giving the $2,500 prize money to the revolutionary student movement. Cries went up that the poet who had written "O Germany, your murders" was intent upon murdering democracy and that he had placed a "cuckoo's egg" in the hands of those who extended him recognition.

Poetry, in our time, can be an act of provocation. Certainly, many of the Group 47 poets have done their best to keep this intent alive.

4

The Radio Play
Life, a Permanently Unanswered Question

It is doubtful if in the near future the German postwar stage will be able to regain the preeminence it once held as a social force and to restore the drama to its traditional popularity as a literary form. Within the last two hundred years, German audiences supported the greatest number of important repertory theaters on the Continent and the pool of gifted playrights seemed inexhaustible, but the economics of the marketplace and the competition of other entertainment media, which bring drama into the home or onto the screen, have become formidable. Besides, playwrights in a drastically changed world no longer see the possibility of heroicizing or humanizing man through theatrical conflicts or the well-worn idea of "fate"; for the most part, they have adopted the mechanics and philosophy of a *drama nouveau*—the parabolic and absurd theater—so that the reorientation of a tradition-minded audience (whose limit of taste is expressionism) and the gaining of a new, receptive audience will take time. The documentary theater, which thrives on political and moral controversy, has fared somewhat better. However, the greatest playground for experimentation, with resultant gains for every medium of drama, has been the radio play.

Although consumer industries are notorious for products with built-in obsolescence, the radio industry with its programming of radio plays achieved an astonishing balance between quantity and quality. A brief index of the popularity and literary longevity of the German radio play may be found in Heinz Schwitzke's critical survey, *Das Hörspiel* (1963), which contains an eight-page list of radio plays aired between 1945 and 1962 and published either singly or in anthologies. Of the authors who enhanced their reputations through the radio play at least twenty-five were associated also with Group 47 at one time or another. The reason for this link is not astonishing given the fact that after a few years of the group's meetings publishing house and radio editors, aside from reporters, began to be present faithfully. As early as 1951, one reporter noted that a writer who had read a story which met with group plaudits was besieged later by three talent scouts from different radio networks; they bought the radio rights to the story. As consumer demands increased, so did the number of authors who would write plays, essays, and features for radio. Not only did the meetings serve as a literary marketplace, but contacts between writers and editors proved valuable. Through the radio play, many writers survived economically difficult times and also were enabled to pursue their careers without compromising their art. In fact, the radio play encourages imaginative technical and aesthetic solutions to the problem of reaching audiences through exclusively auditory and acoustical means. Some, like Alfred Andersch and Helmut Heissenbüttel, combined their writing with posts as radio editors. One has the feeling that the stage suffered because it had few similar attractions to offer potential playwrights; the radio networks actively sought writers while the stage did not.

Aside from economic considerations, the radio play allowed considerable scope for social and artistic expression; Group 47 authors were conspicuous.

The radio play does not stand isolated in time. Its authors are simultaneously authors contributing to the stage, the novel, poetry and more recently to television. Worthy of note is that several of the most creative associates of Group 47 have been attracted to the radio either before the days of the Third Reich—like Günter Eich and Wolfgang Weyrauch—or after 1945—like Ilse Aichinger, Alfred Andersch, Ingeborg Bachmann, Heinrich Böll, Hans

Magnus Enzensberger, Wolfgang Hildesheimer, Wolfdietrich Schnurre and Martin Walser. Despite the range of
differences in their writings, they all are "engaged" writers, people who strive for clarity and a deeper understanding of self and world, finding in the poetic word a key to
what lies beneath the surface of appearances. . . . (E. G.
Fischer, *Das Hörspiel: Form und Funktion*, 1964)

Pioneering broadcasts on German radio began in 1924, but
not until four years later did the radio play come into
existence through adaptations from classical and modern
plays. It took time for radio writers to realize that the new
medium required new orientations and that such naïve
presentations as Friedrich von Schiller's *Wallenstein* (1798)
done in full theatrical regalia before microphones was a misunderstanding of functions. By 1935 sensitive writers were
depressed by political events against which they could not
speak out. As Schwitzke notes, "We preferred to be silent or
to write of other things," as evident, for example in Eich
texts, which were "harmlessly pretty, pleasant, and often
linguistically notable." When the radio play department was
nazified, militant propaganda strangled the new medium.
Perhaps it was fortunate that the Nazi *Reichssendeleitung*
did not understand the potential emotional effectiveness of
the radio play, which was groping for sophistication; as
might be expected, crude propaganda destroys the essence
of any art form. After the war, the radio was the first
medium to be able to satisfy informational and cultural
needs, giving radio writers an opportunity to extend the
fledgling efforts of the thirties into mature expression.

The unabashed desperation of the homefarers—the stream
of the uprooted, the defeated soldiers, prisoners of war
internees—was most eloquently expressed in Wolfgang
Borchert's radio play *Draussen vor der Tür* (1949; *The Man
Outside*, 1952), which was first broadcast over the Hamburg
network in 1947. In the play, one hears echoes of the early-
century theater of expressionism as Borchert's exclamatory
lines cry out for human contact and a new, compassionate
world. Like Bertolt Brecht, he believed in the possibility of

a new man in a new society. As an artistic effort, the play stands as a lone reminder of a phase which quickly passed because most writers and critics were embarrassed by the old expressionistic pathos and sentimentality, the ecstatic language in protest against the world, and the subjective distortions; instead, more indirect means were sought to comment on the past and to capture contemporaneous experience. Günter Eich, who was to become the dean of radio playwrights, gave implicit direction to the medium for almost a decade with the broadcast in 1951 of his *Träume* [Dreams]. The dominant tone and intent are clearly recognizable as we look, for instance, at the play's first and last lines:

I envy all those who can forget,
who can rest becalmed in sleep and have no dreams.
I am envious of my own moments of blind content:
the vacation goal, North Sea bathing, Notre Dame,
a glass full of red burgundy and pay day.
Yet basically I feel that even a good conscience is insufficient,
and I doubt the goodness of sleep in which we all rock ourselves.

. . . .

No, do not sleep while the world's administrators are busy!
Be suspicious of their power and the pretense that they must gain it for your sake!
Be wakeful so that your hearts are not empty when it is counted on that your hearts will be empty!
Do the unprofitable, sing those songs which no one expects from your mouth!
Be discomforted, be sand, not oil, in the machinery of the world.

Here is one of the many techniques used by most of the Group 47 writers to remind and alert listeners, viewers, and readers to social and political realities and to keep their hearts and minds open. Eich exerts power through lyricism, without cosmic wailings or expressionistic pathos, in an attempt to broaden conscience and consciousness. Writers who frighten no one, Eich notes, are worthy only of parlor talk. Eich seeks out the audience's nerve endings and encourages emotional identification with those who suffer in the world. In *Traüme*, Eich categorically says, "Everything which happens concerns you." While Borchert was accepted as an attorney for the dispossessed, four years later a relatively settled audience did not wish to have its mental peace disturbed. Through letters, they vociferously protested against Eich's play. Apparently, they wanted to "rest becalmed in sleep," but, more and more, writers like Eich felt it their duty to disturb and provoke audiences. Of Eich's many radio plays, *Die Mädchen aus Viterbo* [The Girls from Viterbo] (1952), *Das Jahr Lazertis* (1953; *The Year Lacertis*, 1968), and *Die Brandung vor Setúbal* (1957; *The Rolling Sea at Setúbal*, 1968) are modern classics. Fantasy and reality merge in *Die Mädchen aus Viterbo* as two Jews, a girl and her grandfather, hide from their hunters in the Berlin of 1943. While in the apartment, they imagine for their own diversion, and for the radio audience, the fate of schoolgirls from Viterbo who are lost in cavernous catacombs. To be discovered would have opposite results for each pair; while the audience is momentarily distracted and hopes for the rescue of the girls, the apartment door is torn open suddenly—the reality of capture is overpowering. Eich cunningly enlists the pictorial imagination of the listeners as happenings shift from one plane to another and subtly merge. The double time narration and flashbacks within flashbacks are exquisitely threaded and tragic resignation in the face of imminent death is simply delineated in such lines as, "I think that one can only begin to pray when one no longer wishes for anything from God."

The strange modulations of life—entwined in reality, the imagined, and in language—are felt during the search by Paul, a painter, for the meaning of an overheard but indistinct word which sounds like "Lazertis." Throughout the play, *The Year Lacertis*, he follows Laparte, a specialist on lizards (lacertae), and meets a shy, lizardlike girl and a father-figure (Laertes) who dies of leprosy in a Brazilian jungle; Paul is placed in a lepers' home (called *La Certosa*) and becomes a Lazarus figure. Despite the "certitude" that he is leprous, it is discovered that he is free of the disease and could be freed from the home; yet, he decides to stay not because he has discovered the unspoken word *charity* but because he needs those to whom he has ministered. Although Paul has not exhausted all the assonances and associations of the word Lacertis, he is content to rest, perhaps because he thinks of himself as an homo *lacero*, torn and mangled, who can be healed by helping humans who are doomed. The dialectics of the human heart are deftly caught with musical nuances; the difficulties of the plot, briefly given here, vanish through Eich's superlative grasp of techniques in the service of aesthetics.

Eich's implicit idea that language can become a medium for self-healing, as well as a means of tolerating the paradoxes of life, is carried even further in *The Rolling Sea at Setúbal*. Dona Catarina, the mistress of the poet Camões, lives in a shell of hallucination for twenty years, refusing to believe his death until a chain of incidences lead her to awareness which, however, is continually cushioned by the language of rationalization. She can face the same plague that caused her lover's death when faith and reality take on equal significance. One may criticize Eich for suggesting that the crutchlike substitution of one illusion for another provides a stoic panacea for facing life and its miseries. Yet, Eich senses a truth of human behavior: Dona Catarina ceases to be afraid of the plague when she realized that it existed: the Jewish grandfather and the painter Paul calmly faced up to terror precisely at the moment they accepted its existence. One cannot view dread without the help of some illusion. Whether terror is of man's or nature's making, the eye of the storm offers temporary refuge.

Few have succeeded better in translating warnings against complacency into gripping dramatic formats than Ilse Aichinger. To be effective, a message must have a provocative and imaginative medium. A startling transformation is slowly wrought in her radio play *Knöpfe* [Buttons] (1953) as, with most economical means, she pictures the identity loss of several characters who comfortably and almost mind-lessly work in a factory producing buttons; they have lost the initiative to meet the challenges of a cold world and they settle for a routine which ironically saps their life. Where realistic ironists, like Charles Chaplin in his *Modern Times*, pictorialize the devastating effect of repetitive work, Aichinger extends her logical fantasy to the point of Kafkaesque parable as her characters turn into glowing buttons. *Knöpfe* is her most influential radio play, while her others became increasingly esoteric by artfully avoiding action.

Fantasy is also anchored in reality in Ingeborg Bachmann's *Die Zikaden* [The cicadas] (1955), a play about insects who formerly were humans but who now live on an island, a questionable utopia where they do nothing but sing; they have discarded love, longing, material needs: "magically transformed, but also damned because their voices have become inhuman." Escape into song or escape into aesthetics are synonymous damnations. While the "cicades" abjure human love, Bachmann's two lovers—Jan representing the "old" and Jennifer the "new" world—seek an ideal fulfillment in *Der gute Gott von Manhattan* [The good God of Manhattan] (1958). The play received popular and critical acclaim. Werner Weber wrote: Bachmann "unfolds a web of broad experience with effortless earnestness and a tone of a hymnic wedding song mixed with the dryness of everyday presentation—a mystic-orphic expression of beatified yearning." Indeed, Bachmann invokes the lovers of King Solomon's song, Dante's lovers damned in hell, and Shakespeare's star-crossed lovers, and lards her scenes with woebegone *Liebesleid*, but the radio play strikes me as a peculiar hybrid between Austrian operetta and Wagnerian metaphysics. The good God, envious of lovers who strive for sublimity and disapproving of those who disrupt conventional patterns, sends his dowry, a bomb, to Jennifer's Manhattan apartment; Jennifer is blown to smithereens, a fate which may not be underserved considering her painfully stilted language. That God or fate is a spoiler and deliberately frustrated the possibility of ideal love is the gist of the author's highly personal fantasy, which simply remains mired in pathetic lyricism.

Social concerns strike the dominant notes in the *Hörspiel*

of the fifties, and the radio playwright took craftsmanlike
pride in the well-constructed drama; above all, like Wolfgang Weyrauch (b. 1907), he wished to communicate with
his unseen audience. In *Die japanischen Fischer* [The Japanese fishermen] (1955), which portrays the consequences of
atomic fallout, Weyrauch speaks directly to the radio
audience: "I don't in the least know who you are or to whom
I am talking. But even if only one listens to me, that is
sufficient." Though belonging to an older generation of
writers, Weyrauch gained the ear of younger writers in 1949
when he proposed the idea of a stylistic *Kahlschlag*, a drastic
pruning of verbal underbrush, in order to clear the way for a
language free of reprehensible association with Third Reich
terminologies as well as a language free of luxuriant metaphysics and frills. His readings at Group 47 sessions since
1951 demonstrated that practice cannot always follow theory
in every detail. Yet, while social themes were still popular
and reaction to this trend was still disorganized, Weyrauch's
lyrical realism found acceptance. Along with Heinrich Böll,
he was among the few writers to reconcile successfully art
and reality. The critic Fritz J. Raddatz was deeply impressed
with Weyrauch's fifty-minute radio play *Die japanischen
Fischer* at the group session in 1955; it was allowed a full-
length reading, an opportunity accorded only on rare
occasions and to rare persons. Raddatz thought Weyrauch's
play to show congruence between a timely, topical problem
and a form reduced to stylistic essence. If the audience had
not been supersaturated with other readings, Raddatz felt
that the play would have been in contention with a Martin
Walser story for which its author received the group's prize.
(Interestingly enough, Walser had been the radio producer
for Weyrauch's *Hörspiel*, *Die Minute des Negers*, adopted
from Weyrauch's ballad by the same name [1953], which
sympathized with the social plight of the Negro.) Weyrauch's choric, balladistic, and poetic radio plays temporarily
revived methods used by the expressionists of earlier decades.
His rhetorical phrasing of questions and answers, filled with
despair and naïve optimism, are on the emotional side:
"Does God consent to what man is doing to man?" ask the

Japanese fishermen. "I have set the rainbow between myself and the earth; as long as the earth endures, there will be no surcease of sowing and harvest, frost and heat, summer and winter, day and night," is the answer of the God of the Old Testament in Weyrauch's radio play *Totentanz* [Dance of death] (1961) — man will survive even nuclear holocaust.

Not only was the question of language and style an on-going concern in the critical discussion at the Group 47 meetings, but also the relation of message and content or how to dress up a theme in one's writing. Heinz Huber's radio play *Früher Schnee am Fluss* [Early snows at the river] (1953) was rigorously analyzed. Huber shows the insulation of an average family: during dinner time the news that the Korean war has broken out is shunted aside as unappetizing. If the world is headed for ruin, runs Huber's message, it is the consequence of people's boundless indifference to what goes on in the world. Some listeners at the group reading felt that the author's protest contained too much *Welt-schmerz* and too little background material of substance; others thought that "scare" literature prompted by fears of catastrophe was being overworked. That Huber's appeal to conscience through the form of the radio play was criticized as being too obvious speaks for the continuing changes of aesthetic criteria within the heterogeneous Group 47 and the rejection of idealistic pathos that marked the early writings of many associated with the group.

Yet, messages continued to come through loud, clear, and with artistic integrity in the radio plays of group associates Walter Jens, Horst Mönnich, Heinz von Cramer, Christian Ferber, and many others. Schwitzke has noted that Jens's three radio plays fall into the realm of "aggressive actuality," another way of saying that they struck sensitive nerves in their clear, dramatic exposition of moral dilemmas. Among the painful situations during and after the Third Reich was the relationship between the intellectuals who left the country — voluntarily or because of threats to their lives — and those who compromised in order to stay. The émigrés were rarely made to feel welcome after the war, and most, like Herbert Marcuse, were never offered academic posts suited to their distinguished backgrounds; many simply decided to stay with the universities abroad, which had given them shelter and recognition. In Jens's *Der Besuch des Fremden* [The visit of the stranger] (1953) a postwar dialogue ensues between a professor who declined to take an oath of allegiance to Hitler and left the country and another who stayed. The former claims that "one cannot sell one's conscience" and the latter counters with, "it was not easy, but now we have survived it." The irony of the matter is that the émigrés for the most part did not have it less "easy." The émigré is convinced that if half of the faculty had followed his example, justice would have prevailed in Germany and that they would have made the world a better place to live in for their children. Against this moral absolutism the other professor, who compromised, registers a protest: "Justice, what do you mean by justice? You always talk in abstractions. You thought of justice but I thought of doing what was right under the circumstances." The ideological lines are drawn with a firmness reminiscent of Ibsen and Galsworthy, and Jens does not shun their emotional devices; the result is a somewhat old-fashioned melodrama, which perhaps still forms a good platform for debate of important issues. The theme of the man without a country is given more symbolic treatment in Jens's *Ahasver* (1956), and the narrator unfolds a story of persecution, employing a liturgical tone of sorrow rather than of indignation.

Among the sharpest indictments of the economic miracle or the new prosperity for its materialistic detriment to spiritual and social values, we find Horst Mönnich's *Kopfgeld* [Money per capita] (1958). The lines are drawn between the new economy which has its own implacable laws, demanding the individual's subjection to "progress," and private morality. As in the message-dramas of the period, Mönnich declares through one of the characters that if the truth about ourselves will provide insights there is hope for change. Although the comforts provided by the new economy can easily narcotize memories of the past, Heinrich Böll's radio plays, especially *Klopfzeichen* [Knock-codes] (1960), shows the unavoidable intrusion of past memory into the present, causing mental anguish to those who ironically least deserve to be plagued by their conscience. Böll's stories about the little man whose acts of humanity were punished during the Third Reich are so skillfully told that sympathy is elicited through events and fate rather than debate.

Submission to authority and genuflecting to superiors, which have been seen as particularly German traits, find dramatic representation in Heinz von Cramer's *Die Ohrfeige* [The slap in the face] (1959). In the radio play, a bank employee spots a general who had abandoned his men to death during the last stages of the war. In a moment of rage he slaps the now prosperous general, but under the none-too-subtle pressures of his superiors at the bank he hides his damning knowledge during the trial. The underling's rebellion is squelched, his inner conflict is resolved in favor of expediency and reward, and the myth that a military general can do no wrong is upheld. Not only the little man but also certain writers have sold their souls to the establishment, as portrayed in von Cramer's novel *Die Kunstfigur* [The artist] (1958); what is needed in our world, endangered by cybernetics, is a new type of responsible human, a cry expressed with lyrical and expressionistic fervor in his novel *Leben wie im Paradies* [We live in paradise] (1964). Von Cramer (b. 1924) was drafted into the German army in 1945, promptly deserted, and hid in Berlin until the arrival of the Allies. For seven years he worked as a radio director for the American-sponsored radio station RIAS and then, in 1953, he took up residence on the Italian island Procida near Naples, visiting Germany every so often to produce radio plays; Nelly Sachs's *Eli* was one of his successes. Not until 1961 did his association with Group 47 begin and not until then did most members of the group pay attention to his writings, which had already been favorably compared with the powerful social literature of Heinrich Mann. Von Cramer is an underrated writer probably because in his writings the didactic element frequently overpowers the artistic. Generally he gives the impression of being a critical outside observer.

An effective attempt to show that complexities of human

behavior lie beneath the surface of events was illustrated by Christian Ferber (b. 1919, pen name of Georg Seidel) in *Gäste aus Deutschland* [Tourists from Germany] (1962). A mother and son visit a French island sixteen years after her late husband had been the German commandant and there, contrary to superior orders, had surrendered to the Allies, sparing the town from certain devastation. Although the son is aware that some German tourists are accompanied by a bad conscience when visiting European countries, he feels that in his case the islanders might remember gratefully his father's individualistic act for which he and his family were stigmatized by the German military. Yet his father's motives were misconstrued by most villagers, and those Frenchmen who persuaded him to violate orders were hounded as collaborators. The question of moral decision and immoral results, despite a highly hypothetical situation, is given a multiple perspective. In his radio plays, Ferber demonstrated lucid lines of thought which have also gained him a reputation as an essayist, and incidentally as an objective commentator on various Group 47 meetings in which he participated.

The radio play of the fifties served its writers and audiences extremely well as entertainment and art; it covered a wide spectrum of social and political issues and afforded writers almost unrestricted opportunities to perfect acoustical narratives in the dimensions of time and space and to develop the potential of dramatic, epic, and lyrical expression. Many of the writers were imbued with the optimism of Bertolt Brecht in regard to literature's role in changing man and bringing about a new sense of communality. They felt that the experiential relationship of the inner and outer world of the figures of the radio play could induce listener empathy through directness of appeal. However, the time when one of Günter Eich's radio plays could attract two million listeners had passed, and the air time being allotted to the radio play by stations was hovering at about two percent. The large audience shift toward television severely affected radio programming, with new emphasis on the housewife and the motorist. It was time for reevaluation for other reasons as well. Significant changes were taking place in the fields of fiction and poetry writing, and the question was raised as to whether or not radio writers had become enslaved to commercial requirements—as well as to radio technology—and had fallen into ruts. Fortunately, the momentum for change was coincident with a lessening of audience pressures as listeners dwindled to those who were receptive to radio play experimentation. Art content and forms must be flexible or they risk becoming redundant, even for a tolerant audience.

Again, members of Group 47 were catalysts in the transition toward the radio play of the sixties. Toward the end of May 1960, a special two-day meeting was called; also, guests influential in the radio networks were invited to the city of Ulm, with the avowed purpose of thoroughly discussing the fate of "The Literary Radio Play." Several authors, including Ilse Aichinger, read works, and shop talk centered on such problems as coping with pressures to resist rewriting by producers and editors who worried more about public rather than artistic taste and intent. Günter Grass tried to put the radio play in the perspective of a special art form which he did not practice because it offered him little resistance and would exploit his weaknesses. Incidentally, he asked, what would a writer stranded on some South Sea island write— a radio play? A rhetorical question deserves a rhetorical answer, but to approach the underlying question seriously would be to call to Grass's attention that some authors sharpened their talents on the whetstone of the radio play and gained their craft and discipline, which served them well in other writing media. At the same time, they created open forms of radiogenic drama with authentic power and contemporaneous validity; its technical dimensions—stream of consciousness, monologue, reportage, verbal play, fantasy, objective and subjective reality—are as extensive as those in other arts. The group meeting apparently spurred a number of published studies and helped to clarify the new directions.

A considerable number of radio plays were contributed by writers from England, America, and many of the continental countries, either in German or through translations, giving a cosmopolitan aspect to the medium. Yet few except Dylan Thomas (whose *Under Milkwood* was translated by Erich Fried, *Milchwald*, 1955), Beckett, Ionesco, Max Frisch, and Friedrich Dürrenmatt made any lasting impression or assisted in the transition to the sixties. A marked change of tone, a dominance of pessimism, became noticeable. One need only look at Eich's radio play *Man bittet zu laüten* [Please ring the bell], written and performed in 1964, and compare it with his earlier work. The play's title is taken from the directions posted in several languages at the entrance of a Protestant graveyard in Rome, but it would take strenuous interpretation to relate the title to the action of the play for there is almost no action. Through an almost Joycean flow of monologue—composed of clichés, colloquialism, and pseudoliterary scraps—which wells up from the underworld mind of the narrator, a porter at a home for the deaf and dumb, we get the impression of a pitifully corrupt and opportunistic mentality at the mercy of atavistic instincts; his experiences do not lead to constructive insights. The hopes which Eich had for the little man have vanished; there is no moral regeneration and he has no goal beyond ridding himself of "poverty which weighs like asthma." The collage effect is heightened by interspersed poems from the works of seventeenth-century German writers and recited by a chorus of school children. The words of the poems with their brimstone terror and naïve expression of pleasure at the simplicities of life and faith in God seem like anachronisms. With the quoting of lines which attribute to the artist-poet the power of rendering the wonders and visual delights of the world, it may be that an ironic contrast is intended between the world view of the baroque and the modern poet.

A typical representative of other radio playwrights in whose work the transitions are quite evident is Peter Hirche (b. 1923). Only one reading is recorded at the Group 47 sessions, in 1955, but he had already established himself in the field with such radio plays as *Die seltsamste Liebesgeschichte der Welt* [The World's strangest love story] (1953), in which realistic interior monologues show the irreconcilable distances between two people. Twelve years and several other effective plays later. Hirche, in a foreword to his *Miserere*, makes evident a drastic reorientation: "The entire play must wind down rapidly. . . . No full development of situations. No sentiment. Everything is matter-of-fact." Further there were to be no messages, no criticism, the author's position might be centered solely in the title, the basic form is to be the collage, and no value is to be placed on the creation of theatrical illusion or resemblances to reality. Many of the characteristics of the new radio play are sounded here, including an attempt to be freed from tangible purpose and engagement.

Dream and reality, parable, surrealism, and the absurd have a common fountainhead in the theater of Strindberg; since then the grotesque and the macabre have become its modern offspring. Eich, Bachmann, and Wolfgang Hildesheimer (b. 1916) were among the leading practioners of these forms. Since 1951, Hildesheimer has been among the most active members of Group 47 and has distinguished himself as a storyteller. Some of his novels, short stories, and theater plays originated as radio plays. He was born in Hamburg and during his youth received schooling in Farnham, England; in exile he engaged in free-lance art work and scenic design and served as a British Information Officer in Palestine, 1940–45; at the Nuremberg trials he was an interpreter, and later as a free-lance writer decided to remain an expatriate by taking up residence in Poschiavo, Switzerland. Personal reticence marks his work—even the memoir sketches of his youth in Cornwall, *Zeiten in Cornwall* (1971)—in the sense that no specific experience or direct expression of opinion or emotional reaction come through. Much seems to be hidden behind the masks of his figures, symbolized in his eerie surrealistic line-drawings, or sublimated in his version of the theater of the absurd. At various times he has explained his preference for parable which deliberately avoids the explicit message: "The theater of the absurd serves in the confrontation of the audience with the absurd in that it censoriously shows the audience its own absurdity." Moreover, the theater of the absurd is not a protest against theatrical forms but it is philosophical theater which protests against conventional views of the world: "Life is a permanently unanswered question." In his memoir he sees the landscape of Cornwall as a backdrop for the staging of *Lear* and Beckett's *Godot* but it could serve also as the mental setting for his own plays.

For Hildesheimer perhaps literature is a flight from life, but the literary vantage point allows an objective and symbolic representation of life; his state of discomfort, caused by an imposed homelessness, darkly colors all of his writings. From Dürrenmatt and Frisch, Hildesheimer learned to generalize sociopolitical problems and from Beckett and Ionesco he learned to use language which perfectly mirrors the emptiness of existence. A streak of sardonic satire, however, gives his work a distinct flavor as the neuroses of civilization take on specific similitude in the characters of his fiction: they are all forced to look into the abyss and they are shocked by the realization that there is no way back. Descriptively appropriate is the collective title for some of his dramas influenced by French surrealism, *Spiele in denen es dunkel wird* [Plays in which darkness falls] (1958), with particular affinity to Marcel Aymé. One of his deservedly popular radio plays *Herrn Walsers Raben* [Mr. Walser's ravens] (1960), displays an utterly black sense of humor. Mr. Walser keeps a huge family fortune intact by turning his fortune-hunting relatives, one by one, into ravens. At the point he feels completely secure, he learns in no uncertain terms that his housekeeper is a potential sorcerer's apprentice who has learned his magic; his own prospects become grim. Similar disillusionment faces a married couple in *Unter der Erde* [Below the ground] (1962) who crawl through a hole in their garden in the mistaken belief that they have found an underground castle. They are almost buried by a slide, manage to escape with a whole skin, but have learned nothing and return to their old, stupid quarrels. Not so lucky is the intellectual in the one-act drama *Nachtstück* (1962; *Nightpiece*, 1966) who deteriorates into madness to the same degree that he slowly immolates himself in his ivory tower and devises locks to keep out the evil burglars of the world; his failure to cope directly with forces of destruction leads to the same catastrophe pictured by Frisch in his *Biedermann und die Brandstifter* (1958; *The Firebugs*, 1963), a radio drama before it was adapted for the stage. With his radio play *Monologue* (1964) Hildesheimer radicalizes his philosophic approach in favor of speech collages, exposing language as a veneer for misguided conscience, and adopts the newer methods of the "speech play," which became one of the principal forms of the radio play in the sixties.

Several tendencies which were already latent in the fifties emerged full-blown in all writing media of the sixties. With calculated pessimism, Dürrenmatt ended his dramas at a point where the action could take only a turn for the worse; in the radio play, particularly, this seemed to become the starting point for most dramas. No longer was it possible for the main figures to gain ethical insights through inner and outer experience; the possibility of being a hero or protagonist vanished absolutely, and instead he became a victim, a nonentity, a confused voice struggling against a mass voice. There is no possibility for the listener to identify with the hero because there is no hero. The listener no longer is addressed directly; instead he becomes someone who overhears talk, as one might at a street corner, on a bus, a telephone line. The drama is rendered through collages and an assault upon the senses with impressionistic fragments which the listener may or may not be able to assemble. As a result, the listener's mind must work strenuously to make sense out of what seems nonsense; he must feel more intensely than ever before. Nothing is presented to him on a platter. If, as the new dramas imply, the system or the establishment has crushed the individual, only chaos can picture the facts. An act of assertion to pull meaning from this chaos may help to reestablish the listener's own sense of individuality. Gone is the lyrical realism of the fifties, sentiment is purged, and the artificiality of art is emphasized at every turn in order to destroy the illusion of drama. Many of the writers of drama, poetry, and fiction flatter themselves with having ushered in a new phase of literature whereas it seems to me to be a wholesale regression to the principles of Dadaism of the twenties; what we see is one form of illusion, the artist's sleight of hand, substituted for another which often makes it difficult to sort out craft from craftiness.

Grotesque stylizations, mordant satire, kaleidoscopic play with language found in everyday life or in books, the positioning of possibilities, and natural associations of ideas become the fabric of the new radio drama. Just as the world of Hildesheimer's Herr Walser slowly was hemmed in by the increasingly ominous cries of the ravens so is the world defined by other characters who feel the periphery of their existence shrinking through fear and the approach of voices. The purely acoustical means of the radio make such nightmares real. This is particularly evident in the radio plays of Jakov Lind: *Anna Laub*, 1964, *Hunger*, 1966, *Angst*, [Anxiety] 1967. All of Lind's creatures are caught in the web of a present consciousness, and without the ability to orient themselves to past or future they become unredeemable, Dantesque figures whose unrelieved fears brutalize them even further; the possibility of regeneration through insights is denied them. The disembodying of figures and the removal of possible identification in terms of background and social status is carried even further by others writing for the radio so that the entire aural-play is concentrated on themes and language. The thematic approach is artfully illustrated through the radio plays written in 1969 by Jürgen Becker: *Bilder* [Pictures], *Häuser* [Houses], *Hausfreunde* [House guests]. Almost everything which can be said about houses is said and the failure of the speakers to sort out the significant from the trivial becomes the author's unspoken comment on contemporary mindlessness or inattentiveness to the implication of spoken words. It is the vacuous mind and the insensitive tongue which level everything to a common denominator so that the specter of Nazi victims smoked out of ghetto houses in *Häuser* is submerged in the cauldron of colloquial talk.

While some of the radio plays contained enough concrete words in their texts to allow the listener to make associative sense, others deliberately confuse language and reality or attribute a computerlike function to language; indeed, in Peter Handke's radio plays, language resembles the output of a computer gone beserk. The fact that Handke's *Hörspiel* [Radio play] (1968) results in a crosspurpose or disfunctioning dialogue between questioner and the one questioned is explained by the latter: "I use every word as a means of avoidance." The deliberate avoidance of the straightforward response or action is his only means of forestalling boredom. Whether the radio listener can do likewise is a question Handke seems not to have asked himself. Typical of the game play are the lines: Questioner: "What occurs to you when I say this sentence, 'The children of the dead person cuddle in the bed of the neighbor.'" The one questioned: "No one has a spot remover at hand." In *Hörspiel Nr. 2*, 1968, Handke pastes together scraps of conversation overheard mainly between taxi drivers and their fares—a technique that was run into the ground long ago by followers of Eliot's *The Waste Land*. The most devastating comment on the contents of the play occurs in the following dialogue: "Tell me something. Does nothing occur to you? Don't you have anything to tell me?" "*You* tell me something." "Nothing occurs to me." "Tell something." "Really, nothing occurs to me." "Come on, tell me something already!" "Nothing occurs to me! For the death of me, nothing occurs to me." And indeed little occurs to Handke in his last two radio plays *Geräusche eines Geräusches* [Noise of a noise] (1969) and *Wind und Meer* [Wind and sea] (1970) in which variations of sounds *are* the plays. Meaning is reduced to kinesthesia; action and story are dead, as is the individual in fiction.

The same incoherence which marks much of the avant-garde poetry, ostensibly to reduplicate the incoherence of life, has pushed the radio art form into the same impasse. Incommunicability or the failure to communicate among humans, banality and emptiness, cannot for long remain the contents of any art form without destroying itself. With the seventies, the radio play, like all other forms of fiction whose lines have become fluid and indistinct from one another, has reached a point of crisis which every so often overtakes literature. It will take time to overcome the crisis, but until then we can expect little more than experimentation. Experimentation, in my vocabulary, means unsuccessful art.

5

Documentary
The Playwright as Preacher and Teacher

The international furor attending the various productions of Rolf Hochhuth's *Der Stellvertreter* (1963; *The Deputy*, 1964) gave new impetus to the documentary theater of the sixties. The play was directed first by Erwin Piscator (1893–1966), who was the midwife of the earlier version of the German documentary theater in the twenties, which embodied the expressionistic mechanics developed by Max Reinhardt and employed the sociopolitical strains of Marxist philosophy. Piscator had broken with a long family line of Protestant ministers to found a political church, his theater, with the trinitarian slogan of "knowledge, perception, commitment" (*Kenntnis, Erkenntnis, Bekenntnis*). The choice of politically inflammatory material, supported by documentary data and shaped by partisan viewpoints into a theatrical format, lends similarity to the documentary theaters separated by some forty years. While the debates among playwrights on the question of art-and-pedagogy remain, the modern documentary theater has broadened the aesthetic and ideological premises beyond Piscator's "direct action" theater. Although all recognize the potentialities of history not merely as background events but as contemporaneous political realities, Piscator's short-lived proletarian theater with its call for a classless society, a revolutionary communality, and a socialistic art has found translation in its simplistic forms only in Communist countries. In the documentary theater of the West, scorn and indignation directed against the worst features of capitalism has not abated, but there has been a shift from attempts at political persuasion to moral persuasion. The shift of emphasis has resulted in a larger audience. In the twenties Piscator easily managed to incur the vicious epithets of the right-wing press, which heralded the vocabulary of the Third Reich, but he enlisted neither the proletarians nor the demoralized middle class. Many of the modern writers within and outside of Group 47 have largely transferred agitation for political change to the essay, journalism, and the electioneering platform. Yet, despite all their fervor, few were able to penetrate the shell of the comfortable audience and touch it to the quick.

The career of Rolf Hochhuth, born 1931 in a small Hessian town, was cited as one proof by Heinrich Böll that Group 47 was not the only possible forum for success and that it did not inhibit other literary directions. And perhaps it was to the good that the young man did not belong to the group in whose atmosphere of literary and critical sophistication his basic questions might have sounded naïve and where, as a self-taught man, he might have been made uncomfortable by all the high-powered writer-academicians. One must look far to see the function of the writer so clearly and unequivocally stated as in Hochhuth's dictum: "Authors must articulate the bad conscience of their nation because the politicians have such a good one." Hochhuth noted, "I was fourteen in 1945, and the total collapse of Germany was a great emotional shake-up for me. I considered it my responsibility to study the shameful history of the Third Reich. Again and again I came to think, 'What would you yourself have done if you had been old enough to act?'" While for him this was a deeply personal and hypothetical question, it was not so for older writers who waltzed around the question to avoid painful self-examination. With the extermination of Jews and other Europeans brought into the German concentration camps, all Germans incurred shame and guilt, but in Hochhuth's view, there also is a hierarchy of guilt from the active top down to the majority of the nation which brought Hitler to power legally and supported him positively or passively practically to the end. Furthermore, the whole civilized world shares guilt by association, particularly England and America, for inaction to stop the exterminations. Hochhuth, like Günter Eich, equates inaction with silent complicity. An examination of the role of those in power led Hochhuth to the study of Pope Pius XII who, in 1958, "was virtually canonized by world opinion on his deathbed," and, more and more, he came to the conclusion reached by historians who like Gerald Reitlinger felt that the Pope was obsessed with neutrality and diplomatic immunity; "I do not think," said Reitlinger, "that this need have happened had there been a better Pope." Indeed, whatever the reasons for the Pope's failure to assert moral leadership in the name of Christ, the church's credibility suffered irreparably.

Hochhuth's intentions crystallized around symbolic and specific points: "I wished to show Pius XII, a historical figure . . . the Deputy of Christ who remained silent; each spectator, Catholic, Jew, or Protestant—who did not take a position should see reflected his own guilt . . . 'What part of the responsibility is yours?'" Hochhuth also wished to make it clear that he wanted to attack each person to his profoundest depth, "to attack *living* Christians, not solely to criticize Pope Pius XII, who is dead now and belongs to history." With these intentions, Hochhuth has defined his version of the documentary theater. Whether, as Piscator hopes, it will be a force for change or whether it will only remain as a basic primer for our times, which gives the postwar generations a text unequaled in frankness, remains a moot point. I don't think that Hochhuth fully realized what the consequences would be when he dramatized a subject which was taboo or when he ripped off the scabs of healing wounds or antagonized those who have a bad conscience. At first he wrote the play for his friends and his wife, whose mother had been killed at Auschwitz, and with the idea of fixing responsibilities for moral crimes, but the storm which resulted turned him into a crusader. He had been an editorial assistant at the Bertelsman publishing house, which submitted to church pressures and did not publish *Der Stellverträter* although it already was in galleys. As a result, Hochhuth resigned and moved to Basel, Switzerland, to become an assistant director of the Municipal Theater.

Much has been said about the literary deficiencies of Hochhuth's *The Deputy*, but whatever these may be—the large sprawl of scenes in the "epic" tradition, flat characterizations, and stilted verse—anyone who has seen the play staged has no difficulty in sensing its theatrical power. It has brought out the worst behavior and the best reasoned reaction in people. Some Parisians tried to storm the stage, shouting anti-Semitic epithets. But, on the other hand. Friedrich Heer, a professor of Catholic history at the University of Vienna, spoke for many Catholic theologians and churchmen, who felt that Hochhuth succeeded in realizing the descriptive subtitle of his play, "a Christian tragedy"; they hoped that the play would have a cleansing and liberating effect. It should be remembered that Hochhuth dedicated his play to two martyred Catholic priests and paid tribute in the play to the spirit of anguished resistance and the memory of thousands of priests who fell victim to Hitler; and, by the same token, he found it reprehensible that the Pope and the upper clergy did not lift a finger to help any one of them. Yet—and this is rare in a documentary play—oppositional attitudes receive a considered hearing in the play through the confrontations which help to create dramatic tensions and give documentary evidence a tangible shape.

Among the drawbacks of the documentary drama is its tendency to present surfaces of events and people, outer characterizations rather than inner tumult and psychological depths. Most writers of this genre use the stage as a pulpit, platform, and as a tribunal to indict the accused. In Hochhuth's next play, *Soldaten: Nekrolog auf Genf* (1967; *Soldiers: An Obituary on Geneva*, 1968) Sir Winston Churchill was indicted for his decision in 1945 to level the city of Dresden and his disinclination to agree with the Red Cross for a Geneva covenant that would prohibit saturation and fire-bombings of open cities. The extraliterary effect of the play was the abolition of the English Lord Chamberlain's office of national censorship, resulting from a public uproar when Hochhuth's play was first denied a production permit. The play's moral thesis—the condemnation of all aerial bombings—overshadows the convolutions of historical figures.

In his play *Guerillas*, 1970, he abandons careful research and projects a science-fiction plot centering on a doomed revolution during which idealists—led by a senator—attempt to infiltrate key positions of power in the United States in order to bring about sweeping social reforms and a political utopia. Attacks on the military-industrial complex, the FBI, and CIA are not new, and the vast social and economic reforms needed in the United States are part of vital debates in public life; despite all this, to equate the United States with Russia as police states is a patent absurdity which Hochhuth—as well as several radical writers of Group 47— have hysterically adopted. The outlandish plot inundated those significant ideas which Hochhuth emphasized in an interview about the play (which some have mistaken for a Marxist extravaganza). He criticizes Marx for not having established an oppositional element in his system, which would be a safeguard against tyranny, and he suggests that it is not the ownership of wealth but the possession of power—in the United States and Russia—which becomes the instrument of social oppression. Here he restates his basic and valid premise that power, political or spiritual, without concomitant morality may lead to social crimes. With *Guerillas* Hochhuth illustrates his thesis that the political or documentary theater "does not have the task of reproducing reality—which is always political—but to oppose it through the projection of a new one; and, only when it agitates in a moral rather than political sense does it make an impact on the viewer."

Hochhuth, like Günter Grass, is a literary Ralph Nader with his exposés which gain public attention and spur debate. In 1965 the former German Chancellor Ludwig Erhard, stung by the political attacks of writers, particularly of Group 47, flayed their "idiocies" and called them "intellectual snobs." He heaped particular scorn upon Hochhuth, "There the writer ends, and there begins the Pinscher." Erhard's dog epithet was an acknowledgment that these writers could effectively "bite," and this they continued to do with all the more gusto. The documentary theater possessed that kind of potential.

Peter Weiss manages a balance of ideas and art in his plays, giving the concept of the documentary theater new dimensions; he, like his work, is complex and brilliant and probably one of the most representative artists of our age of anxiety through his translation of inner and outer autobiography into visual and dialectic art. If in his novels and stories up through 1962 the question of personal identity and direction are paramount, Weiss's experiences account for the questing and confessional aspect of his works. Born in 1916 near Berlin and brought up in Lutheranism, he was the son of a converted Czech Jew, who became a textile manufacturer, and a Swiss mother. With terrorization by German storm troopers, the family migration began in 1934, progressively deepening Peter Weiss's feeling of isolation. In England, where Weiss studied photography, he was insulted as "Fritz," in Czechoslovakia he was called a German, in Switzerland he was arrested as a suspect alien, but finally he was allowed residence and citizenship in "the politically placid" Sweden where his parents had established a factory. A sense of estrangement from life—even from his family and later from his wife and child—prompted him to hazard a writing career (encouraged by his literary idol Hermann Hesse) and avant-garde film directing, where everything was "alive." For a time, art was a flight into aestheticism but it also afforded a vantage point for viewing life, using his pencil to give life its contours and gaining clarification of what he saw; and much of his work showed affinity for Strindberg (whose *Dream Play* he translated into German), Kafka, and the surrealists.

Weiss seemed to have ensconced himself in a cocoon, but several experiences during the early sixties exploded him out of it. Probably his contact with Group 47 was one of his main encouragements for a social redirection of energies, and he became a most active member. He read a philosophical story *Das Gespräch der drei Gehenden* [The conversation

of the three ambulators] (1963) to the group in 1962 and
came in second to Johannes Bobrowski in a polling to deter-
mine the group's literary prize, which had not been awarded
since 1958. The recognition was salutary, at any rate. Still,
he shied away from German internal political matters by
declining to sign the resolution, drawn up by many Group
47 members, protesting the government's role in the "Spiegel
affair." A year later, Weiss again participated as a reader and
also criticized some readings as too esoteric, a view which
departed from his own earlier stance. For his text, Weiss
chose some songs and monologues from his play *Die Ver-
folgung und Ermordung Jean-Paul Marats dargestellt durch
die Schauspielgruppe des Hospizes zu Charenton unter An-
leitung des Herrn de Sade* (1964; *The Persecution and As-
sassination of Jean-Paul Marat as Performed by the Inmates
of the Asylum of Charenton under the Direction of the Mar-
quis de Sade*, 1965). He accompanied his reading of political
ballads with the beating of a drum, reminding one of
Brecht's theater; features of the *Threepenny Opera* and
Mahagonny are evident. Weiss readily acknowledges
Brecht's influence: clarity, the necessity for making plain
the central social question in a play, and stylistic lightness
instead of a typical German psychological ponderousness.
Hans Mayer, the most potent of the group's critics, gave a
fiery interpretation of Weiss's reading, and later in his critical writings ascribed to Weiss a greater literary influence
than to Grass. The prediction made by group members that
the *Marat/Sade* play would cause a stir was fully justified
when it was performed in Berlin; the Swiss writer Emil
Staiger attacked it as the epitome of the sickness in modern
literature. Subsequently it was produced in more than thirty
countries and translated into seventeen languages. Weiss
revised the play five times and the last published version has
attained the sharpest political orientation. Of all modern
plays, it emerges as an example of "total theater," borrowing
elements from surrealism, Dadaism, the theater of the absurd, and the cruel; yet it also is theater with a documentary
slant. Retrospectively, Weiss defended the documentary
theater as principally an art form. If it were to be a political

forum mainly and shun artistic accomplishment, said Weiss, it would put its function in question: "In such a case, practical political action in the outside world would be more effective."

Through his possession of film and art techniques, Weiss produces a panoptical spectacle that integrates music and pantomime into intricate patterns of sound and colors—costumes are meticulously prescribed as are the actors' style of movement and motion. Very likely, Weiss took a cue from Jacques Louis David's masterful painting *The Death of Marat*, 1793, in which Marat, one of the political leaders of the French Revolution, lies slumped in a bathtub and holds in his hand a personal petition by Charlotte Corday, who had also plunged a knife into his chest to eliminate one she felt to be a bloodthirsty tyrant. Marat, in the tub during most of the play, suffers from a psychosomatic skin condition which he alleviated by sitting in water. In a detailed note to the historical background of the play, Weiss discusses his theatrical combination of fact and fiction. Sade was interned for thirteen years, until 1814, in the asylum of Charenton, the hiding place for the moral rejects of society, where he occasionally produced declamatory plays with a cast of patients and took a role himself. Although Sade's encounter with Marat in the play within the play is fictional, it is designed to portray a conflict of ideology between extreme individualism as expressed through counterrevolutionary sentiments and the justification of violent political and social upheaval. Some critics saw the play as a victory for Sade and others as an open-ended discussion of the meaning of revolution, forcing the audience to seek its own answers; consequently, Weiss instructed directors of the play to put the accent upon Marat as the moral victor. Weiss interprets Marat's writings as suggesting that he wanted to avoid a bourgeois victory as a consequence of the French Revolution and wanted to push to goals beyond a "slave and master society" but that he overreached himself. Sade is characterized as a supporter of the revolution who is prevented by his futile individualism and propertied orientation from going all the way. Marat is extolled as "one of those who were in the process of building the socialist image" and for the acuteness of his ideas. In sum, the need for revolution is preached and the asylum becomes symbolic of capitalist-bourgeois society; the inmates become representative of the masses and their rebellious leaders, while the asylum keepers are the oppressors. In the Epilogue or scene 33, there is Dantesque bedlam as the marching inmates shout "Revolution Revolution/ Copulation Copulation" and one of Marat's followers exclaims, "When will you learn to see/ when will you learn to take sides." Although Weiss does not intend that the message ridicule itself, it does so by the aura of madness, perversion, cynicism, and self-righteousness which bathes all the characters. The play is set in 1808; the play-within-the-play portrays Marat's last hour during July 13, 1793, and by implication it also represents the viewer's time. While the reading version allows one to follow the ideological and documentary content of the play, the performance subdues the thought-content in favor of the shocking and often brutal spectacle of reason submerged by uninhibited and cunning emotion. Though the demented ballet of the inmates is a mirror image of certain historical events, it does nothing to enhance the desirability of revolution; on the contrary, the notion shows repelling consequences. Biographically, we have seen a strange progression here from Weiss's fears, when he was a child, of "power and soldiers and force" to the adult who became fascinated with precisely the same elements.

Although one can easily infer from Weiss's narratives that the postwar viewing of films which graphically recorded the horrors of the German concentration camps brought into his existence something that could no longer be dismissed, it took a long and painful period of disattachment from personal involvements before he could transfer his emotions to social engagement. The transition from isolation to communication with the world and his ardor to change it was also the road from the theater of illusion and inwardness to the literature of commitment. The critical change occurred when he found emotional identification and a place with epiphanic significance: "It is a place for which I was destined but which I managed to avoid. . . . my name was on the list of people who were supposed to be sent there for ever." In an essay called *Meine Ortschaft* (1965; *My Place*, 1967), Weiss describes with taut simplicity his visit to the former German concentration camp in Poland, Auschwitz. Although he spent only one day there, in his memory it was the only place that remained constant. His orientation is slow, almost numb, as he identifies the black execution wall, the medical experiment building, the torture rooms, the gallows, the ovens, and the other objects which like the "ramp" have since the forties assumed a horror beyond their simple name-signification. He hears in his mind the screaming of the millions of naked victims, some of whom were sluiced into furnace rooms and arose as brown sweetish-reeking smoke while others were exterminated by phenol injections into the heart. He also saw the large painted words *Obedience, Industriousness, Cleanliness, Honesty, Sincerity, Sobriety, Love of the Fatherland*, slogans and virtues made obscene by those who wrote them. Weiss's answer on how to deal with these monstrous facts in a communicative way was given in his drama *Die Ermittlung* (1965; *The Investigation*, 1966), an oratorio to be recited—not acted—by the victims and the accused in a bare courtroom staging. There is no other play like this one, which had its premiere in seventeen theaters, nor will there ever be one like it. For, having been done once, it remains a primer, a memorial to the sub-Neanderthal instincts of modern man abetted by his technology. It is a summation of the documentary materials gathered during the 1964 War Crimes Trial in Frankfurt and is condensed into eleven scenes. Weiss relies on dry recital of the facts in order to stimulate the mind's vision of the audience because realistic portrayals would be unbearable. Weiss had faith in the ability of the documentary theater "to construct from the fragments of reality a usable pattern, a model for the actual happenings" and to achieve theater art. Others disagreed, and Max Frisch noted that the immediacy of documents fails to replace theatrical vision, which requires a distancing.

The documentary theater, despite its semblance of objectivity, shows the playwright to be partisan. In Weiss's case, *The Investigation* takes on an editorial slant when he accuses German big industry of having benefited from the gas chamber experiments and he charges that many in the trial audience associate themselves with the accused in claiming that they were merely doing their duty as concentration-camp death-dealers, that everything has been atoned for, and that attention should be paid to other things than the past. Weiss's political thinking became more radical in his call for a "socialist ordered society," but it seems to me that he went too far in 1965 in favoring the East German regime and indirectly slighting those West German authors who were honestly striving for reform. A debate ensued between Weiss and Enzensberger, another Group 47 writer, in which the question of the relative aspects of commitment and political independence received no satisfactory resolution. However, Weiss showed in later plays that he was no slave to Communist party lines.

Weiss's rising fame and the rediscovery of his earlier fiction, I am afraid, blinded many critics and audiences to the increasing political superficiality and theatrical thinness of his last plays, perhaps because of the popularity of their themes among intellectual progressives and the assumption that art and Weiss's writing were always synonymous. *Gesang vom lusitanischen Popanz, The Song of the Lusitanian Bogey,* and his *Viet Nam Diskurs,* full title, *Discourse on the Progress of the Prolonged War of Liberation in Viet Nam and the Events Leading Up to It as Illustration of the Necessity for Armed Resistance Against Oppression and on the Attempts of the United States of America to Destroy the Foundations of the Revolution* were plays written in 1967 and translated in 1970. Both plays end with the crescendo of the choruses: ". . . the liberation which is near"; "the fight goes on." In the first instance, Weiss sketches conditions which led to native uprisings against Portuguese oppression, and in the other he posts a series of skits depicting the entire revolutionary history of Vietnam, extending into the present intervention by imperialist-racist-capitalist-etc. American forces. Both are designed to be realistic in speech and manner, with some effective Brechtian doggerel ballads, but the pamphleteering notes and the condescending use of "educational" material to illustrate class struggle dogma, and to condemn capitalist imperialism make for argumentative theater which swallows up some of the occasionally brilliant and emotionally touching scenes. During Weiss's discussion of the Vietnam problem with Americans while attending the Group 47 sessions at Princeton in 1966, he steadfastly verified only his preconceptions and saw little of the anguish which tears at many Americans. His statements to the press bordered on invective and were consonant with the zeal of one who confessed to having been "converted from the somnambulism of self-enclosed art to an attempt, through writing, to make the world more habitable."

Trotzki im Exil [Trotsky in exile] (1970) is a combination of portrait and thesis play, based heavily on documentary sources; here he begins to be less dogmatic about the schematic separation of the socialist and capitalist worlds and sees more complicated structurings within each. As in *Marat/Sade*, Weiss shows how the revolution devours its children, yet "what has happened here does not prove the falsity of socialism but the brittleness and inexperience within our revolutionary actions." Probably here is an echo of Weiss's disillusionment with the Russian invasion of Czechoslovakia and his rejection of the resurgence of Stalinistic totalitarianism. He poses Trotsky as a model of the sound revolutionary thinker, takes liberties with Trotsky's writings for the sake of stage-performance condensation, and postulates as the ultimate wisdom Trotsky's prophecy that students will lead the world revolution. The essentially deleterious consequences of unfocused student movements has apparently escaped Weiss's attention. Undigestible, too, is the steady phrase and slogan mongering, the prolonged argumentations, the unconvincing effusions about human solidarity, and the exaggerated linking of Trotsky and Lenin. How quickly weather vanes can change direction is evident by the attacks upon him as an agent of imperialism by Communist critics who previously hailed him as a laureate of Marxism; they simply could not tolerate deviations from current and simplistic propaganda lines. Group 47 critic Marcel Reich-Ranicki lampooned the theater audience which tamely accepted Weiss's dramatized preachings for a revolution of which they would be the first victims, but he also feared that Weiss's simplifications endangered any credibility which the political theater might have in West Germany. Further controversy died when the play fell flat after performances in two West German cities.

Linked to the portrait of Marat and Trotsky is an almost legendary figure in Weiss's play *Hölderlin*, performed in 1971. Friedrich Hölderlin (1770–1843) is remembered for his superb hymns and elegies, some of which bore the imprint of optimism engendered by the early stages of the French Revolution, and his idealism and faith in the humane possibilities of man. Weiss saw in all these figures a similar conflict, namely, "the dualism between Utopia, wish-projection, dream, humanism, drive for changes, and, on the other outer-realities, dogma, ossification, force, compromise, repression. Always it concerns humans who stake their entire person upon a basic transformation of existential relationships and who are pushed by reality into a corner, to the brink of destruction, or are actually destroyed." Weiss does not see them as tragic figures but incorruptible ones who do not betray their ideals; though Hölderlin lived in a twilight of madness for forty years, not his mind but the mind of the world was clouded. As an alternative to the looming possibility of jail for his "revolutionary consciousness," Hölderlin took refuge in a tower in Tübingen, which also, according to Weiss's thesis, saved him from being broken on the wheel as were Marat and Trotsky. Because of the main figure, *Hölderlin* develops into the most poetic and least combative—in a documentary sense—of Weiss's plays; it also retains many of the song-and-dance devices and choruses of *Marat/Sade*.

Increasingly, Weiss has begun to feel and to portray, in *Hölderlin* for example, the pressures of conflict and dualism in his own person, a fact forcibly impressed upon him by the reaction to his plays in the East and the West; he has found no overwhelming comfort or reciprocity in either world. The last scene of the play imagines a dialogue between Hölderlin and Marx, in which the young economist says, "Two roads are usable/ for the preparation of/ basic changes/ The one way is/ the analysis of the concrete/ historical situation/ The other way is/ the visionary formulation/ of the deepest personal experience." As a writer, Weiss obviously cannot devote himself to time-consuming political activism or theorizing so that his affinity lies with the visionaries: Marat, Trotsky, Hölderlin. The path fulfills his creative needs but it is intellectually dangerous: all visionaries have shattered against the wall of reality.

A tendency toward demythologizing great literary figures of the past and to evaluate them in terms of socioliterary contributions has caught Goethe and Hölderlin in the nets flung during debates by German critics. Martin Walser, with whom Weiss became acquainted through Group 47, put the contrast between the poets succinctly by charging that in treason against the human spirit Goethe allowed his art to be tamed by an aristocratic court, rejected the chance to reorient bourgeois culture in a democratic direction, and became "an appalling phrase-monger," while Hölderlin preserved his personal and artistic integrity. Weiss expressed indebtedness to Walser for helping to clarify lines of thought. Weiss also owes his ideas to a book by the French Germanist Pierre Bertaux, *Hölderlin und die französische Revolution*, which sees Hölderlin not as a proponent of national Germanism but as a Jacobin idealist of the French Revolution. Yet again, through Weiss the political and documentary theater showed itself engaged in translating the contemporaneous ferment of ideas into dramatic visualizations.

In two instances severe criticism was leveled against playwrights for having abused the spirit of authenticity which had been a claim of the documentary theater. The widow of the playwright and social revolutionist Ernst Toller (1893–1939) protested that Tankred Dorst had distorted the facts in his play *Toller*, 1968. Dorst's rejoinder shows an attempt to reject the concept of the documentary theater despite his obvious use of its techniques. He noted that "truth in the documentary sense would, without doubt, consist only of the reality of the documents themselves." Further, theater is "arranged fiction" and anything else is a swindle. Although he claims that theater must operate "without damaging truth," truth—by whatever definition—is the mote in the eye of the playwright. His avowed aim is to denounce the self-dramatizations of Toller, to portray him merely as a prototype of those who convert social revolution into literature and politics into theater, and to show him as a model of naïve, political coquetry.

The other instance concerns the documentary play *In der Sache J. Robert Oppenheimer* [In the matter of J. Robert Oppenheimer] (1964) by the noted playwright and novelist Heinar Kipphardt (b. 1922) who draws upon the 1954 transcripts of the Atomic Energy Commission to show that Oppenheimer, like Galileo in Brecht's theater version, repented of having turned over his scientific findings to a state which used them for destructive purposes. The real Dr. Oppenheimer pointed to unacceptable improvisations in the play, which distort facts and personalities; above all, he had not opposed the making of the atomic bomb in view of the terror unleashed upon the world by fascism in the thirties and forties. One of the elements of the sweeping success of Kipphardt's play is the blanket indictment that not only Germany but others too were responsible for the holocaust visited upon cities during the war. Dr. Oppenheimer's criticism validates the reservation one occasionally has about the responsible use of documentary materials in the theater.

Hans Magnus Enzensberger, one of the leading firebrands of Group 47, released in book form and presented on stage his *Verhör von Habana* [Inquest at Havana] (1970). His intent is to reconstruct an event and indicate its wider meaning through the self-portraiture of the Cuban counterrevolutionaries captured during the misfired invasion in 1961 at the Bay of Pigs. The confessions, on stage, are culled from the actual thousand-page Cuban document of the tribunal interrogations. Not only are these bourgeois counterrevolutionaries put on the stand but also their counterparts in the West. All of them, in Enzensberger's reconstruction, condemn themselves as ideologically naïve persons molded into conformity by the pressure of the ruling classes, and they fail to understand either the true nature of the workers' oppression by capitalist imperialism or their own criminality. The "educational" aspects are so heavily weighted in favor of the Castro regime and doctrinaire leftism that the play becomes an example of pure agitation propaganda. On a huge placard facing the audience is the dictum that "either you are a part of the problem of imperialism or you are part of its solution"; Black Panther Eldridge Cleaver's name is appended to the slogan. This ominous prejudgment hovers over the proceedings and one wonders if Enzensberger himself is fully aware of its "final solution" implications. The drama deliberately reduces the characters to types, a technique which, I am afraid, relegates them to something less than human. Of course, in a theater where politics becomes a weapon we cannot expect polite or in-depth reasoned argumentation.

Enamored of the Cuba he visited, Enzensberger failed to show the Stalinistic repressions that existed; yet, events can strew ashes on radical politics blinded by exotic utopianism. The version of Enzensberger's play published in 1970 was dedicated to Heberto Padilla, one of Cuba's most notable poets. Ironically, one year later Padilla was arrested for writing poetry which lacked revolutionary zeal, was tortured during thirty-eight days of interrogation, and then publicly recanted with humiliating self-criticism for having written counterrevolutionary verse, namely, poetry not quite complimentary to the Castro state. One of his poems begins,

> Cuban poets dream no longer (not even at night).
> They close the door to write alone
> when suddenly the wood creaks;
> the wind buffets the garret:
> Hands seize them by the shoulder.
>
> *Fuera del Juego*, [Out of the game] 1968

Cuba as a model in the realm of socialism is somewhat tarnished, except in such "inquests" as represented by Enzensberger. Because of subsequent disagreements with Castro, Enzensberger no longer may visit Cuba. Closed or public trials and confessions have been greater theaters of the macabre than anyone could invent. By comparison, Enzensberger's *Verhör von Habana* is a drab political revue. He dislikes both the designation of "documentary" and "theater" for his play, but what else can this tract be called when it relies on actors, a script, documents, and a stage; its spontaneity is as illusory as all theater which relies for potential effect upon selective representations.

The documentary theater thrives on controversy, but only Peter Weiss, so far, has been able to also push it toward an art form. Only art can move the mind and emotion with integral impact. Despite the defects of Weiss's *Lusitanian Bogey*, the harrowing experiences and humiliations of the Lusitanians came through in the Broadway performance by the Negro Ensemble Company. Critic Clive Barnes wrote, "By far the most horrifying moment—for a white man at least—comes when the various industries of Angola and Mozambique are impassively listed on the side of the stage, naming all the great European and Anglo-American corporations that have substantial holdings in them, and at the same time, while women moan and a saxophone wails, someone on the other side of the stage describes the wages of the workers. I felt ashamed, and shame is not something I often feel in the theater." If the documentary theater can raise such feelings in the spectator, it has fulfilled its intent, despite—or possibly because of—the contrivances it has inherited from expressionism, the protest theater of the twenties, the political cabaret, the Living Newspaper of the thirties, and the theater of argumentation and social protest generally. Its playwrights not only are moral executors but often take too stridently a role as moral executioners. The form of the documentary theater may vary, but its social consciousness and partisanship does not. Often the playwrights seem to be talking only to other converts or partisans in their uncritical and hysterical acceptance and espousal of anything which carries the label of "Revolution." Still, the documentary playwrights through their use of text montage, biographical-historical portraiture, ritualistic play, and in some cases "total" theater have enlivened awareness of critical issues as no other art form was capable of doing in the sixties.

6

The Stage: Of Dialectics and Bedlam

Not until the sixties did Group 47 members begin to take more than a sporadic interest in writing for the theater. Most of their literary energies were absorbed by the radio play, belletristic writing, poetry, and fiction generally. As a reading forum, Group 47 was inadequate for play manuscripts, and any attempt to read from plays to the group was more difficult than the presentation of excerpts from other types of literature; further, the time had not been ripe for innovative technical perspectives or radical subject contents. The market, however, expanded through the system of municipal or state support of theaters, more than one hundred throughout West Germany. This has meant the growth of repertory companies but also has placed programming somewhat at the mercy of local politics, pressure groups within and outside of the theater, and of bureaucrats who provide the subventions. Especially during the fifties, the German stage of necessity went through an astonishing phase of cosmopolitanism with plays imported wholesale from America, England, and France; revivals of classics from Shakespeare to Ibsen; revivals of expressionists from Wedekind to Toller; the resurgence particularly of Brecht plays written during the twenties and during his exile; the realistic problem-plays by such émigrés as Carl Zuckmayer, Günter Weisenborn (who had worked with Brecht in the thirties and later survived Nazi internment); and the importation of powerful plays by the Swiss Fritz Hochwälder (Swiss by adoption after his 1938 exile from Germany), Max Frisch, and Friedrich Dürrenmatt.

The popularity of such plays as Thornton Wilder's *The Skin of Our Teeth* (1942; translated as *Wir sind noch Einmal davongekommen*) and Zuckmayer's *Des Teufels General* (1946; *The Devil's General*, 1962) was accounted for by a national mood which was receptive to plays with stark pathos expressed in general philosophical or parable form and naturalistic melodrama. Some plays adopted the varieties of Brechtian parable ranging through sociorealistic didacticism, historical portraitures intended as audience-think pieces such as *Mother Courage*, grotesque ballad operas and oratorios, as well as the legendary and mythical. For a while, Brecht held court with his epic or dialectical theater and its loose episodic scenes; he attempted to create distance between play and audience in order to force thinking based on observation rather than emotionalism—the so-called alienation effect. Gradually, some playwrights departed from Brecht's optimistic views about the possibilities of changing society through art; their pessimism emerged in the representation of the world as subject to amorphous forces, pointing to a nonutopian future.

In the sixties, the number of playwrights increased significantly, but Group 47 was not as dominant in the theater as it had been in other literary fields. Still, the group made signal, and sometimes provocative, contributions through the plays of Martin Walser, Hildesheimer, Weiss, Grass, and Handke. The pendulum had swung toward a more critical, and even condemnatory, view of the present; in some cases an anarchic restructuring or dismantling of theater as an art form was envisioned.

The deepened sociocritical content of plays in the sixties was a direct reflection of sharp political controversies. Martin Walser, a prominent Group 47 member, clearly outlined targets of major discontent and fears in a widely-read book, which he compiled with an introduction, called *Die Alternative* [The alternatives: do we need a new government?] (1961). The authors raised a set of troublesome questions which intended to shatter the public complaceny engendered by the economic miracle, resulting in West Germany's relative affluence (the recovery was unlike anything ever seen in Europe and stood in ironic contrast to the economies of the "victorious" European countries). The salient questions involved the atomic alliance with the United States and potential atomic disaster, the sharpened appetite for *Revanchismus* or the drive to reclaim territories lost during the war, the wave of anticommunism, the political power concentration, the rebuilding of the army, the resurgence of the old Fascists—some of whom only had a thin coat of whitewash—and their entrenchment in public office. In general, there was concern about the appearance of a refined form of dictatorialism behind the mask of democracy and through the political emasculation of the public by a reactionary governmental system; they feared the consequences of explosive big business profits and the tentacular growth of monopolistic capitalism with its possible effect on economic and social life. Of singular psychological impact was the Eichmann trial in 1961 in Jerusalem and subsequent criminal trials in West Germany. One of the virtues but also points of abrasion in a free society is the inevitability of raking up the past. Debate grew in respect to lengthening the time limit for prosecution of war criminals under the existing legal statutes, and pressure mounted against those who played along with the Nazis or those who still were in hiding.

In this atmosphere there was receptivity to, but also resentment against, many playwrights who saw it their task to combat complacency. With his play *Eiche und Angorra* (1962; *The Rabbit Race*, 1963), Martin Walser was among those who spearheaded the attack. For Walser, the meaning of a work should grow out of it and be sensed by the viewer or reader instead of being built into the work. By adhering closely to this premise, Walser avoids the argumentative and didactic clichés of the documentary theater and the postwar theater of realism. Walser's play puts into motion an idea which allows an audience to laugh at the bumbling failures of a little man to keep in step with the "German chronicle" from the Third Reich to the present; but, for some, there is retroactive choking at the realization that Walser also satirizes the successful keeping in step, the preservation of one's own skin, by most of the population who had been intoxicated with the early victories of the Hitler machine and then succumbed to a mechanistic fatalism which absolves one of blame and places it instead on the workings of history. The rapidity with which attendance at the play wound down after the initial performances, when word had gotten around, is sufficient commentary. Central to the play is Alois Grubel whose slow wits render him an anachronism in rapidly changing times. When others had exchanged the red flag for brown uniforms, he still was a Communist and was put into a concentration camp where, as a victim of medical experiments, he was castrated; there he was converted to Nazism. While others kept in step and expediently converted to democracy, nazified Alois became a leper to his denazified fellow citizens who for reasons not obvious to poor Alois wanted to forget the past. In the camp, Alois had raised Angora rabbits which the camp officials cynically named after the murdered Jews. These ingrained habits and the business of skinning the Angora rabbits were carried over by Alois into the postwar years until the symbolic reminders and the stench of slaughtered rabbits, as well as Alois's castrato voice, became unbearable to the citizens and Gorbach, the ex-Nazi mayor of the town; Alois is put into an asylum which previously had failed to cure his "backward" ideologies. Walser departs from playwrighting which indignantly exposed perverted ideologies and actions, and he relies on black satire to make his points. He holds up to ridicule both the owners and the ideas which were abandoned not because of their essential idiocy or corruptness but for the sake of appearances. Perhaps some indication of the macabre reality created by Walser may be seen through part of a dialogue between Alois and Gorbach:

> Alois: The German, Mr. District Leader, stands in jeopardy. Because certainly our race would be destroyed if the subhumans were to conquer us. Party-man Schock has told everyone of us: "Alois' Angora rabbits are superior to ordinary rabbits just as the German is to the subhumans." Because of that he gave the special

order that I could take the breeding pairs out of
the camp.

Gorbach: But why the Jewish names, Alois? That's certainly not fitting.

Alois: That is fitting all right, inasmuch as we destroy
the rabbits. And we strip them of wool, and so
they serve us. For a pound of Angora wool,
today you can get more than for a gold Party-
pin, Mr. District Leader. One first has to have
something to get dressed with otherwise it's
not possible to stick on a pin. . . .

Alois's logic and doctrine of yesterday make Gorbach wince;
the wool which has been pulled over Alois's eyes no longer
can be removed, and he becomes symbolic of the easily
manipulable—and at other times mulish—philistine who is
too obtuse to tell right from wrong or even to lie. Hellmuth
Karasek, a reviewer of the play and guest critic at Group 47
sessions, noted that "German fate was not presented as a
Götterdämmerung but as a shabby prank; with Walser, satire
has won a sharpness not heard since the pieces of Brecht."
To Karasek's sound observation, the name of Grass should
have been added among those who most effectively unsettled
the German feeling of *Gemütlichkeit*.

Just as the force of an idea exaggerated the figure of Alois
into the satiric, in Walser's next play *Überlebensgross Herr
Krott* [More than life-size Mr. Krott] (1964), subtitled sarcastically "Requiem for an Immortal," he draws a caricature
of a modern industrialist, this time, on the topside of the
social spectrum. The intriguing idea here lies in the industrialist's view that his underlings passively move from one
condition of conformity to another with the same shabby
tricks of adjustment used by Gorbach. Bored by the spine-
less nonresistance of those who suffer under his almost
sadistic oppression, the aging industrialist tries to needle
people into rebellion. When this fails, he commits suicide.
Walser overshoots the mark, a danger every satirist faces,
because the basic idea is more grotesque than the play which
develops from it.

Veering between realism and satire, Walser's *Der schwarze*

Schwan [The black swan] (1964) portrays the consequences of the shock felt by a youngster who finds out that his father had an organizational role in the mass exterminations carried out by the Nazis. The son formulates the premise, "What a father does, that too the son would have done," and after severely probing his father and himself, he no longer can face life. Ironically, the father had been able to effect a cure for his own conscience, but the son cannot. The important question of the attitudes of the younger and the older generation in respect to sins committed during the Third Reich has been forced by Walser into an extreme psychological dilemma, unresolvable in fact and salutary only if the premise can be denied. Why the son identifies so strongly with the father's shame is not made plausible. The more common question really, if faced up to, is how to proceed constructively from an ineradicable past. All too often the question has been pushed under the rug or answered in an aggressively negative and defensive fashion. While the disillusioning aspects of the discovery by some of the younger generation of the weaknesses of the older have been real and sobering, the outcome in life has rarely been as tragic as in Walser's play. Indeed, there is danger that Walser's fiction sails against the facts and becomes a melodramatic hypothesis. Reports indicate that by and large the children of former top Nazis appear to be prospering and have fond memories of their fathers. In response to whether Reinhard Heydrich, the Nazi boss of Czechoslovakia, was an evil man, his daughter said that she had watched herself a long time without feeling this within herself. It is a reflective attitude similar to the one Walser's fictional character adopts, but the conclusion is significantly different. Heydrich's son, an engineer, refuses to judge the Third Reich and, in pursuing a career, he does not want to be "held up by the past." Others regard themselves as "burnt children." G. M. Gilbert, a psychologist at the Nuremberg prison, suggests that they see their fathers as personalities split by good and evil, a rationalization which makes memory tolerable but not always free from pain. There is one exceptional case on record. Hans Frank, who died on the gallows, had admitted his guilt in the extermination of millions of Jews and Poles while he was governor-general of Poland. His son, probably as a result of the confession, has declared, "I feel a sense of responsibility that we, as Germans, never become guilty again." By spreading the base of guilt, he has made history tolerable.

Walser's reliance on talk at the expense of action on the stage at times gives some of his plays a static and declamatory quality. Walser is often hobbled by the complexity of his own talent while lesser playwrights, such as Erwin Sylvanus, Günther Michelsen, Martin Sperr, Wolfgang Bauer, and Siegfried Lenz, have more linearly and effectively dramatized social and political issues. Lenz, a Group 47 novelist and playwright, has been consistently popular with theater audiences through his realistic parables and existential themes. In the *Augenbinde* [The blindfold] (1970), for instance, several explorers are caught by blind tribesmen who offer them liberty only if they would choose to join the tribe and allow themselves to be blinded. The equation can be readily drawn between the tribe and the demands for conformity by modern society, and Lenz allows his speculative mind considerable range.

What seemed to be Walser's turning away from the political drama toward what many West German critics derogatorily call "entertainment for the culinary theater" has been explained by the possibility that Walser had the first act for his *Die Zimmerschlacht* [The battle in the room] (1967) in his drawer for about ten years. Several Group 47 critics took their colleague to task for a frivolous rather than a social-conscience use of the theater, and Walser subsequently tried his hand at more acceptably avant-garde experimentation that found publication in the smaller periodicals. Audiences, however, greeted the play, subtitled "Exercise for a Married Couple," with the same stormy pro and con reaction as Edward Albee's *Who's Afraid of Virginia Woolf?* If high seriousness is absent in the play, Walser does to some extent indicate broader social contexts and neuroses which give rise to the crises, malaises, battles, and battle fatigues with which many couples in any audience can identify. Walser has a flair for the bon mot; neither Strindberg nor Albee had greater verbal finesse in their mayhem-scenarios: "Marriage, after all, is a serious battle. No, no—an operation. Two surgeons operate upon each other continually. Without anesthetic. But continually. And progressively they improve their understanding of what hurts." Obviously, the battling couple is comfortable in the self-created hell, and the surface lacerations, as psychologists point out, cannot sever the deep ties that ultimately bind the couple; in fact, their verbal duels hint at the deep concern for each other.

Wolfgang Hildesheimer, discussed in connection with the radio play, has written many plays whose obliqueness in rendering reality may have had some influence upon the younger playwrights who carried his absurdist ideas to greater extremes; certainly, during the fifties, Hildesheimer brought French surrealism to the German stage. During the sixties his sardonic, "nonsense-is-life's essence" approach culminated in a one-act study of a person who goes mad trying to keep the world from his door, *Nachtstück* (1962, *Nightpiece*, 1966); but since this last attempt at the philosophical drama, he has devoted himself mainly to adaptations and translations into German of plays by Sheridan, Goldoni, and Shaw.

Although Günter Grass, the best-known member of Group 47, has tried his hand at every literary form, his comic exploitation of ideas has been least suited to the restrictions of the play format, primarily because his dialogue is not as strong as his prose. From 1954 to 1969, he has written eight plays which show a movement from the theater of the absurd to that of contemporary politics. Almost uniformly his plays of the absurd are three-ring circuses in which people bumble away the opportunity of straightening out their lives by failing to communicate with each other on a responsible level and to establish sensible life values; at points of crises, their failures become most evident. A modern Noah's family, symbolic of German postwar society, when threatened by a flood quibbles about inessentials and afterward the older and younger generations become hope-lessly separated; Noah's son comments sarcastically upon his father's trivial ambition to save his prized family photo-album, "Anyone without a photo album is like a coffin without a lid" (*Hochwasser*, 1963; *The Flood*, 1967). When a crew of cooks fails to gain a recipe for an extraordinary soup from a certain count—despite threats, cajolery, and bribery—it becomes morose; ironically, the recipe is simple but like the recipe for living, one must find it on one's own (*Die bösen Köche*, 1961; *The Wicked Cooks*, 1967). In various episodes a would-be killer botches jobs he has set for himself and becomes a grotesque failure in a society where crime is a daily occurrence. He is dispatched by children so that the act becomes a macabre "child's play" (*Onkel, Onkel*, 1965; *Mister, Mister*, 1967); the language is lyrical and almost parodies itself. Enmeshed in impractical dreams some engineers try to devise ways of getting a loco-motive moving; a realist hops onto the locomotive and dis-appears with it (*Noch zehn Minuten bis Buffalo*, 1959; *Only Ten Minutes to Buffalo*, 1967). Trying to escape from a teacher, an authoritarian hygiene crusader (symbolic of life) who insists on brushing his student's teeth, the student always finds himself trapped (*Zweiunddreissig Zähne* [Thirty-two teeth], radio performance in 1958 but unpub-lished). These plays remind me of a storyteller who spins out a joke interminably and then falls flat. Critics, including Group 47 stalwart Joachim Kaiser, reminded Grass that he had not as yet come forward with the "epic theater" he had promised and that his plays lacked sufficient "sociological pertinence." Although social content was greater in his subsequent plays, the criticism is symptomatic of certain re-viewers who would forgive aesthetic flaws if the ideas are "right." Grass's plays of the fifties show originality of con-ception and iridescent wit, which one can savor better on the printed page than on stage. In *The Flood* one survivor rat views the rainbow with rapture while another says, "I'd much rather nibble," illustrating in a flash the contrast, which Grass so often uses, between the idealist and realist. Ideas are toys and not bludgeons in his hands; they become a blend of cold precision and inspired imagery. If no single

or simple messages can be drawn from the plays, it is because they provide the allure and frustration of trying to
grasp quicksilver. His novels, however, showed where his
power lay.

Grass's aim of writing a resounding play was finally realized in 1966 with the performance of *Die Plebejer proben
den Aufstand* (*The Plebeians Rehearse the Uprising*, 1966),
reflecting the spontaneous workers' revolt on June 16–17,
1953, in East Berlin, which was crushed by the military
forces of the Soviet occupation. This critical event worsened
relations between East and West until the treaties of 1972
which recognized postwar East European frontiers and the
autonomy of East Germany. The uprising had not been converted to theatrical use possibly because West German
writers felt that any high-pitched treatment of the subject
might endanger future prospects of reunification. East
German writers were told to regard the incident as the work
of counterrevolutionaries. The dilemma for most writers was
so obvious that for the most part they avoided it; Grass did
not. Some critics have been tempted to call the play documentary, yet Grass's departures disallow the designation; his
play does not ride herd on a political thesis. The subtitle,
A German Tragedy, suggests Grass's concern with the more
general issues of which the revolt was a part; he does not
display partisanship, and he does not draw up a specific bill
of indictment. A documentary play on the subject would
have had to deal more explicitly with such background
materials at the class structure in East Germany, the decree
which raised workers' production norms (an economic
squeeze which triggered political discontent and the revolt),
the Ulbricht-Kremlin axis, the intraparty conflicts, the Four-
Power politics, and the like. Grass is interested in the role
of the writer and politicians and the impulses of the in-
surgent workers who were joined by thousands of sympa-
thizers. Not only, as Grass says, does "each side's tenacity
contribute imperceptibly to its guilt," but also the gulf between theory and practice widens when both the workers
and the intellectuals are unrealistic.

Grass has described the peripheries of his play:

. . . the construction workers petition the boss or theater director for a document [summoning a general strike] with his important signature. . . . In my play the theater director does not flatly refuse. . . . He intends to draft it as soon as the masons and carpenters have demonstrated to him how people behaved on the Stalin Boulevard at the beginning of the uprising. For him the main thing is to utilize a current issue for his staging of Shakespeare's *Coriolanus* and the uprising of his plebeians.

. . . While the workers in the play regard the attack of the Soviet tanks as fate which they at the most can oppose with stones or not oppose at all, the theater director holds an extemporaneous discourse on the subject of whether and how armored vehicles can be used on the stage. For him, whatever happens becomes a stage-scene—slogans, spoken choruses . . . everything becomes an aesthetic question—his is an unmixed theatrical nature.

Not only are these ironic comments on Brecht's strenuous attempts to turn Shakespeare's *Coriolanus* into a Marxist showpiece of the class struggle while he was director of the East Berlin Ensemble, but Grass also portrays in general the writer's isolation and entrapped position between politics and art, ideological consciousness and reality. He was less concerned with being absolutely fair to Brecht and more occupied with the moral question of the possibility that even a socialist writer with sympathies for working men could ignore their pleas for help and turn their plight into useful materials for his aesthetics and art. He was worried about the solipsistic gravity of art.

Since 1965, Grass has taken to the political stump by making campaign speeches for the Social Democratic Party and has shown that the engaged writer not only can envigorate public debate, but that he also must engage in the necessary "hackwork for democracy." The dual position of artist and political campaigner has prompted some self-analysis. At the Group 47 meeting at Princeton in 1966, he gave a talk with the baroque title "Concerning the Lack of Self-confidence of Authorial Court Jesters in Consideration of a Non-existent Court," which concluded with the following idea: "Let us be aware of this: The creative work knows no compromises, but we live through compromises. Whoever actively endures this tension is a fool and changes the world." The writer as a "court jester" preserves his freedom to write without compromising his art, yet when he participates in the democratic process he should be ready for compromise. Among Group 47 writers such a statement of position is almost unique. If Grass's play seems to portray Brecht as a prototype of aesthetes who sacrifice socialist ideology on the altar of expediency, it also shows Grass's indebtedness to the brilliant theatricality and the satiric language of Brecht's plays. I don't think that Grass could have bettered Brecht's poem "Die Lösung," "The Solution":

> After the uprising of June 17,
> the secretary of the Writers Union
> had leaflets distributed on the Stalin Boulevard,
> which read that the people
> have lost the Government's confidence
> and that only through redoubled work
> might they regain it. Would it not
> be simpler, though, if the Government
> would dissolve the people and
> elect another?

A live stage and live audiences continued to prove irresistible to Grass and he converted his political novel *örtlich betäubt* (1970; *Local Anaesthetic*, 1970) into a thirteen-scene play called *Davor* (1969; *Max*, 1972). The basic situation of the play involves the teacher Starusch who wishes to dissuade his student Philipp (Flip) Scherbaum from publicly burning his dachshund, Max, in order to publicize his protest against the use of napalm in Vietnam and to castigate German politics. Starusch succeeds with his arguments that his pupil ought to use the school newspaper to sound his alarms instead of burning an innocent dog, a macabre Grassian joke at best. As usual, Grass's approach runs the risk of making caricatures of peoples and events, especially of student radicalism and protests. Disarmingly, he submits his alter ego, the teacher, to comedy as well; nevertheless, his own politically moderate stance and appeal to reason through psychological argumentation ring clearly through all the theater burlesquing.

Although the "culinary" theater attempts to balance classical, modern, and first-run plays in most subsidized German theaters, there have been running battles between those who want to radicalize the drama and the traditionalists, between those who feel that a play should primarily entertain and those who want it to preach social commitment; and the cultists of "alienation" have taken on all comers. Since the late sixties another type of playwright has insisted upon being heard and having his "happenings" viewed. Some of the "happening" playwrights have gone so far as to attempt anarchical obliteration of the theater as an art form and paradoxically to use it as an instrument for its own destruction. Of these playwrights, Peter Handke has been able to stand the theater on its ear and to gain international attention. Again, the value of Group 47 as a publicity forum became spectacularly clear.

During the Princeton meeting of Group 47 in 1966, a pall of boredom had begun to settle over readers, critics, and audience when the youngest angry man, the twenty-four-year-old Austrian-born Peter Handke, rose to the attack. Probably he was encouraged by the example of Peter Weiss who a day earlier raged against prose fantasies which ignored the realities of the present. Shaking his Beatle-mane, Handke seemed like a youngster among grandfatherly types and in a tone of displeasure he railed against what he had been listening to: impotent narrative; empty stretches of descriptive (instead of analytical) writing pleasing to the ears of the older critics; monotonous verbal litanies, regional and nature idyllicism, which lacked spirit and creativeness. The audience warmed up to the invectives with cheers, and later even those whose work had been called idiotic, tasteless, and childish came over to congratulate the Group 47 debutant and to patch things up in brotherly fashion. The privileges of youth had been served. Handke's blast against "literary parades" was greeted as a sign of freedom of expression within the group and was likened to the rebellions more than a decade earlier by Martin Walser and Hans Magnus Enzensberger, who had attacked the long trend of postwar realism. As he stood among a circle of interviewers—a thin, energetic figure with thick, dark sunglasses—it became clear that he had arrived as a spokesman for the young and hitherto silent clique and reestablished confidence in the rejuvenating capacity of the group. Ignoring those who saw Handke's behavior as that of an ill-tempered beatnik, Günter Grass and Hans Werner Richter asserted that Handke's protests were well taken. Instead of showing outward annoyance at the disruption of the usually well-ordered group ritual, Richter yielded to Handke's upstaging by noting wrily that he had fabricated something newsworthy. Handke remarked that this was precisely what he had intended.

If Handke were no more than a publicity-seeker, he would not be worth talking about; but through his writings he has seriously concerned himself with the questions of how to deal with our times and how to use the writer's arsenal of provocative measures. As a nonconformist, Handke, the son of a bank employee, gave up a potential career in law, for which he studied at Graz, Austria, between 1961 and 1965, to seek an audience for his sociophilosophical ideas. His audacious harangue to the group in April was more extensively presented to a small theater audience in October of the same year in Frankfurt through a *Sprechstück* called *Publikumsbeschimpfung* (1966; *Offending the Audience*, 1969). By *Sprechstück* Handke means "speak-ins," speaking pieces for the theater, "spectacles without pictures, a world consisting of words which give the audience a concept rather than pictures of the world; the actors are instructed to use colloquial expressions and gestures to achieve naturalness. Much of his short speak-in harangue tries to persuade the audience to be natural and to experience without barriers of time and stage artificialities a plotless, actionless, inventionless situation in which the persons of the audience *are* the play. The actors use Pavlovian tricks on members of the audience to shock them into self-awareness and to break down barriers that normally exist between them and the stage;

then, the actors launch into a catalog of invectives, mostly foul, invented by modern man to denigrate his fellowman. However, at the end of this happening or sensitivity session where only words make contact, the playwright is conciliatory by calling the audience brothers, sisters, fellow humans. Whether the peaceable note is dictated by sentiment or expediency, the fact remains that a playwright needs an audience. While German audiences took the invective play fairly calmly, Spaniards at the performance in Barcelona rose to the bait and traded insults with the actors. The event proved to be a triumph for Handke—life had spilled over onto the stage.

In a similar vein, the same year Handke put on his *Selbstbezichtigung* (1966; *Self-Accusation*, 1969), another short speak-in backgrounded by beat music, in which he charts a personal progression: "I came into the world" (first sentence) to "I wrote this piece" (last sentence). The string of declarative sentences of deliberately erratic length again catalog happenings—the sins of commissions and omissions, commonplace universalities, the sins of Everyman, and varieties of commendable or tasteless conformities and nonconformities. If nothing else, the unrelenting atonement speeches point to man's awesome abuses of free will. Yet, the excesses of the confessional catalogs become absurd and negate any meaningful grasp of the relation between truth and reality; instead, the narrator seems to enjoy the act of cerebral see-sawing. Self-flagellation becomes a substitute for dignified self-assertion.

If words fly like ping-pong balls in Handke's dialectical games, it should not obscure his basic purpose of seeking clarifications through verbalization rather than through action. Verbalization becomes the action, and the process itself leads to awareness and acute self-consciousness. We are inundated daily with mass communication verbiage consisting of clichés, colloquialisms, warmed-over ideas, and other anesthetizing word-sounds. One's first step should be to recognize the problem and the second to find a way of coping with it. In his five-page *Hilferufe* [Cries for help] (1967), Handke's speakers repeat and reject and continually

reduce the mountain of everyday clichés while they search
for the word *help*, a search for which they need help. Once
they find the word, they no longer need help; they are re-
lieved because they have found it possible to say the word
and to recognize their need but, at the same time, the word
has lost its meaning. Yet, is it possible ever not to need help?
Verbalized discoveries create new dilemmas for the speakers
who have been drinking coca-cola during their "natural" performance; they keep substituting one illusion for another.

Through his first several speak-ins, Handke consolidated
some workable ideas about theater performance: the reduction of language to primitive building blocks; the potentials
of invective in stirring up audiences; the radicalization of
theatrical action into mimetic gestures; surprising turns in
verbal processes; and the substitution of the acoustical and
colloquial—cement-mixer sounds, everyday words—for expected theatrical illusion. His rhythmic sense of style and
ideas for the integration of words, sounds, and pantomime
come from his attention to rock, pop, and other modern
music.

These devices were put to work in his discussible full-
length speak-in *Kaspar*, (1967; translated by Michael Roloff,
1969), first performed in 1968. The title alludes to the real
Kaspar Hauser who as a child was supposed to have been
kept in a small, darkened room and was to have learned
how to speak only later in life. Kaspar pushes his way
through the curtain and is born on stage and the stage becomes his world. He appears as a "Frankenstein robot" possessing one sentence which he utters over and over: "I want
to be a person like somebody else was once." With this
elementary capacity and with progressive "speech torture,"
he moves through sixteen phases of increasing enlighten-
ment until he reaches the level of all other normal Kaspars,
and even begins to "sing like a true believer," like the other
clownish Kaspars in the cast. With phase 16. Kaspar has
reached the sophistication of existential despair: "Who is
Kaspar now? Kaspar, who now is Kaspar? What is now, Kaspar, Kaspar?" Through a command of language, Kaspar is
able to relate to his surroundings, to reduce his fear of the un-

known, to engage in question and response, to analyze himself. At the same time he learns that "everyone must not forget to care for others"; he feels the contrasts of pride and shame. Handke charts the history of the species and the individual—as ontogeny recapitulates phylogeny—through speech. Language becomes an instrument made flexible through repeated drills and then becomes an instrumentality of life. When Kaspar becomes aware of the dual process of language which means using language and being used by it, manipulating it and being manipulated by it, Kaspar's self-awareness and the condition of absurdity become so acute that he cries, "I cannot rid myself of myself any more." The world had become a "poem with rhyme and reason," but when Kaspar begins to question everything, his language turns to chaos and meanings are lost. Language is creative and paradoxically can incur its own destruction. Handke in his myth of language points no way out—one is trapped by existence, neither conformity nor nonconformity seems satisfactory.

Originally, Handke's Kaspar concluded his sentimental education with the exclamation, "I: am: only: accidentally: I," inverting the boast by Shakespeare's Edmund, Gloucester's bastard, "I am what I am" and for that we *cannot* blame the stars; but Handke struck out this sentence in subsequent editions. Instead, Kaspar ends by repeating five times, "Goats and Monkeys," echoing Othello's bitter indictment of human lechery. The phrase intimidates the other Kaspars and may also be directed against the audience. Through Kaspar, Handke has brilliantly demonstrated man's creativity in raising himself from the elemental to the awareness that choices are illusory (a thesis to which Sartre now subscribes) and that alienation is simply the exception which proves the rule of conformity. Both Kaspar and Handke stand helplessly before this dilemma. Critical attempts have been made to raise Handke's *Kaspar* to the level of plays by Beckett and Ionesco, and to include it in the repertoire of the theater of the absurd. Qualitatively, Handke has yet to reach that level. Despite many similarities to the theater of the absurd, Handke strains against such inclusion because he avoids lyricism and "literary" quality and does everything possible to prohibit linear action. The result is static "demonstration," catalog speeches, stage props instead of scenic pictures, pantomime, accumulations of words without summary direction; he deliberately aborts the possibility of the well-made play—traditional or absurdist— and imposes his own idea of theater pieces as speak-ins. Philosophically, Handke does not share Ionesco's moralistic affirmation that integrity defines the essence of individual existence and that without integrity man becomes a slave to political state systems.

His play *Das Mündel will Vormund sein* (1969; loosely rendered as "The young wish to be the elders") was written at the time of the student revolts. It is a pantomime acted out by two masked figures, a farmer and his helper, whose quarrels are symbolic of the divided generations. The farmer vanishes and the helper has stepped into his shoes. Is this a cynical comment on the likelihood that the young become like their elders when they, in time, become heirs, or is it Handke's message that emancipation and power come through usurpation? In respect to the disaffected young, he is gloomy:

> What disturbs me is the alienation of people from their own speech. That, too, is the basic ill of the young revolutionaries in Germany: They are alienated from their language, which no longer is language—so that they can no longer communicate. Their speech shows their lamentable self-convulsion. (Interview in Artur Joseph, *Theater unter 4 Augen*)

Social satire sweeps also through his play *Quodlibet*, 1969, in which figures from every strata of society, except the middle and economically lower classes, stroll onto the stage in type-cast dress. They talk past each other with innocuous phrases and then through monologues caress their own egos, oblivious of one another and content with their isolation.

No Continental, English, or American reviewer has been able to say with certainty what Handke's next play was all about. *Der Ritt über den Bodensee* [The ride across Lake Constance] (1970) may well be a warning against looking for order and meanings either in life or on Handke's stage. The title, more intriguing than much of the content, refers to a German poem in which a courier rides over the frozen lake and then drops dead when he realizes the unsuspected danger he has survived. Handke, too, skates on the thin ice of novelty. Handke, like the poetess Ingeborg Bachmann, was stimulated by Ludwig Wittgenstein's *Tractatus Logico-Philosophicus*. Each of Handke's plays, I believe, constitutes a "proposition" which, according to Wittgenstein, "only asserts something insofar as it is a [logical] picture [of reality]." A sampling of Wittgenstein's statements helps us to understand what Handke is trying to achieve through language: "By means of propositions we explain ourselves"; "It is essential to propositions that they can communicate a *new* sense to us . . . with old words"; "Colloquial language is a part of the human organism and is not less complicated than it"; "From it, it is humanly impossible to gather immediately the logic of language"; "Language disguises the thought. . . . The silent adjustments to understand colloquial language are enormously complicated." Ingeniously Handke has put these propositions into practice so that the speak-ins are pictures of life and are identical in form of representation; they aim to communicate a new sense to us. Perhaps most useful to Handke was Wittgenstein's observation in *Philosophical Investigations* that all of us play "language *games*" with infinite potential, "the *speaking* of language is part of an activity, or of a form of life." Hence, Handke's speaking pieces for the theater.

In *The Ride Across Lake Constance*, parodistically styled in the form of an old Hollywood scenario, the actors play themselves and each figure means no more than what he or she is, completely wiping out theater as a form of make-believe; the chitchat flounders in innocuous verbiage and mechanical sexual teasings. By pushing art for art's sake to the extreme, Handke rejects every form of contemporary drama from the parable to the documentary and seeks new equivalents for the representation of life.

Paris has been especially hospitable to Handke's modernistic work and he has taken up residence there. Everything which he has written sells and his plays are performed on many international stages. In proportion to the audiences Handke has been reaching, he has become suspect to some German critics who once heralded him. They massed their strength in one issue of the periodical *Kursbuch*, edited by Group 47 writer Hans Magnus Enzensberger, to pulverize Handke; but he pays little attention to the idea of "committed literature" espoused by the left wing and also avoids the tiresome chestnuts of Marxist philosophy. He has an intelligence and sensibility unmatched by most of the young writers inside or outside of Group 47, but his dry aesthetics and coldly cerebral constructions produce an amalgam of some expressionistic devices, that were stillborn fifty years ago, and modern techniques. Handke's petulance and anger are real and his verbal exercises are provocative. While pop artists humorously see "art" everywhere in life, Handke grimly sees the literary arts imitating life, a situation which he quixotically wishes to destroy. The act itself is quixotic, and regrettably it has found imitators. It seems to me that Handke has not yet either acted or suffered enough in the world to have become so scornful of it.

Playwrights of the sixties, such as Weiss, revitalized the theater and worked within traditions to open up greater theatrical dimensions without loss of social-critical and oppositional contents; at times they succumbed to propagandistic styles. Often, whether humanistic, democratic, or socialistic, the playwrights still kept their eyes on the coordinates of a Fascist past and a politically unpalatable German present with its hosts of problems. Slowly a countertrend developed. In a summary of the intentions which motivate the newer playwrights or nontheatricalists—among them Bazon Brock, Handke (the only one with some Group 47 relation), Martin Sperr, Jochen Ziem—Hellmuth Karasek notes, with gleeful satisfaction, "Calculated ego-dramas, calculated success recipes (to which belonged for some time the 'mastering of the past play') seem finally to have been abandoned; the documentary zeal no longer appears"; instead, they aim at stripping art of ideology and literary qualities and to dip into extraliterary subject areas. It seems to me that their quest is illusory, for theater without art is a contradiction in terms, and theater without some substantial subject matter invites vacuity. In their search for the "new" they have achieved the paradox of calculated improvisation which is synonymous with anarchy for the sake of anarchy. The net "gain" is to dissolve language into a spray of octopus ink and to portray life as a quilt of imbecilities. Generally enough dispiritedness and senselessness exist in life without having them multiplied in the theater. Despite these carpings, the so-called new theater would be redeemable if only it were not so consistently dull. Critics like Karasek seem to be looking for kicks; he suggests that the youngest playwrights have not gone far enough in divesting themselves of every last vestige of recognizable theater tradition. With encouragement like this, descent into further obscurantism should not be difficult.

The dogmatism propagated by the older and the younger playwrights points to no foreseeable benefit to the theater, and their clawing away at the common enemy—the establishment—is pursued without a reasonable alternative. I cannot help but agree with Ernest Borneman's evaluation, in an article in the *Times Literary Supplement*, that despite pretensions to open democratic discussion among all participants—from critics to technicians to playwrights—in the contemporary German theater, there dominates a contempt for democracy. In every respect, the implications have a worrisome ominousness; it is as if the *Götterdämmerung* has been staged in the form of a rock-beat operetta or bedlam theater.

Postscript

In the words of its initiator, Hans Werner Richter, Group 47—a circle of his "friends"—is active or dormant at his pleasure. He regarded the group as always a private matter regulated by his power of invitation. After a quiet celebration in 1967 of its twenty years of agitated existence, Richter decided to call a meeting for September/October 1968 in the castle of the Czech writers' union near Prague. In the meantime, on the historic 21st of August, the Warsaw Pact nations, spearheaded by Russian troops, marched into Czechoslovakia. Richter had to cancel the meeting but, as he pointed out to me in a letter, he made a resolve: "I then promised the Czech writers that we would not again hold group meetings until it would be possible to do so in Prague." It was a gesture so human and political that it typifies the attitude held by Richter and most of Group 47 since its inception. At the heart of the attitude lies political conviction, yet in the literature produced through the reflected and reflecting intellect it is expressed by varied forms of social consciousness with little that is politically overt.

After a five-year lapse of meetings, Richter relented at the urgings of friends and called for a session in May 1972 at his Berlin home. Similar to the 1967 meeting, it was kept to an intimate gathering of about twenty-five persons, yet publicity was held to a minimum and a seminar atmosphere prevailed. Among the critics were such old hands as Baumgart, Höllerer, Kaiser, and Raddatz and among the writers were Grass, Johnson, Kluge, and Weiss. There were newcomers—novelist

Walter Kempowski and the Chilean dramatist Gaston Salva-tore—but young rebels in the pattern of Peter Handke were absent. Richter had been undecided as to whether or not "this would be the final farewell for 'Group 47' and its time or a new beginning." After twenty-five years Richter now finds himself on the other side of the antagonistic genera-tion gap: "What will happen now, I really don't know. On the scene is a new generation which though it hardly as yet has made a literary appearance makes itself instead all the more politically and noisily noticeable. Would it be possible for them to go along with the ground rules of Group 47? I would hardly think so. They, the members of this genera-tion, again love firm organization, the director, the majority decisions, the flag, the cash register, in short, everything which we did not want." Whatever the contributing reasons, the beginning of the seventies marked the end of the post-war literary renaissance and saw the end, according to Richter, of idealistic and optimistic hopes embedded in an unbelievably strong enthusiasm which provided the motive power for literature.

Perhaps it is worth speculating briefly about the end of the renaissance in the light of Group 47's beginning and subsequent history. In the transition from the almost ex-clusively political base of *Der Ruf* to the literary forum of group sessions, a belief was retained in the effectiveness of literature to change society; later this belief was expanded to the potential capability of literature to counter what was believed to be a social, political, and economic restoration of the past. Group 47 literature directly or indirectly assumed an oppositional stance and hoped to encourage a new set of values. The main deleterious aftereffect of the economic miracle, *Wirtschaftswunder*, was a social arrogance and a papering-over of the Hitler past as not having been so bad as it had been pictured. Grass's novels, in particular, tore that complacency to shreds. By the sixties it became obvious that the goals set by *Der Ruf* were becoming even more re-mote than ever before. Far from discouraging some writers, the situation goaded them into more aggressive measures that resulted in documentary literature and the poetry of commentary. The stepped-up politicizing of literature, at best, had a needling effect, but it proved itself incapable of becoming a "useful instrument" in the so-called revolutionary struggle. The ensuing disillusion with what perhaps was a fallacious notion to begin with led either to the idea of abandoning literature or to the latest avant-gardism which seeks to destroy literature as an artificial form that stands between the writer and life. The "new literature" of the avant-garde, with the help of some critics, has succeeded in intimidating audiences rather than in opening new perspectives through mature insights that would expand the reader's intelligence and imagination. The strength of Group 47 for the greatest part of its existence had been its resistance to all "isms."

Another hope of some charter members of Group 47 was to unflinchingly confront the past, to exorcise or master it, and to lay new foundations; literature was to plumb the depths and transform the experience of the past and the present into art without propaganda. These profound and optimistic goals challenged the full moral and aesthetic resources of writers. Only a few of Group 47 writers came anywhere near these goals. It was not a question of "commitment" or "engagement"—in fact, only the dead are disengaged or noncommitted—but a question of courage to go into "the forests of the night" and through creative skill frame the fearful symmetry of evil and deception. Fear of sentimentality, the greatest bête noire of Group 47, fear of "contaminating" literature with the fulminations of polemic and excessively irritating readers, and fear of emotionality, all led to much literature of genteel *avoidance*. In his introduction to a selection of a cross-section of texts read at Group 47 meetings from 1947 to 1961, Fritz J. Raddatz registers his reaction to "something unexpected and almost nimbus-destroying":

In the entire volume the words *Hitler, concentration camp* (KZ), *atom bomb, SS, Nazi, Siberia* do not appear nor do the themes appear. (Enzensberger and von Cramer are the sole exceptions—Weyrauch mentions "camp"—

aside from Nowakowski who in a narrower sense does not
belong to German literature although his books now appear in Germany.) A frightening phenomenon to put it
mildly. The most important German postwar authors
have concerned themselves, in any case, with the nightmare of military boots and corporals; however, not transformed into poetry or prose was the large room piled
high with hair and teeth in Auschwitz or the guinea pig
mentality of the storm trooper Professor Kremer who
made such diary entries as, "Blueberries have become
more expensive. Dissected sixteen fresh Jew-livers. Yesterday Frau Schulz sent a good pair of woolen socks."
(*Almanach*, 1962, pp. 55–56)

Several years later Professor Joseph Bauke of Columbia University gave his impressions of the Group 47 readings at
Princeton in 1966. He noted that Germany's Nazi past
occasionally surfaced in some texts, but he could not help
feeling that "the vague and unspecified aura of guilt that
permeates the writing of some of them, is an acquired taste,
not unrelated to the sentimentalizing of Anne Frank and
the philo-Semitism now fashionable in some German circles." Bauke also mentions the deadly monotony caused by
minutely detailed nature descriptions, the absence of literary
interest in sex, and the critics' utterances which for the most
part were designed to impress other critics. Tart comments
on the provincialism of current German fiction were made
by Jakov Lind: "Though each member of Group 47 may
be a charming fellow, the literary sum total produced in
Princeton attests to the castration of the German mind. It
is as if the dead suck the life blood from the living."

What the comments by Raddatz, Bauke, and Lind point
to is the enigma of why the raw data of the past—available
through personal, public, or research sources—were not in
any significant measure objectified through literature. The
argument is not that the past should have been detailed
realistically in all its bloody horror but that it should not
have been so impressively sidestepped, and in many cases
forgotten. The ability to forget may be necessary for physical

and mental hygiene, but as Herbert Marcuse notes in *Eros and Civilization,*

> To forget is also to forgive what should not be forgiven if justice and freedom are to prevail. Such forgiveness reproduces the conditions which reproduce injustice and enslavement: to forget past suffering is to forgive the forces that caused it—without defeating these forces. The wounds that heal in time are also the wounds that contain the poison. Against this surrender to time, the restoration of remembrance to its rights, as a vehicle of liberation, is one of the noblest tasks of thought. . . . Like the ability to forget, the ability to remember is a product of civilization—perhaps its oldest and most fundamental psychological achievement.

Perhaps the answer to the question of avoidance of the past lies in the terror, repulsiveness, and complexity of the source materials and experience. Most writers simply found the substances and emotions unmanageable and the inescapable moral indictments unbearable. Realism, in the tradition of Zola or Balzac, some felt, might have reduced the tragic events to Hollywood shockers.

Wolfgang Koeppen (b. 1906) asked himself the purpose of having been a witness to events and why he had remained alive. He answered his own question with a group of novels that stand among the best in modern fiction: *Tauben im Gras* [Doves in the grass] (1951), *Das Treibhaus* [The greenhouse] (1953), and *Der Tod in Rom* (1954; *Death in Rome,* 1960). In 1926, he had read Joyce's *Ulysses* and was pulled completely into its vortex. Readers who are not acquainted with Koeppen's work might prepare themselves for a similar experience. During the Third Reich he wrote two novels, but with "the shudder that blanketed the world," he lapsed into silence and yearned for an end to the tragedy. He was always a loner, and it is surprising to see him listed among Group 47, though only as one of its guests. Koeppen broke his silence because

> . . . who, if not the writer, should play the role of Cassandra in our society? A thankless, a fruitless role. Every

book has its effect in the political world; even if not directly. My vanity goes along the literary path. I wrote *Das Treibhaus* as a novel portraying a wreckage [it concerns the fate and introspection of a Bonn politician during the postwar period]. If I had wished to be effective politically, I would have attempted to become minister of defense, to seize power by controlling power. (Interview with Bienek)

And, his novels deal more unsparingly with social and political aspects of German life than any fellow writer dared. He wrote with Joyce in mind, whose style "expresses our capacity for feeling, our consciousness, our bitter experiences," and he was also aware of the cinematic techniques of Dos Passos and Alfred Döblin. German postwar literature had to overcome a void by tying into the new tradition, an international tradition. Koeppen saw literature as "poetic truth" which needed a more flexible and richer style than the sparse *Kahlschlag* or watery realism briefly fashionable around 1950. Neither the public nor most of the critics were ready for Koeppen's style or truths—one was too demanding and the other too stark. Böll whittled down experience and events of the past and present to narrower literary dimensions graspable and more acceptable to the reading public. Thesis novels and plays also took on polished literary formats during the fifties. No one any longer tried to write a tragedy in any traditional sense; history, it was felt, simply had transcended modern literature's capacity for the tragic. Perhaps the most powerful substitute for tragedy was the combination of the grotesque and satire, particularly in the hands of Grass who brought readers to a pitch of excitement with mixed reactions of rage or approval as rarely before. While no other fictional genre had been able to bring about the confrontation with festering problems, antagonistic satire finally did.

Several internal and external critics of Group 47 have commented that proportionate to the economic affluence of society and writers social criticism progressively lost its edge and that subconsciously some accommodations have been made to reader tastes. One would be hard pressed to prove or disprove these generalizations conclusively. Yet, quite obvious were the huge gaps between the socioeconomic realities and the writings of Group 47 authors, probably because much was alien to their personal experience. The life of the middle and upper classes, as well as the professions, was given major attention while other phenomena such as the foreign "guest laborers," *Gastarbeiter,* remained largely untouched, with such notable exceptions as Böll's novel *Gruppenbild mit Dame* (1971; *Group Portrait with Lady,* 1973). Aside from such massive help during the early postwar years as the Marshall Plan and the German passion for work, with the remarkable absence of crippling strikes, a contributing factor in the astonishing economic growth has been the imported and cheap labor of Yugoslavians, Turks, Italians, Greeks, Spaniards—herded into substandard nationality ghettos—who now number more than 2.2 million. The economic and social ghettoizing of these people who, subsequent to the Third Reich, essentially replaced the forced laborers has been a steady surfacing of explosive human issues. West Germans are talking about "over-foreignization" of their country, and dangerous race and national-superiority feelings, not unlike those of the thirties, are spreading. Group 47 has been singularly oblivious to such materials for literature; the materials cannot be intellectualized and therefore do not prove attractive aesthetically and technically. For most of the younger writers the past is out of the reach of experience while the present is an incitement to counterculture literary activity.

The three-day cultural and international event which was taking place at Princeton in April 1966 was duly taped for broadcast by a West Berlin radio station; in contrast, Professor Bauke's report appeared modestly on the back pages of the *New York Times Book Review,* indicative of the generally low-keyed publicity effect of the literary forum — a fact which terribly annoyed many Group 47 authors. Yet, Peter Weiss made newspaper headlines with his condemnation of the United States role in Vietnam. Later he claimed to have spoken only as an individual and not for the group. The idea of the group as a noncollective voice had to be preserved. Still, what is striking is the typical separation of public politics and "private" literary forum throughout the life of Group 47. In poetry, the radio drama, and the drama, especially the documentary, the ideology of politics was given an opportunity of playing a controlling role. In the novel, the most popular of art forms, this was rare, with the obvious exception of works by Böll and Grass.

A few further points may be made about the public and political role of Group 47 writers compared with the subject matter of their art. The noise which resulted from public controversies by individuals—in respect to domestic and foreign politics—was generally louder than that in their literature. The pronouncements by Group 47 members on the actions of the U.S. in Vietnam, for instance, are similar to that of their counterpart American intelligentsia; both castigate the South Vietnamese as "U.S. clients" and glorify the heroes of Hanoi who only wish to liberate their brothers, an immoral oversimplification of a tragic situation in which power and politics play corrupting roles on all sides. For some Germans the situation affords a welcome opportunity for finger-pointing accusations that American actions were no better than those under the Third Reich, an attitude which contains some *Schadenfreude*, shared also by the French who failed in Vietnam, at the uncomfortable and untenable position of Americans. It may all be part of wishing to hang on to the myths, shattered in the postwar world, that reunifications are possible and desirable whether in Ireland, Korea, the Middle East, or the Germanys. Slogans about reunification appear painted on the Wall and on streamers in West German cities, but few German voices will note the possible dangers of reuniting what now are two among the world's greatest industrial powers. Torn between idealistic national hopes and the vision of danger to one's self and Europe, writers for the most part have evaded public debates on such issues and have avoided full exploration of the subject in fiction. It was still possible during the thirties for the intelligentsia to find political utopias and political heroes; both possibilities are shrinking to the vanishing point today, although some still glorify totalitarian states

which they have never visited nor in which they would want
to reside. The days of the antihero in fiction and in politics
finally have converged.

After the Princeton meeting, some of the Group 47 writers
had an opportunity to make or to renew contact with
America. Representing the view of some, Raddatz wrote
about the United States as a country whose language and
gesture were becoming more brutalized daily. He saw New
York as a mixture of things: the art metropolis of the world,
a city with a murderous ecology, provincialism, intellectuality, ugliness, elegance, riches, and poverty. He expected
that the meeting and the writers who fanned out to Texas
and California to give lectures would have an "eminent,
quasi-subcutaneous effect, which will make itself felt literarily
as well as politically." These presumed educative functions
have since then manifested themselves in ways which have
little distinction. Literarily, I have already discussed Uwe
Johnson's America novel in progress, which endlessly cites
American newspaper sources. Politically, the attack was
launched later by Reinhard Lettau's compendious hymn of
hate US *Täglicher Faschismus* [U.S., daily fascism] (1971).
Lettau also uses American news items as documentary
sources and spreads his undiscriminating net wide: Texas's
sole contribution to civilization is "lynch justice," U.S. astro-
nauts are "Apollo-bums," America's tired democrats are fools
who delude themselves about living in a democracy; he
heaps ridicule on the fact that a haberdasher can rise to the
presidency, a Greek to the vice-presidency, and a film star to
a governorship. Professor David Schoenbaum of the University of Iowa has aptly characterized Lettau as an *idiot savant*,
familiar in European literary history, with good intentions
but unshakable political naïveté, and as a radical democrat
who shares with political rightists a deep aversion to a democratic society.

Now, Lettau himself is not a very important writer
(though he has commendable short stories to his credit)
among Group 47, but he does represent the mentality of
others, particularly the homeless Left. The fiction produced
by this group within the Group is reflective of their intellect
and their disillusionment with the politics and sociology of

democracy. Incapable of tolerance, compromise, and dis-
crimination between fact and fiction, scurrility and reason,
they have become frustrated armchair revolutionaries. The
varieties of avoidance of dimensional fiction are fascinating
and point to severe personal disorientation of writers. In
Peter Handke's "America novel," *Der kurze Brief zum
langen Abschied* [The short letter attending a long farewell]
(1972), a dazzling technical performance, the narrator states
the problem of the individual's alienation from self, from
others, and from reality: "Perhaps you know people who
immediately conceptualize everything they see, even the
most surprising, and transfix it through a formulation, and
consequently stop experiencing it." Handke seems to say
that the fictionalizing of experience kills the reality of experience and makes the writing of literature a paradoxical
act destructive of both literature and life. *Freedom* in
Handke's novels usually means the violent disattachment by
any means from human and other relationships, although in
this novel a marital couple parts peacefully by the grace of
what Handke calls his own wish projection. Why the
American setting if, curiously, no hints of social or political
issues occur? Handke replies that he is assailed by an "uncanny disgust" at the idea of making generalized concepts
out of the isolated scenes and people he has observed. For
him America is the foreign territory, "the other world," a
dream world where one can start anew and with relief slough
off one's individuality and become a type. Here is a macabre
self-revealment: the literary intellectual's cerebral con-
gestion, disgust with self, the torment brought about by self-
reflection and self-flagellation, the urge to throw off the ter-
rible burden of psychological, social, and political awareness.

The malaise which has infested the leftist intellectuals of
the dormant Group 47 and the debilitating effects of their
disillusionment is satirized by Martin Walser (who for some
time has wanted to remove the group label which has clung
to him since 1955 when he won its coveted prize). Lest
Walser's intent be misunderstood, he has written his own
jacket copy for the novel *Die Gallistl'sche Krankheit* [The
Gallistic sickness] (1972), a philosophical inquiry into the
social and political sickness of the narrator Gallistl (figur-

atively, bitter as gall) who seeks his cure. He identifies the source of his social sickness as the "competitiveness mentality" which has been drilled into most people since childhood. He refuses to play along and is isolated; he finds new friends who give him a social or socialistic vocabulary and consciousness and offer him a solidarity beyond the competition principle, allowing him to defy the hostile majority of society, a struggle which sensitizes him. Gallistl grapples with reality and necessarily formulates a futuristic socialism. Walser playfully suggests that since all this does not occur within given reality it results in fiction, a novel of conscious human encounter with reality. Walser's novelistic tract is like a fairy tale, yet serious, which converts "once upon a time" to a hopeful "it *will* be thus." The message in this pseudo-novel is so obvious, namely the need for creative analysis of self and world, that it might just as well have been sent by way of Western Union rather than wasted in merely another one of the dreary commentary or "think" novels, poems, plays which locate the seat of fiction in the brain rather than in the gut or heart.

The tendency to reduce experience to statement and excessive intellectualization rather than to expand it fully into literature has become the malaise of many German writers today. At the peak of Group 47's life from the late fifties to the mid-sixties this would have drawn some reproof. As it is, writers who once belonged to the group might remind themselves of the exuberant moments of its history and try to recapture them. Clearly, each age must write its own literature —and this becomes a painful and challenging task—but whatever the state of the world, which has never been better nor worse, nothing justifies the solipsistic and moribund. There is a difference between the moribund and the sense of the tragic, a sense which separates the production of consumer books from the creation of literature. One of Böll's comments is a sensitive summation of the moral vision of literature shared by many writers of Group 47: "Man really does not live by bread alone; he needs consolation, and he finds it in the inconsolability of art."

Appendix

Meetings of Group 47

 1—September 1947, Bannwaldsee, Bavaria
 2—November 1947, Herrlingen near Ulm
 3—April 1948, Jugenheim near Darmstadt
 4—September 1948, Altenbeuern, Bavaria
 5—April 1949, Marktbreit near Würzburg
 6—October 1949, Café Bauer, in Utting near the Ammersee, Bavaria
 7—May 1950, former monastery at Inzigkofen near Sigmaringen, Swabia
 8—May 1951, Bad Dürkheim in the Rhineland
 9—October 1951, Laufenmühle near Ulm
10—May 1952, Niendorf on the Baltic Sea
11—October 1952, Burg Berlepsch near Göttingen
12—May 1953, Mainz
13—October 1953, castle Bebenhausen near Tübingen
14—April 1954, Cape Circeo, Italy
15—October 1954, Burg Rothenfels am Main
16—May 1955, Berlin
17—October 1955, castle Bebenhausen near Tübingen
18—October 1956, Niederpöcking on the Starnbergersee
19—September 1957, Niederpöcking on the Starnbergersee
20—November 1958, Grossholzleute, Bavaria
21—October 1959, castle Elmau near Mittenwald, Bavaria
22—November 1960, Aschaffenburg; May 1960, Ulm (special meeting on radio plays)
23—October 1961, castle Göhrde near Luneburg; April 1961, Sasbachwalden (special meeting on TV questions)
24—October 1962, Wannsee in Berlin

25—October 1963, Saulgau near Ulm
26—September 1964, Sigtuna, Sweden
27—November 1965, Wannsee in Berlin
28—April 1966, Princeton University, New Jersey
29—November 1967, Waischenfeld near Bayreuth
30—May 1972, the Fischerhaus, Berlin-Grunewald

Authors who have read at Group 47 meetings (1947–1972).

*Ilse Aichinger (1952)
Carl Amery
Alfred Andersch
Ernst Augustin

Ingrid Bachér
*Ingeborg Bachmann (1953)
Wolfgang Bächler
Heiner Bastian
Arnold Bauer
Reinhard Baumgart
Konrad Bayer
Enrique Beck
*Jürgen Becker (1967)
Reinhard Paul Becker
Friedemann Berger
*Peter Bichsel (1965)
Horst Bienek
*Johannes Bobrowski (1962)
*Heinrich Böll (1951)
Elisabeth Borchers
Nicolas Born
Uwe Brandner
Hans Georg Brenner
Hans Christoph Buch

Paul Celan
Peter O. Chotjewitz
Louis Clappier
Heinz von Cramer

F. C. Delius
Reinhard Döhl
Milo Dor
Jürgen Dreyer

*Günter Eich (1950)
Armin Eichholz
Carl-Heinz Eickert
Karl-Wilhelm Eigenbrodt
Herbert Eisenreich
Gisela Elsner
Hans Magnus Enzensberger
Ingeborg Euler

Peter Faecke
Reinhard Federmann
Christian Ferber
Hubert Fichte
Humbert Fink
Uve Fischer
Erich Fried
Heinz Friedrich
Barbara Frischmuth
Gerd Fuchs

Christian Geissler
Thomas Gnielka
*Günter Grass (1958)
Gunter Groll

Helmuth de Haas
Peter Härtling
Peter Hamm
Peter Handke
Ludwig Harich
Rudolf Hartung
Rolf Haufs
Herbert Heckmann
Klaus Peter Hein
Hans Jürgen Heise

(Asterisk indicates winners of the Group 47 Prize, with date of award in parentheses.)

Helmut Heissenbüttel
Walter Heist
Wolfgang Held
Siegfried Heldwein
Georg Hensel
Günter Herburger
Kurt Heuser
Richard Hey
Wolfgang Hildesheimer
Walter Hilsbecher
Hans Rudolf Hilty
Walter Hinderer
Peter Hirche
Walter Höllerer
Jürgen von Hollander
Margarete Hohoff
Karl August Horst
Heinz Huber
Günter Hufnagel

Urs Jäggi
Janheinz Jahn
Josef Janker
Walter Jens
Bernd Jentzsch
Uwe Johnson

Robert Kahn
Walter Kempowski
Alexander Kluge
Barbara König
Walter Kolbenhoff
Christine Koschel
Fritz Kracht
Rudolf Krämer-Badoni
F. Kretzdorn
Karl Krolow
Hans Jürgen Krüger
Erich Kuby
Otto Heinrich Kühner
Günter Kunert
Paul Krunterad

Hans Joachim Lange
Hartmut Lange
Rudolf Langer
Dieter Lattmann

Gert Ledig
Hermann Lenz
Reimar Lenz
Siegfried Lenz
Reinhard Lettau
Jakov Lind
Manuel van Loggem
Wolfgang Lohmeyer

Wolfgang Maier
Klaus Mampell
Michael Mansfeld
Walter Mehring
Veijo Meri
Benno Meyer-Wehlack
Karl Mickel
Ulf Miehe
Horst Mönnich
*Adriaan Morriën (1954)
Bastian Müller
Marlise Müller
H. R. Münnich
Thomas Münster
J. Muljono
Hans Josef Mundt

Paul Nizon
Klaus Nonnenmann
Helga Novak
Tadeusz Nowakowski

Günter Oliass
Heinz Olschewski
Gunar Ortlepp

Hermann Peter Piwitt
Friedrich Podszus
Johannes Poethen
Wolfgang Promies

Kuno Raeber
Joachim Rasmus-Braune
Renate Rasp
Ruth Rehmann
Christa Reinig
Stefan Reisner
Hans Werner Richter

Luise Rinser
Klaus Roehler
Rolf Roggenbuck
David Rokeah
Peter Rühmkorf

Hans Sahl
Gaston Salvatore
Ole Sarvig
Paul Schallück
Wieland Schmied
Hans Jörg Schmitthenner
Ernst Schnabel
Franz Joseph Schneider
Rolf Schneider
Ilse Schneider-Lengyel
Wolfdietrich Schnurre
Mathias Schreiber
Rolf Schroers
Max Walter Schulz
Hans Dieter Schwarze
Günter Seuren
Johannes Mario Simmel
Hans Jürgen Soehring
Villy Sörensen
Nicolaus Sombart
Willy Steinborn
Jörg Steiner

Klaus Stephan
Klaus Stiller
Michael Stone
Albin Stuebs

Albert Vigoleis Thelen
Franz Tumler

Heinz Ulrich

Guntram Vesper

*Martin Walser (1955)
Dietrich Warnesius
Heinz Weder
Hans Weigel
Peter Weiss
Dieter Wellershoff
Aar van de Werfhorst
Wolfgang Weyrauch
Erwin Wickert
Gabriele Wohmann
Ror Wolf
Karl Alfred Wolken
Dieter Wys-Sonnenberg

Barbara Zaehle
Gerhard Zwerenz

Selected Bibliography

Most of the sources and texts specifically cited in the book itself have not been repeated in the Selected Bibliography.

Books which contain substantial bibliographical materials are marked with an asterisk.

Sources, Group 47 Portraits, Origins and Activities

Bauke, Joseph P. "Group 47 at Princeton." *New York Times Book Review*, 15 May, 1966, pp. 43–45.

"Group 47: Nation's Conscience." *Newsweek*, 16 May, 1966, pp. 67–70.

"Gruppe 47 at Princeton University." *German-American Review*, Special Supplement, April 1966. Contains a profile of the group by Professor Theodore Ziolkowski and a list of anticipated authors and guests at the Princeton meeting.

Höllerer, Walter, ed. "Kunst und Elend der Schmährede: Zum Streit um die Gruppe 47." *Die Sprache im technischen Zeitalter* (Oct./Dec. 1966).

*Lehnert, Herbert. "Die Gruppe 47: Ihre Anfänge und ihre Gründungsmitglieder." In *Die deutsche Literatur der Gegenwart*, edited by Manfred Durzak. Stuttgart, 1971.

*Lettau, Reinhard, ed. *Die Gruppe 47: Bericht, Kritik, Polemik*. Neuwied/Berlin, 1967. Contains valuable first-hand accounts of meetings and polemical articles pro and contra the group. In the editor's appendices (Section III) and in the register of persons, information at times is either whimsical or incorrect.

Meyer-Brockmann, Henry, illus. *Dichter und Richter*. Munich, 1962. Reports on Group 47 meetings and a collection of M.-Brockmann's brilliant caricatures of numerous group participants.

Richter, H. W. "Literatur in unserer Zeit." *Merian* 1/XXV (January 1, 1972), pp. 84, 86.

*Richter, Hans Werner, and Mannzen, Walter, eds. *Almanach der Gruppe 47: 1947–1962*. Reinbek/Hamburg, 1962. A cross-section of texts read at group meetings. Other and later texts read may be found in various issues of the periodical *Akzente*.

*Schwab-Felisch, H., ed. *Der Ruf: Eine deutsche Nachkriegszeitschrift*. Munich, 1962. Contains a retrospective introduction by Richter and a variety of writings by the precursors of Group 47.

*Trahan, E. Welt, ed. *Gruppe 47: Ein Querschnitt—An Anthology of Contemporary German Literature*. Waltham, Mass., and Toronto, 1969. Selected German texts with a brief introduction to Group 47.

Wapnewski, Peter. "Einst hiessen sie Gruppe 47," *Die Zeit*, 9 May 1972, p. 10.

Anthologies

*Dollinger, Hans, ed. *Ausserdem: Deutsche Literatur minus Gruppe 47—wieviel?* Munich and Bern, 1967. With an introductory letter by H. W. Richter. This anthology seeks to complement the list of contemporary German authors who by choice or lack of invitation did not belong to Group 47 at the time of publication. Several authors who declined to contribute to this volume expressed their distaste for *any* literary group activity or anthologies; the poetess Hilde Domin, for instance, refused to play the game of *Literaturpolitik*. Some joined the group later.

*Hasenclever, Walter, ed. *Prosaschreiben: Eine Dokumentation des literarischen Colloquiums Berlin*. Berlin, 1964. A compilation of discussions and creative writing which resulted from one of the Berlin workshops for young writers led by established Group 47 authors. Some of the young writers later were invited to read at Group 47 meetings. A collectively written novel was published also and unintentionally proved the absurdity of the attempt.

*Middleton, Christopher, ed. *German Writing Today*. Baltimore and London, 1967. An anthology of translations of short pieces—prose, poetry, essays.

*Wagenbach, Klaus, ed. *Lesebuch: Deutsche Literatur der*

sechziger Jahre. Berlin, 1968. An unusual reader with socio-literary orientation, which includes many selections by Group 47 writers of the sixties.

Backgrounds

Brandt, Heinz. *The Search for a Third Way*. New York, 1970. An autobiography, highly informative and sobering, by a trade-union figure who intimately knows both East and West Germany, with a personal account of pre-Third Reich politics.
Dichgans, Hans. *Das Unbehagen in der Bundesrepublik*. Düsseldorf and Vienna, 1968.
Jaspers, Karl. *The Question of German Guilt*. New York, 1947. A candid, probing study of a problem which confounded the postwar generations.
Lust, Peter. *Two Germanies: Mirror of an Age*. Montreal, 1966.
Leonhardt, Rudolf W. *This is Germany*. New York, 1964.
*Rauschning, Hans, ed. *Das Jahr '45: Dichtung, Bericht, Protokoll deutscher Autoren*. Gütersloh, 1970. A cross-section of writings in 1945, which includes some authors later known through Group 47; it affords a complementary view of the contents of *Der Ruf*.

Interviews and Interpretations

Bienek, Horst. *Werkstattgespräche mit Schriftstellern*. Munich, 1962. Includes interviews with Andersch, Böll, Johnson, Koeppen, Martin Walser.
Bender, Hans, ed. *Mein Gedicht ist mein Messer*. Heidelberg, 1955. Interpretations by poets of a poem in progress, including works by Walter Höllerer, Krolow, Weyrauch.
Böll, Heinrich. *Aufsätze, Kritiken, Reden*. Stuttgart and Hamburg, 1967, pp. 537–53. Three interviews with Böll.
Bucher, Werner, and Georges Amman. *Schweizer Schriftsteller im Gespräch*, I. Basel, 1970. Includes an interview with Peter Bichsel.
Krolow, Karl. "Lesen." In *Nichts weiter als Leben*. Frankfurt/M., 1970. An explication of one of the author's new poems.
Schulz, Uwe, ed. *Fünfzehn Autoren suchen sich selbst*. Munich, 1967. Autobiographical reflections on writing style, including essays by Böll, Krolow, Siegfried Lenz, Schnurre.

*Speck, Josef, ed. *Kristalle*. Munich, 1968. Holds interest for the lesson-plan interpretations of poetry in German schools.

Cross-genre critiques

Becker, Rolf, ed. *Literatur im Spiegel*. Munich, 1969. Includes some book reviews by and of Group 47 authors, which appeared in the *Spiegel*.

Blöcker, Günter. *Literatur als Teilhabe*. Berlin, 1966.

*Demetz, Peter. *Postwar German Literature*. New York, 1970. Contains information about the political and social scene as well as numerous literary portraits.

*Durzak, Manfred, ed. *Die deutsche Literatur der Gegenwart*. Stuttgart, 1971.

Haenicke, Dieter H. "Literature since 1933." In *The Challenge of German Literature*, edited by H. S. Daemmrich and D. H. Haenicke. Detroit, 1971.

Heissenbüttel, Helmut. *Über Literatur*. Olten, 1966.

Jaeckle, Erwin. *Der Zürcher Literaturschock*. Munich, 1968. Polemics and literature.

Jarmatz, Klaus, ed. *Kritik in der Zeit: Der Sozialismus—seine Literatur—ihre Entwicklung*. Halle (East Germany), 1970. A compendious collection valuable for the official East German line on writers.

Jens, Walter. *Deutsche Literatur der Gegenwart*. Munich, 1961.

Mayer, Hans. *Zur deutschen Literatur der Zeit*. Reinbek/Hamburg, 1967.

―――. *Das Geschehen und das Schweigen*. Frankfurt/M., 1969.

Moore, Harry T. *Twentieth-Century German Literature*. New York, 1967.

*Nonnenmann, Klaus, ed. *Schriftsteller der Gegenwart*. Olten, 1963. The 53 literary portraits of contemporary writers include 35 who have read at Group 47 meetings.

Reich-Ranicki, Marcel. *Deutsche Literatur in West und Ost*. Munich, 1963.

―――. *Literarisches Leben in Deutschland*. Munich, 1965.

―――. *Lauter Verisse*, Munich, 1970. Also contains a reprint of Handke's sharp attack on Reich-Ranicki.

*Weber, Dietrich, ed. *Deutsche Literatur seit 1945 in Einzeldarstellungen*. Stuttgart, 1968. Of the 25 authors discussed, 18 were associated in some way with Group 47.

Weber, Werner. *Tagebuch eines Lesers*. Olten, 1965.

Fiction

Bauke, Joseph P. "German Writing," On Contemporary Literature, edited by Richard Kostelanetz. New York, 1964.
Baumgart, Reinhard. Aussichten des Romans oder hat Literatur Zukunft? Neuwied/Berlin, 1968.
Heitner, Robert R., ed. The Contemporary Novel in German: A Symposium. Austin, Texas and London, 1967.
Mandel, Siegfried. "The German Novel: In the Wake of Organized Madness." In Contemporary European Novelists, edited by S. Mandel. Carbondale, Illinois, 1968. Includes discussion of Böll, Grass, Johnson.
*Waidson, H. M. The Modern German Novel. London, 1959.

Poetry

Bridgwater, Patrick, trans. Twentieth-Century German Verse. Baltimore and London, 1963. Contains some sharp and provocative judgments.
*Enzensberger, Hans Magnus, comp. Museum der modernen Poesie. Frankfurt/M., 1960. World poetry since 1860 in German translation, with original texts, which indicated the growing postwar exposure to cosmopolitan influences upon the young generation of German poets; with many distinguished translations by Group 47 poets.
*Hamburger, Michael, and Middleton, Christopher, trans. and introd. Modern German Poetry: 1910–1960. New York, 1962.
Krolow, Karl, Aspekte zeitgenössischer deutscher Lyrik. Munich, 1963.
*Schwebell, Gertrude C., trans. and ed.; Contemporary German Poetry: An Anthology, introduction by Victor Lange. New York, 1962. Professor Lange's 25-page essay sensitively analyzes key figures and trends.

Radio Play

Fischer, Eugen K. Das Hörspiel: Form und Funktion. Stuttgart, 1964.
*Frank, Arnim P. Das Hörspiel. Heidelberg, 1963.
*Goldberg, Frederick G., ed. Spiegel und Echo. New York, 1965. Professor Goldberg provides a brief introduction to

radio plays in German texts by Cramer, Eich, Ferber, Jens, Mönnich.

Hörspiele, with an introduction by Ernest Schnabel. Frankfurt/ M., 1961. Radio plays by Aichinger, Bachmann, Böll, Eich, Hildesheimer.

*Schwitzke, Heinz. *Das Hörspiel*. Cologne and Berlin, 1963.

————. "The Radio Play: Its Form and Significance," trans. R. R. Read. *Dimension* 1 (1968), 94–111.

The Stage

Anderson, Michael et al. *Crowell's Handbook of Contemporary Drama: A Critical Handbook of Plays and Playwriting since the Second World War*. New York, 1971. Contains informative essays on West and East German dramas and playwrights by Professor Jack D. Zipes.

Benedikt, Michael and Wellwarth, George E., eds. and trans. *Postwar German Theatre*. New York, 1967. Professor Wellwarth provides an incisive introduction.

[Borneman, Ernest]. "The German Theater in the 1960's." *Times Literary Supplement*, 3 April 1969.

*Braun, Karlheim, ed. *Deutsches Theater der Gegenwart*. 2 vols. Frankfurt/M., 1967. Vol. 1, with an essay by Henning Rischbieter; vol. 2, essay by Helmuth Karasek.

Kautz, Ernst-Günter, intro. *Stücke*. Berlin, 1970. Contains an informative survey.

Piscator, Erwin. *Das politische Theater*. Reinbek/Hamburg, 1963.

Individual Authors

*Alldridge, J. C. *Ilse Aichinger*. London, 1969. Contains biographical information and English translations of several short stories and poems.

*Baumgart, Reinhard, ed. *Über Uwe Johnson*. Frankfurt/M., 1970.

*Beckermann, Thomas, ed. *Über Martin Walser*. Frankfurt/M., 1970.

Blomster, Wesley V. "The Documentation of a Novel: Otto Weininger and 'Hundejahre' by Günter Grass." *Monatshefte* 61 (Summer 1969): 122–38.

Böll, Heinrich. *Aufsätze, Kritiken, Reden*. Stuttgart and Hamburg, 1967.

Böschenstein, Bernhard. "Johannes Bobrowski: 'Immer zu benennen.'" In *Studien zur Dichtung des Absoluten*. Zurich and Freiburg, 1968.

*Canaris, Volker, ed. *Über Peter Weiss*. Frankfurt/M., 1970.

*Hilton, Ian. *Peter Weiss*. London, 1970. A critical monograph with English translations, in a separate section, of excerpts from plays and novels.

*Kaiser, Joachim, et al. *Ingeborg Bachmann: Eine Einführung*. 2nd ed. Munich, 1968.

Kelletat, Alfred. "Accessus zu Celans 'Sprachgitter.'" *Der Deutschunterricht* 18 (1966): 94–110.

*Kreuzer, Ingrid. "Martin Walser." In *Deutsche Literatur*, edited by Dietrich Weber. Stuttgart, 1968.

*Meinecke, Dietlind. *Wort und Name bei Paul Celan*. Berlin, 1970.

*Migner, Karl. "Heinrich Böll." In *Deutsche Literatur*, edited by Dietrich Weber. Stuttgart, 1968.

*Müller-Hanpft, Susanne, ed. *Über Günter Eich*. Frankfurt/M., 1970.

Neumann, Peter H. *Zur Lyrik Paul Celans*. Göttingen, 1968. An excellent, compact study.

Richter, Hans Werner. *Bestandsaufnahme: Eine deutsche Bilanz*. Munich, 1962. A social and political balance sheet.

———. *Die Mauer oder der 13. August*. Hamburg, 1961. Contains a collection of appeals to East German writers to resist official repressions despite the erection of the Berlin Wall.

———. *Menschen in freundlicher Umgebung*. Berlin, 1965. Richter's satires include some directed against Group 47. Socialistic in politics and somewhat conservative in literary tastes, he was annoyed at the rapid appearances of new and fashionable trends.

Thomas, R. H. Hinton, and Will, W. van der. *The German Novel and the Affluent Society*. Manchester, 1968.

*Schwarz, Wilhelm J. *Der Erzähler Uwe Johnson*. Bern and Munich, 1970. Also contains a survey of English and American criticism.

Sokel, Walter H. "Perspective and Dualism in the Novels of Böll." In *The Contemporary Novel in German*, edited by R. R. Heitner. Austin, Texas and London, 1967.

*Tank, Kurt L. *Günter Grass*. New York, 1969. With a useful bibliography compiled by W. V. Blomster.

Walser, Martin. "Berichte aus der Klassengesellschaft." *Bot-*

troper Protokolle, compiled by Erika Runge. Frankfurt/M., 1968. A brief essay on the writer's relationship to the working classes.

*Weinrich, Harald. "Celan." In *Deutsche Literatur*, edited by Dietrich Weber. Stuttgart, 1968.

Weissenberger, Klaus. *Die Elegie bei Paul Celan*. Bern and Munich, 1968.

*Yates, Norris W. *Günter Grass*. Grand Rapids, Michigan, 1967.

Index